AF292344

THE
MAN
WHO SOLD
HONOURS

THE MAN WHO SOLD HONOURS

THE FIRST MODERN CASH FOR HONOURS SCANDAL

STEPHEN BATES

Published in the UK in 2025 by
Icon Books Ltd, Omnibus Business Centre,
39–41 North Road, London N7 9DP
email: info@iconbooks.com
www.iconbooks.com

ISBN: 978-183773-027-8
eBook: 978 183773-207-4

Typeset by SJmagic DESIGN SERVICES, India

Printed and bound in the UK

Appointed GPSR EU Representative: Easy Access System Europe Oü, 16879218
Address: Mustamäe tee 50, 10621, Tallinn, Estonia
Contact Details: gpsr.requests@easproject.com, +358 40 500 3575

CONTENTS

Introduction: The Man in the Brown and Yellow Taxi   ix

1. A Land Fit for Heroes   1
2. Bum Cheeks   9
3. Mayfair and Town Topics   23
4. The Chief at War   37
5. Squiffy and The Goat   47
6. The Man who Won the War   67
7. The Honours Tout   81
8. Honours Abounding   99
9. An Insult to the Crown   115
10. Indispensable No More   135
11. An Act for the Prevention of Abuses   145
12. The Ambassador Club   155
13. A Death in the Family   179
14. Nemesis   191
15. The Whole Story   207
16. Monsieur de Gregoire   219
17. Cash for Honours   229

Bibliography   239
Endnotes   245
Index   267

INTRODUCTION: THE MAN IN THE BROWN AND YELLOW TAXI

One of the most noted figures in the distinguished pageant of Whitehall.
DAILY EXPRESS, 22 FEBRUARY 1933

Arthur John Peter Michael Maundy Gregory was many things in his life: an actor, teacher, a theatre manager, a newspaper editor, blackmailer, a police informant, a self-proclaimed spy master, a club owner, a hotelier, a prisoner, a bankrupt and an exile, and some of the claims made by and about him were even true. It was lucky he had so many Christian names to cover his multiple identities. But what he was chiefly, memorably and most profitably was an honours tout.

He sold knighthoods and baronetcies for money, and he was rather successful at it. Maundy Gregory indeed may well have sold more honours over a longer period than anyone else has ever done, before or since. Moreover, he was an equal opportunities tout: selling for both the Liberal and Tory parties until the law caught up with him – and only him in the hundred years since the Honours (Prevention of Abuses) Act of 1925 has been on the statute book. After that he sold papal and other foreign honours instead.

In the years immediately after the First World War, those wealthy and vain enough to wish to add a knighthood to their name could pay a visit to a discreet townhouse at 38 Parliament Street, almost directly opposite the entrance to Downing Street and only a few paces down Whitehall from Parliament itself. They would enter through glass panelled double doors with the words *The Whitehall Gazette* – Gregory's paper – picked out in gold lettering. There they would be met by a uniformed usher wearing a livery so very similar to that worn at the time by House of Commons messengers, right down to the brass buttons, that they could be mistaken for their counterparts. They would be escorted upstairs to a waiting room, whose sepulchral calm was enhanced by stained glass windows, before a buzzer would sound and they would be summoned into the presence in the next room of the man who could make their wishes come true.

Maundy Gregory would be sitting on a large red leather upholstered armchair, behind an enormous desk upon which were several telephones and telephone consoles with switches – this at a period when many companies still had no telephones at all – and bell pushes, an array of small coloured electric lights, a Morse tapper key to summon his secretary and a series of red dispatch boxes looking exactly like those government ministries used. On the walls around the room were portraits of the crowned heads – and recently deposed heads – of Europe, all of whom he claimed to know personally. On a side table were signed photographs in silver frames, among them the Duke of York – the future George VI – at whose marriage to Elizabeth Bowes-Lyon in 1923 Gregory had been an usher. Next to it was another picture of a famous figure, the Tory politician and former Lord Chancellor Lord Birkenhead – F.E. Smith as he was – who quietly borrowed money from the man he called the Cheerful Giver to subsidise his drinking and gambling debts and underwrite his young mistress, Miss Mona Dunn.

Gregory himself would rise graciously to greet the supplicant. He was slightly below medium height, a little on the portly side, his hair neatly pomaded and parted in the middle. His dress was immaculate – likely a three-piece, purple-shaded suit and a wing-collar to his shirt – and his shoes were highly polished. Around his neck hung a ribbon to which a monocle was attached.

His manner was confiding and softly spoken, almost obsequious, and, as the conversation continued, it was likely that he would, apparently absent-mindedly, pull a large heart-shaped, rose-coloured diamond that was allegedly once the possession of Catherine the Great from his waistcoat pocket and fondle it between his fingers.

The conversation would be desultory, but names would be dropped. Occasionally, the telephone might ring, and he would excuse himself to answer it, confiding that it was 'Number Ten' on the line, without admitting that he himself lived at Number Ten, though Hyde Park Terrace, not Downing Street. Ben Pengelly, Gregory's accountant, suggested that the address had been chosen specifically for that reason.

An anonymous *Daily Express* correspondent wrote admiringly of Gregory: 'One met him at Ascot and at the first nights of West End plays whose stars were frequently his intimate friends. One saw him again in Whitehall entering his palatial offices between Scotland Yard and the prime minister's residence in Downing Street. His distinguished presence would catch the eye at once. The diamond watch chain displayed on a suit of subtle purple was in keeping with his aristocratic features ... those who were privileged to visit these offices were always struck by the grave atmosphere of decorum.'[1]

Getting down to business, Gregory was sure he could help his visitor. The man would likely explain that of course he did not want an honour for himself, but it would please his wife. Gregory would probably intimate that he had heard very good things about the man's patriotism and sterling business achievements and how he would be only too pleased to be of service. Of course, these things did not come cheap, unfortunately. Wheels needed to be greased to ensure that the name would make it onto the next honours list in a few months' time, or at the very least the one after that. The normal tariff for a knighthood was £10,000, a baronetcy would be somewhat more: £40,000 because the title could be passed on to one's heirs and successors.[2] Neither gave a right to sit in the House of Lords – peerages were more expensive again at £50,000 – but putting 'Sir' in front of one's name and 'Lady' for the wife back at home was not to be sneezed at. The purpose of the sale of titles was to raise money, particularly for the Prime Minister David Lloyd George's political fund: perhaps those willing to buy a title were not too choosy where their money went. If they were, they could always go to a Conservative honours tout like Harry Shaw.

And, of course, part of the consideration went to Maundy Gregory himself. In the early 1920s, it has been estimated that he was making £30,000 a year in commission,[3] six times the salary of a senior cabinet minister of the period. It enabled a comfortable lifestyle, a large apartment in St. John's Wood (later to become the Abbey Road studios) before moving to the property overlooking the north side of Hyde Park, and, not least, a distinctive brown and yellow taxi and its driver, Tom Bramley. Gregory claimed that the cab was his own, though this seems doubtful since it could not be a licensed taxi and yet employed solely for his personal use, but Bramley did receive a salary. It was useful, he said, for zipping through the London traffic and for escaping from would-be Bolshevik assassins: it even had a peephole cut in the back so he could see if they were being followed. It was not clear why he thought such a taxi would not stand out or be easily spotted in the bustle of London's black cabs by any terrorist who wanted to bump him off. Probably none did.

Maundy Gregory's self-image as someone who knew everyone and had easy access to the rich and influential while still operating discreetly in the shadows was one that he obviously liked. He could call up anyone he wanted: dukes and duchesses, exiled kings, the Lord Chancellor himself, government ministers and MPs, the Dean of Westminster Abbey or West End stage stars, and they would take his call. It all fed his ego, and it was no wonder his staff called him the Chief to his face: just the same as the newspaper tycoon, Lord Northcliffe, proprietor of the *Daily Mail* and *The Times,* was known to his employees at the same time. Naturally, Gregory called his office the Chancellery. It was, said Colin Coote, then a young Liberal MP who wrote articles for Gregory's newspaper, but much later became editor of *The Daily Telegraph,* like 'a cross between Downing Street and MI5'.

Coote left a recollection of his first meeting with Gregory and his modus operandi in his memoirs. It came about probably in 1919 or '20: 'I received one day a letter on imposing notepaper headed *The Whitehall Gazette* asking me to call on the editor and signed "J. Maundy Gregory" … The word "editor" had an irresistible attraction. I called … and was ushered into the presence of an impeccably dressed personage who could not by any possibility live up to his trousers, but who possessed a kind of ingratiating flamboyance. He laid it on with a trowel. "It was always useful for brilliant young politicians to get publicity … if I paid him fifty guineas he would produce a cartoon of me which would be the sensation of Westminster!"

'I did not need to be told the answer to that one. I said that I had not got fifty guineas but if he would pay *me* that sum I would write him an article which would be the sensation of the periodicals. This tickled him; to my astonishment he agreed; and to my even greater astonishment he paid. I soon saw that the magazine was a cover for something. Nobody could flaunt so many appurtenances of wealth, including a fountain pen with a twenty-two-carat nib half an inch broad, a taxi perpetually engaged and an infinite capacity for champagne on the profits of a rag like that.'[4] A £50 fee then would have been immensely generous for a freelance article – as would its equivalent of more than £2,350 today.

Maundy Gregory would arise late in the morning at his apartment, dress fastidiously – always important to make a good impression – have breakfast served by his housekeeper, Mrs Kate Wells, and then leave quietly through a back entrance where the taxi would be waiting. It was his practice always to leave and arrive unseen, via the garden. A succession of different routes to Whitehall was followed every day, just in case. Maybe the brown and yellow cab would rattle along Oxford Street and down to Whitehall, or else past Marble Arch and Buckingham Palace, along Birdcage Walk to Parliament Square for him to be dropped off at the back of his office. On days when he was not lunching or entertaining in the evening, often at the club he owned, the Ambassador in Conduit Street, Mayfair, Gregory might stay late at work, writing an article for his newspaper *The Whitehall Gazette and St. James's Review* or interviewing more clients. On occasions like that, a red light would shine from the office window to indicate that he was not to be disturbed. Would-be supplicants could see it if they stood on the street corner opposite.

Gerald Macmillan, who wrote a biography of Gregory in the 1950s, stated that: 'His figure might be against him but now that money was no object he set out to clothe and decorate it as best to distract attention from its essential meanness … to many he gave the impression of being too perfectly dressed and of an opulence rather too pretentious, such as would be expected of a nouveau riche.' He goes on to itemise the highly polished boots, high wing collar, long cuffs and silk tie, gold and jewelled cufflinks and tie pins, never the same set worn two days in a row, gold rings on his fingers and a fresh orchid in his button-hole every day.[5]

Gregory said – and for once there is no reason to doubt it – that he drank champagne every day, though he once told a dinner guest that he customarily dunked a piece of toast in the glass first to get rid of the bubbles, which seems a rather déclassé thing to do especially as he served vintage Krug.

Gregory's charm, however, did not work on everyone. The former Scotland Yard detective Superintendent Arthur Askew was still alive when Tom Cullen, author of *Maundy Gregory: Purveyor of Honours*, interviewed him in the early 1970s. Askew had investigated Gregory in the 1930s, sometime after his prime, into his connection to a possible murder, and he did not like him at all. 'I have met many villains in my lifetime but none whom I distrusted more than Maundy Gregory,' he told Cullen. 'There was an air of the bogus about him. He was too well-dressed, used too much oil on his hair, wore too many rings – one, a green scarab ring had belonged to Oscar Wilde, or so he said. I said to myself: "Hello, here's a crook, if ever I saw one."'[6]

1. A LAND FIT FOR HEROES

What sort of Britain did Maundy Gregory look out upon as his taxi carried him around Belgravia, Westminster and the West End? In the first years after the war, he might well have seen troubling scenes of unrest. The Great War had not only killed 880,000 British service personnel – 6 per cent of the adult population and one in eight of those in the military – and wounded 1.6 million, many grievously for life. But the war's ending caused a much wider social and economic dislocation. Four million men were discharged and looking for work, three million munitions workers and others engaged in the war effort were now without jobs: 11 per cent of the workforce was unemployed in 1920 and mostly living in abject poverty in squalid conditions.[1]

Tens of thousands of families were mourning their fathers, brothers, sons and fiancés. The 1921 Census would reveal 109 adult women for every 100 men. The politicians had promised everyone a better life: a 'land fit for heroes' would be built, jobs and rates of pay would be restored. But it was not as easy as that.

The latter stages of the war had been accompanied by the worldwide influenza pandemic, the erroneously named Spanish flu, which killed a further 228,000 in Britain, many of them young. It came in waves through 1918 and 1919, infection spreading through the military and to their families, unhindered by a government whose attention was elsewhere and overstretched medical facilities which were unready and, in any case, ill-equipped to deal with the virus. Vaccination was not a possibility, and transmission was not well understood. There were not even enough grave diggers to bury the dead or horses to lead the hearses, and bodies remained unburied for days. It was a cruel and fearful time on top of everything else.[2]

The mood of anger, grief and disappointment had bubbled up almost as soon as the Armistice had been signed in November 1918. When King George V, mounted and in full dress uniform, inspected a parade of 15,000 wounded soldiers who had already been demobilised in Hyde Park a couple of weeks later, the Prince of Wales – later Edward VIII – said he detected 'a sullen unresponsiveness' in the crowd. There were cries of 'Where is this land fit for heroes?', and they pushed forward towards the King and crowded round him in gestures not of anger but appeal. It was a tense moment, only a year of so since Czar Nicholas II, the King's cousin, had been overthrown in the Russian Revolution and less than six months since he and his entire family had been executed by the Bolsheviks. The King rode back to Buckingham Palace from Hyde Park and remarked phlegmatically: 'Those men were in a funny temper.' His son, by contrast, wrote: 'It dawned on me that the country was discontented and disillusioned.'[3]

That discontent did not manifest itself in revolution as in Russia – as Maundy Gregory and many others obviously feared – but it did produce strikes and demonstrations in the docks, on the railways, among bakers and even, most alarmingly, in the Metropolitan and Liverpool police forces whose pay rates had fallen lower than factory workers and even street sweepers. The strikes were brought off by large pay increases: police pay doubled; and also by speeding up demobilisation, reducing the Army from 3,500,000 to 900,000. Attempts to form trade unions for police and troops were banned by legislation, and the drives to create militant veterans' groups such as the National Union of Ex-Servicemen were headed off and the organisations replaced by the avowedly non-political British Legion. In any case, most servicemen were not interested in fomenting revolution: they just wanted to get home to their families and resume their old jobs and lives. In the end, the only uprising was in Ireland and the only terrorist incident in England was the assassination of Sir Henry Wilson, the Chief of the Imperial General Staff, on his own front doorstep in Eaton Place by two English-born Irishmen, one of whom was hampered in his attempt to escape because he had lost a leg while serving on the Western Front.[4]

What was more consequential in the longer term were changed social attitudes following the war and the attempted reimposition of an Edwardian social hierarchy. There were drastic economic changes during and after the war for the landowning and aristocratic classes, and many of them found themselves considerably worse off than they had been before the conflict. Those living off investments, as most did, found their incomes eaten away by inflation, and taxes remained much higher than earlier to pay off the war debts: one study suggests that an average estate's taxes which took 4 per cent of its income in 1914, absorbed 25 per cent by 1919. An agricultural slump reduced incomes further, and many landed families had lost their sons and heirs during the war. The young subalterns, who had led their men over the top on the Western Front, suffered proportionately worse than the ranks of enlisted men. The overall death rate of all troops during the war has been

calculated at 11.5 per cent, but of officers who had been educated at Oxbridge in the four years before the start of the war,
the comparable statistics were 29 per cent of Oxonians and 26
per cent of those who had been at Cambridge, bearing in mind
that almost all of them had become officers (only 3 per cent
of the 1,000 Balliol men who joined up served in the ranks.)
Approximately 19 per cent of peers under the age of 50 who
served were killed.[5]

It has been estimated that a quarter of all the land in Britain
changed hands in the four years between 1918 and 1922.[6] The
old, landed families were not exactly dying out, but they were
not flourishing and were retreating from the shires to their
townhouses in London. In their place, in the seats of power
at Westminster, would come the men who Stanley Baldwin
famously described in 1918 as 'a lot of hard-faced men who
look as if they had done very well out of the war'.[7]

The affluent class expanded as a result of the war. In the
words of the historian Gerard DeGroot:

> 'If we include in the upper class those with the means
> to mimic its ways, we can see how the class expanded
> during the war. A significant number of men made vast
> fortunes. Lloyd George's tendency to draft business lead-
> ers into politics gave them the essential ingredient of
> service to the state which had always distinguished mem-
> bers of the upper class … the composition of the upper
> class changed, but its essential nature, its position in soci-
> ety and its power remained fundamentally intact.'[8]

That, of course, was where the sale of honours came in.

The war had other consequences. There was an expansion
of middle-class, white-collar jobs, from 12 to 22 per cent of the
work force between 1911 and 1921. Such workers were drawn
from the section of the population who had volunteered most
enthusiastically to join up and had suffered consequently more

heavy casualties. Now that the war was ended, to personal and family grief was added a sense of resentment that their status was being reduced and disregarded. The same thing happened to the millions of young women who had volunteered for war work but then found themselves out of jobs when the men came back.

The old pre-war social deference had been eroded in the trenches and would not be restored. As Arthur Gleason, an American journalist, recorded: 'An old Oxford friend said sadly to me: "Ten years ago when I came into a crowded bus, a working man would rise and touch his cap and give me his seat. I am sorry to see that spirit dying out."' Deference might have been slowly expiring, but the old social order remained unchallenged.

Shortages of officers as the war ground on led to the promotion of men from the middle classes to fill the gaps: grammar schoolboys and non-university men replacing all those higher-class subalterns who had been killed. To ensure they did not get above themselves, such men were given the demeaning status of 'temporary gentlemen'. They were, according to the war poet Wilfred Owen when he wrote home to his mother, 'privates and sergeants in masquerade', which was rich considering he himself was the son of a Shropshire station master and had been educated at the Birkenhead Institute. Alfred Burrage, an author of cheap fiction who had been educated at a minor public school, was also dismissive: 'Judging by the manners and accents … they were nearly all "Smiffs", late of Little Buggington Grammar School who had been "clurks" in civil life.'

After the war, the 'Smiffs' found they were expected to revert to their old status as non-gentlemen: they had only been promoted on sufferance. 'I try hard to remind myself that the three stars which I now wear are only the temporary marks of proficiency that the war will in ending wipe out and that I will step back into that drab old life,' wrote one captain, who had been a pre-war salesman. Another added: 'We have got to wipe this "war record" clear off our minds, drop the "captain" and "lieutenant" … and regard ourselves as fit young civilians who have had a "jolly fine holiday" for four years.'[9] Nevertheless, it seems many did retain their wartime ranks to prove that they had once been officers and gentlemen. Think drunken Captain Grimes, one of the schoolmasters in Evelyn Waugh's *Decline and Fall*, first published in 1928, though Grimes of course also claimed to have been an Old Harrovian – there were numerous other examples, too, in fiction and in real life.

Almost perversely, as if to rub in the temporary nature of gentlemanly status, those who had been officers found they received neither rehabilitation nor training to reintegrate into civilian life, nor were they entitled to unemployment compensation, or to use a labour exchange to seek work. 'When it is borne in mind that in a very large number of cases this class of officer did not ask for a commission but was nominated by his commanding officer the fact that he should be worse treated on discharge than if he had remained in the ranks seems almost impossible to defend,'[10] wrote one researcher.

Many temporary gentlemen must have found themselves in the same position as George Coppard, who was unemployed after leaving the army aged only 21. Coppard had enlisted at the age of sixteen in 1914, served as a machine gunner on the Western Front for much of the war, and would have been promoted to sergeant had he not been seriously wounded. He wrote in his memoirs 50 years later: 'Although an expert machine gunner, I was a numbskull so far as any trade or craft was concerned. Lloyd George and company had been full of big talk about making the country fit for heroes to live in, but it was just so much hot air. No practical steps were taken to rehabilitate the broad mass of demobbed men and I joined the queues for jobs as messengers, window cleaners and scullions. It was a complete letdown for thousands like me … there were no jobs for the heroes who haunted the billiard halls as

I did … it was a common sight in London to see ex-officers with barrel organs, endeavouring to earn a living as beggars.'[11]

About a quarter of those returning to civilian life had disabilities for which pensions of up to 25 shillings a week were payable (£1.25 in modern parlance, equivalent to £58 a week in notional spending power), with an extra 2/6d for each dependent child (approximately £5.80) – but recipients had to be severely disabled to qualify for this: those with single missing limbs received less, and those with not immediately visible injuries such as shell shock (now known more widely as PTSD: Post Traumatic Stress Disorder) did not qualify at all. The size of such pensions also depended on the rank of the claimant and the generosity of the board making the award, conscious that the rules erred on the side of cruelty. Wounds, mental or physical, which emerged after the war generally did not count and women who married injured former servicemen were not entitled to widows' pensions if he subsequently died from his wounds: it being held that they ought to have known better than to marry a wounded soldier at the time.

Such living conditions were a world away from the hard-faced men who had done well out of the war, the men to whom Maundy Gregory was selling honours for sums that would have taken a lifetime to earn for the people on the street. Some of these would-be honourands were men who were not even temporarily gentlemen: they just had money to spare. Gregory himself had had what the veterans would have called a cushy billet in England, though he had at least joined up. Did he ever think of the war's victims as Tom Bramley steered his taxi through the streets of central London each morning, past men wearing their medals as they played their barrel organs on the corners of Oxford Street and Piccadilly, or the disabled ex-servicemen who were steering their bath chairs down Whitehall? The money he was accumulating for the Prime Minister's political campaigns was going precisely to telling voters like them that the land was indeed fit for heroes.

2. BUM CHEEKS

Gregory always claimed, somewhat improbably, to have been descended from a line of at least eight English kings that stretched back to William the Conqueror on his mother's side and even had a four-foot long scroll to justify his lineage, compiled by the College of Heralds and signed by Garter King of Arms. The pedigree apparently took in both John of Gaunt and Harry Percy, who rebelled against Gaunt's son Henry IV and died at the battle of Shrewsbury in 1403. Indeed, Gregory's mother, Ursula, did have aristocratic connections, being a cousin of the Vernon family whose recent scion Robert Vernon had been elevated to the peerage as Lord Lyvedon in 1858.[1] She was the daughter of Lieutenant Colonel George Wynell Mayow of the 4th Dragoon Guards, who had survived the Charge of the Light Brigade at the Battle of Balaclava.

Hers was clearly a more distinguished family than that of her husband, the Rev. Francis Maundy Gregory, who became vicar of St. Michael's parish church in the middle of Southampton in 1870 and remained there until his death nearly thirty years later. It was, however, scarcely a rich parish and the stipend of £183 a year was low for such a benefice. The church, right in the middle of the Old Town, near to the docks, still dominates the landscape with its 165-foot high steeple, the top of which was added during Gregory's incumbency. By the late nineteenth century, the building had been renovated, but the arrival of a High Church Tractarian Anglican vicar, appointed by the Lord Chancellor with scant regard to the decidedly low church character of the parish, was a source of considerable controversy.

It was only two decades since the church vestry had petitioned Queen Victoria to put down the pretensions of the Pope and remove clergy who would destroy the great principles of the Reformation, but the new priest not only wore vestments at services and a black cassock and Canterbury cap[2] when walking round the parish but also introduced papistical practices in church such as holy days of obligation. In the doctrinal furore of the Victorian Church, this was heretical stuff and some priests even went to jail for reintroducing the old traditions. *The Southampton Times* in September 1870 noted disapprovingly that Gregory had turned his back towards the congregation in reciting the Apostles' Creed at services, preached in a white surplice and 'contrary to all precedent here' pronounced the benediction from the communion rail. Gregory was met with whispers of disapproval, heckled in the street and threatened with violence, but gradually seems to have won at least some of his parishioners round with his sincerity and pastoral care.

What Ursula Maundy Gregory thought of her husband's calling is hard to say. She had left an agreeable family estate at Old Park, Devizes in Wiltshire to marry an impoverished clergyman and live in a rough, rowdy and unwelcoming town centre parish. There, she gave birth to four sons: the eldest, Michael, died of acute bronchitis aged nine in 1882; another son, Edward, was born in 1875; Arthur came along on 1 July 1877 to be followed by Stephen two years later. If not wealthy, their father's stipend still allowed for the employment of a maid and cook and to have the boys educated at a local private day school.[3]

Banister Court in the Southampton suburbs was a large Georgian villa in substantial grounds which had been leased as a school for the sons of merchant navy officers in 1867 and clearly took a muscular attitude to games and physical development which would be suitable for their future careers at sea. Admiral Jellicoe, the future Commander of the Fleet during the First World War, was an old boy. Such a regimen does not seem to have suited young Arthur at all. He had no interest in games or their effect on the 'spirited part of a boy's nature being turned to good whereas it would otherwise expend itself in evil', in the words of its headmaster Christopher Ellaby. Consequently, the young Gregory appears to have been bullied and was nicknamed 'Bum Cheeks', in reference to his rubicund, hamster-like facial features, and 'Pope Lover' because of his father's reputation.[4]

The school did, however, bestow one long friendship in the shape of another local vicar's son called Harold Davidson, a diminutive figure, who, inevitably, was nicknamed Jumbo, and who would grow up to be one of the most notorious, though irresistibly comic, figures of the 1930s. It was indeed an extraordinary coincidence that one small school should produce two such men at the same time. Davidson went on to graduate from Oxford, be ordained and become for many years the rector of the Norfolk coastal village of Stiffkey, from where he was ousted and defrocked in the early 1930s for alleged immorality to the evident entertainment of the newspaper-reading public. For many years he had deserted the parish every week to catch the train down to London and befriend showgirls, sex workers and waitresses in order to rescue them from the danger of immorality, before returning to his parish briefly only on Sundays to conduct services. Davidson liked to think of himself as the prostitutes' padre and inevitably fell foul of the local squirearchy, his naivety (and probable chastity) no protection from the majesty of the Church of England and the prurience of the national press. After being defrocked he would turn to preaching from the inside of a barrel on Blackpool pier and come to a sticky end in 1937 in the jaws of an elderly circus lion named Freddie, who he somehow annoyed while preaching as a modern Daniel from inside his cage at a showground in Skegness. He likely trod on the lion's tail. The classical Christian martyrdom it was said at the time.

That was all many years away in the mid-1890s, when Gregory and Davidson bonded over a joint love of the theatre, though the latter was eventually removed to complete his studies at Whitgift School in Croydon. Davidson, who sounds like the more charismatic performer, used his enthusiasm as a drawing room entertainer, performing comic songs and routines at supper parties successfully enough to fund his degree at Exeter College, Oxford. Gregory followed him to the university in 1895 as a non-collegiate student,[5] apparently to tread in his father's footsteps towards ordination, but abandoned his degree course in 1899, two terms short of his final examinations, following the death of the Rev. Gregory.

Whether the church ever really appealed as an occupation seems doubtful, but the theatrical element certainly did. He was already emulating Davidson as an after-dinner entertainer while at Oxford, and started writing plays there, one of which is said to have upset his father in his dying months. It was called *Self-Condemned* and was about a priest who rejects the church and its rituals, hypocrisies, falsehoods and fallibilities, which would have been distressing enough for the Rev. Gregory but was worsened by the fact that his son apparently borrowed his vestments and the church's sacramental ornaments and arte-facts without bothering to ask permission first.[6]

Self-Condemned was sufficiently well thought of, by Gregory at least, to go on tour, though it went down less well with Northern working-class audiences. The money then ran out and the actors had to make their own ways home. His father's bequest of a little over £3,300 was not enough to sustain his widow and three now grown-up sons: Ursula ended up in a home for 'matrons' or, more strictly, the impoverished widows of former clergymen at Morley College in the cathedral close at Winchester where she lived well into the 1930s, apparently unvisited by her son who could presumably have afforded to set her up in more affluent accommodation if he had wanted to do so. Of the other sons, Edward was an accountant who briefly and unhappily worked with his brother in his theatrical business and Stephen emigrated to Canada and served in the Army during both the Boer and First World Wars, rising from the ranks to become an officer.

Arthur threw in his lot with the theatrical profession, start-ing with the drawing room entertainments, including comic monologues, readings from Dickens, songs, turns at the piano and as 'Signor Gregorio, ventriloquist and his talking dolls'. And it was in doing this that he got his first big break, which came when he met and befriended a family called Loraine who lived at Yew Tree Cottage at Lyndhurst in the New Forest, a dozen miles outside Southampton.

The Loraines had theatrical connections: the three daughters of the family, Ida, Vivien and Florence, were all stage struck, but more importantly they were related to a professional actor-man-ager called Harry Loraine and his son, Robert, who was already starring as a leading man in the West End, despite being only eighteen months older than Gregory. Apart from appearing in Shakespeare and Strindberg productions, Robert would go on to star as Jack Tanner in the first London production of Shaw's *Man and Superman* – the Don Juan role – in 1905. He had also gone out to South Africa as a volunteer to fight the Boers, temporarily giving up his stage career, and he would later become a pioneer aviator, the first man to fly between Britain and Ireland in 1910 in a Farman III biplane.

There may be a hint that the Loraines in Lyndhurst were quite keen to get rid of the importunate young Gregory, since he kept borrowing money from them and neglecting to pay it back. They were only small loans of a few shillings but mounted up until one of the daughters accompanied him to the shops and pretended that she had no money, so he had to stump up. Gregory was known in the family as 'Oh, Mabel' after one of his performance catchphrases.[7] It was also perhaps a comment on his character. If that was the tactic it does not seem to have taught the young man a lesson: in later years those who loaned him money rarely got it back. As one of his subordinates said in 1933, 'Once we get money, we never return it.'

Probably through Harry Loraine, Gregory got taken on by the Ben Greet Players, a touring company, in 1900, which was no mean break because Greet was one of the leading actor managers of the day, specialising in the classical repertoire, from Shakespeare to melodramas, and pioneering open air theatre productions: he would be knighted in 1929 for his work in schools. Despite this and an early part as a comic butler in a play called *The Brixton Burglary*, Gregory did not stay with Greet for long. He claimed later to have toured under eighteen different managements, seemingly in five years, since he then became the manager of the Prince of Wales Theatre, a burlesque and pantomime house in Southampton, but that didn't last long either.

By 1903, he had set himself up as an agent for would-be dramatists, though that was a struggle, too, and he was soon back on the stage working for an Irish-American manager called William Wallace Kelly, playing the wily Prince Talleyrand in a play called *A Royal Divorce* by the Irish dramatist William Gorman Wills about the Emperor Napoleon's love life.

If Talleyrand did not give him insights into deviousness and double-dealing, then Kelly certainly seems to have done so with his talent for hustling and self-promotion. Apparently, Kelly would plaster the towns where the show was being presented with posters telling the audience to choose sides between the Empress Josephine (played by Mrs Kelly, the actress Edith Cole) and her rival Marie-Louise, Bonaparte's mistress and second wife, resulting in cheers from audiences for Josephine and boos for the unfortunate actress playing Marie-Louise. Cullen says that Kelly was an early master of the Madison Avenue advertising technique of 'selling the sizzle, not the steak'.[8] Nonetheless, Gregory's engagement lasted only six months, and he left, perhaps after a disagreement. But probably he had learned some useful non-theatrical lessons for the future.

Gregory was certainly hustling as he went from company to company, cast to cast, playing small character parts as the companies he was engaged by and the venues they toured grew bigger. From small seaside resorts to larger city venues in Birmingham, Manchester and then the suburban London circuit such as the Duchess Theatre, Balham, and the Grand at Woolwich. In June 1903, his mother's cousin, Percy Vernon, the third Baron Lyveden, who was himself an actor (having dropped his first name, Courtenay), secured Gregory an interview with one of the most prestigious of the touring troupes, the Frank Benson company. Frank Benson was a name to conjure with, partly for the modesty of his own acting ability but much more importantly for his enthusiastic commitment to tour Shakespeare around the country and particularly at Stratford-upon-Avon, where his company's summer residencies made them a predecessor of the Royal Shakespeare Company. Many former Bensonians went on over the years to become stars in their own right, including Isadora Duncan, Henry Ainley, Harcourt Williams and Nigel Playfair. While there may only be an apocryphal basis for the stories that Benson, a keen sportsman and former Oxford blue himself, liked to recruit actors who were good cricketers and rugby players[9] to boost the company's off duty teams, that could not have been the reason for Gregory's recruitment. He seems anyway by now to have decided that management rather than acting was more lucrative, and he was appointed manager for the Benson northern company at the steady salary of £5 a week, responsible for organising the venues and paying wages and expenses for the cast around the Lancashire and Yorkshire circuit.

That lasted for about three years until he was suspected by members of the company of misappropriating money. Benson sent Bill Savery, his assistant general manager who had actually hired Gregory, north to Birkenhead to see what was going on. Benson's biographer reported what happened next: 'He found that Gregory, a natural poseur, had rented for an office an empty room next door to the theatre. There "to give a good impression", he explained airily, he had distributed about the room ten letter baskets. Although as Savery knew well, he received a salary of five pounds a week, he had a buttonhole, a rose or an orchid, sent up daily by train from Covent Garden. A cabman in a shiny silk hat would meet the buttonhole at the station, carry it back to Gregory and drive him in full evening dress to the theatre where he had reserved the best box. Arriving a little late, Gregory would sit and scrutinise the company – a habit detested by all and especially by one member to whom he proposed marriage three or four times a week. Except for this window dressing, repeated wherever he went, Gregory had nothing to show but disorder. His accounts were in a mess, his writing was unreadable.'[10] The outcome, of course, was that he was dismissed at once.

Gregory was probably lucky to escape prosecution. As it was, he shamelessly promoted his involvement with the Bensonites the following year. A profile of him in *What's On* magazine in September 1907, which he probably wrote himself, brazenly asserted: 'For some years Mr Maundy

Gregory was prominently associated with the Bensonian management and was instrumental ... in developing the Benson company into four companies ... His well-known red carnation buttonhole and a smile that will not wear off are personal hallmarks, which conceal a disconcerting shrewdness.'[11]

He was making a habit of skating close to the wind, but he could not be faulted in self-promotion. An article in *The Era* newspaper earlier that year showed that William Wallace Kelly's example had not been wasted on him, now he had become an agent: 'Mr Maundy Gregory is a firm believer in the hustling principle and thinks nothing of dictating in the train 40 or 50 letters to his American manager, who types them all on the journey. He frequently travels the length of England for half an hour's interview with someone and then gets straight on the train again for another journey which may possibly last through the night.'

The agency for dramatists, operating out of Gregory's small flat at Burleigh Mansions in St. Martin's Lane off Charing Cross Road, was in fact not going terribly well. He wore a shirt with a detachable cellulose collar which could be wiped clean, pinned back to the shirt and secured with a bow tie when he was expecting clients. The 'American manager' was actually a nineteen-year-old youth named J. Rowland Sales, who Gregory used to get to tap on a broken Underwood typewriter noisily in the bedroom next to the sitting room to give the impression of frenzied activity when there were visitors. Sales was interviewed by Cullen shortly before his death in 1972 and told him how he had answered an advertisement for a manager in *The Era* and been interviewed in the flat: 'I remember thinking to myself, oh dear, this is rather dingy for a man of such importance ... whenever he was expecting important visitors, potential angels to back his shows or actors he was considering for parts, the stage had to be set to impress them, with cut flowers on the table and so forth.' Sales told

Cullen that Gregory promised him a salary of £5 a week, but he rarely saw more than £3.

Eventually, things seemed to be going better for him as an impresario in conjunction with his brother, Edward. At Christmas 1907, they staged the pantomime *Little Red Riding Hood* at the Lyceum, Ipswich. It was a big show with a cast of 60 and was billed as 'The Largest Pantomime Ever Travelled'. Its star was a young girl billed as Barbara Alleyne (her real name was Elise Barbara Alleyne Barrett): 'the smallest solo dancer in Europe' playing Baby Innocence in a ballet sequence, and the only problem was that she was too young to be on the stage. The Prevention of Cruelty to Children Act of 1889 forbade youngsters under the age of eleven from appearing in circuses or shows for which admission was charged, and Barbara's age, eight, quickly came to the notice of the local police. 'Maundy Gregory knew the law as well as anyone,' Barbara Benjamin, by then in her mid-seventies, told Cullen at her home in St John's Wood a decade or so before her death in 1983. 'But he assured my parents that everything would be all right. I was the hit of the show and got rave notices in the local papers, Unfortunately, this brought my tender years to the notice of the police.'

Gregory was fined £5 by the local magistrates ('Winsome Barbara … shed tears of anger and disappointment,' claimed the *East Anglian Daily Times*) and the show moved on to Peterborough, where Gregory, anxious about the money he had invested in the pantomime, again used Barbara, this time singing from a box by the side of the stage rather than acting or dancing on it. But if he thought that would get round the law, he was mistaken. The police stepped in, and Barbara's mother withdrew her from the show.

Far from waiting until she was eleven, however, the following Christmas, Barbara, by now nine, got an even bigger billing in a West End play at His Majesty's Theatre put on by the famous actor manager Sir Herbert Beerbohm Tree. It was called

Pinkie and the Fairies, and Barbara was to perform alongside Ellen Terry, one of the biggest stars in the country. This was too big an opportunity for Barbara's family to miss and, so, to get round the law, they used her older sister's birth certificate and changed her name to Elise Craven. She was a huge hit: 'a marvel of Terpsichorean training and cool self-possession,' said *The Era,* 'The Child who earns £100 a week' headlined another paper.

Maundy Gregory spotted it, however, and decided to engage in a little blackmail, because he knew how old she really was. Barbara Benjamin told Tom Cullen that Gregory's then secretary, a woman called Audrey Jekyll, called on her mother ostensibly to warn her that the little girl's welfare was a concern. 'For a certain consideration – I don't recall what the exact amount was – she was prepared to forget that I was under-age and using a forged birth certificate. After a stormy passage Miss Jekyll left the house empty-handed, for my mother was a very astute woman.' Mrs Barrett was prepared to play that game, too: 'What she did was threaten to expose Maundy Gregory if anything was said about my age. There was no doubt in her mind that the blackmail scheme had originated with Gregory who had put Miss Jekyll up to the whole unsavoury business.'

Gregory must have been desperate for money even to try such a scheme, but it would have been about then that he fell in once more with Harold Davidson, the vicar of Stiffkey, who apart from his mission to rescue fallen actresses and waitresses in the West End had also become chaplain of the Actors' Church Union, based at St. Paul's, the actors' church in Covent Garden, in 1906. As such, he had a wide circle of contacts, aristocratic, ecclesiastical (the Bishop of London had conducted his wedding to his wife Molly) and theatrical, and he advised his friend how to make contacts with potential investors for his shows on his own account.

Mr Sales told Cullen that he came to know Davidson very well. Gregory always insisted that he was eccentric and naïve, not a sexual predator or abuser. 'Believe me he was entirely innocent of any immorality with those girls he was accused of consorting with. He only wanted to help them. He was the most generous and kind-hearted man I ever met. We would walk into the Lyons Corner House [then a well-known chain of tea shops] in the Strand and right away Davidson would accost some pretty waitress with: "What is a lovely girl like you doing here? With your looks you should be on the stage." He meant it. He got many of these girls walk-on parts by badgering the theatrical producers.'[12] Sales said he also took some of them back to stay at the vicarage in Stiffkey, proof that Molly knew all about his activities in London.

Davidson's strategy to boost Gregory's career was to pick up a telephone and call Wyndham's Theatre, asking for a box to be reserved for him that evening because the well-known theatrical producer would be entertaining the Duchess of Somerset.[13] When Gregory protested that he did not even know the Duchess, Davidson told him: 'You will, my boy, you will. Like all the aristocracy, she's simply mad about the theatre … if you want to attract investors it's important that you be seen in such company.'

The result of such networking was the launch of a company called Combine Attractions Syndicate, in which Gregory was managing director and Davidson was its main fundraiser and promoter, and the object was to import stage hits from the US to tour the British provincial theatre circuit. The first project was to have been a play called *Cleopatra* by the 27-year-old British dramatist Reginald Kennedy-Cox, which would have featured the glamorous young starlet and Gaiety Girl Ruby Miller in the title role, but that never got off the ground.

Gregory then turned to a revival of a popular Victorian comic opera called *Dorothy* and persuaded a matinee idol with the distinctly unromantic name of Charles Hayden Coffin to star in the production, though other commitments meant he could only do so for a limited period. The original production had run for three years following its premiere in 1886 – the longest in West End history to that point, far exceeding the contemporary Gilbert and Sullivan operas – and its signature song, *Queen of My Heart*, had been a huge hit, especially in saloon bars and drawing room concerts.

Gregory even secured a fortnight run at the New Theatre (now the Noel Coward Theatre in St. Martin's Lane) over Christmas 1908, but, with his weakness for extravagant productions, it was a much too lavish affair for his resources. He employed a number of young rising stars and veterans, who had played in the original production, and recruited a chorus of 60, the Gaiety Theatre's orchestra and a pack of foxhounds for a hunting scene. The show was competing with 24 pantomimes in London that season, and once Coffin left to appear in another production, *Dorothy* was bound to falter despite the good reviews it had received. After the run at the New Theatre was ended, the show was moved to the Waldorf Theatre (renamed as the Novello in 2005) on the Aldwych, but the venue was less central and less popular, and takings began to slide.

Davidson suggested a charity matinee should be organised to raise relief for the survivors of an earthquake which had just devastated the Sicilian city of Messina three days after Christmas, causing 100,000 deaths. He thought it would be great publicity for the show and would revive its fortunes – as it did, for one performance only. Despite the matinee being on a Tuesday afternoon, 26 January, the Lord Mayor, the Bishop of London and the Lord Chancellor were in the audience, as were the American and Russian ambassadors and royalty in the shape of Prince Alexander of Teck, the brother to the future Queen Mary and Princess Anne Lowenstein-Wertheim-Freudenberg.[14]

The matinee was a great success: 'The fire from the diamond tiaras in the boxes was enough to put your eyes out,' Sales told Cullen more than 60 years later, and the theatre was full, even at £10 a ticket. But it could not save the show.

It came to a bathetic end just ten days later, on 6 February 1909, when the musicians in the orchestra went on strike after the Saturday matinee because they had not been paid. Gregory panicked, and rather than pay up, threw the theatre's electric switch, telling the customers queuing outside for the evening performance that there had been a blackout.

It was a transparent excuse, and when the cast arrived back for the show, they had to grope around in the dark by candlelight to retrieve their possessions. They had not been paid either, and, when he heard of their plight, Coffin borrowed money to pay them himself, leaving him, as he said in his memoirs, a heavy loser. So was Davidson, who lost his £2,000 savings on the show, the equivalent of two and a half years' stipend as rector of Stiffkey. Gregory's excuse was soon shown up for what it was. The electricity company denied that there had been a power failure that night and the newspapers blamed Gregory's 'speculative and insolvent management' for the fiasco. The trade paper *The Stage* accused 'the adventurer and the swindler … collapse and scandal are inevitable in their wake'. It added that the law ought to prevent irresponsible persons from renting theatres.

The show closed that night, Combine Attractions Syndicate was wound up the following week and Gregory would never again attempt theatrical management. He did not stay around to front up or apologise for the disaster. 'It was entirely characteristic of Maundy to walk away from the scene of the crash leaving someone else to pick up the pieces,' Sales told Cullen. Gregory expunged all reference to his theatrical career in the memorandum he gave to his future clients.

3. MAYFAIR AND TOWN TOPICS

Money's no object now: Clean shirt every day!
GREGORY TO THE LORAINES

One lasting relationship came out of the *Dorothy* fiasco for Maundy Gregory, and that was, perhaps surprisingly, with the conductor of the Gaiety Theatre orchestra, Fred Rosse, and his wife, Edith. They had been married only a few weeks earlier, during the rehearsals for the show. They made a slightly ill-matched couple: Edith Marion Davies, whose stage name was Vivienne Pierpont, was a large and emotionally forceful, auburn-haired woman who had been a contralto singer, mainly in the chorus line in light operas of the period such as *The Quaker Girl* and *The Arcadians,* before she would eventually give up the stage in 1914. She had first been married to a ship's purser named Harry Sheppard, but he had drowned at sea in 1900, four years into their marriage, forcing her to return to her previous career.

Fred, six years older than she was (and so ten years older than Gregory), was a small, dapper figure who had made quite a name for himself not only as a musical director but also a song writer and composer of incidental music for West End shows, his most enduring being the Doge's Song for a production of *The Merchant of Venice* at the Garrick Theatre in 1905. His family name was Lichtenstein, indicating their German Jewish origins, but he himself was born in Jersey.[1] He had been educated at Harrow, but then studied music in Germany and Austria where he shared lodgings with Frederick Delius. Now he was in charge of one of the best show business orchestras in London, the Gaiety Theatre's, and was also musical director for several other theatres, all of which kept him out in town most evenings.

It is not really known why the Rosses became such close friends with Gregory, but in the years that followed he stayed with them frequently, and in 1922 the three of them moved into separate flats at Abbey Lodge, a large Georgian villa fronted by an in and out drive in St John's Wood. Gregory had the top floor and the Rosses were downstairs. They were large apartments, each had room for grand pianos, and each had a separate housekeeper. Fred Rosse would have needed his piano for his work, and perhaps Gregory felt he needed one, too. He also apparently invested in a drum kit to tap along with the Paul Whiteman Orchestra on the gramophone, though it is hard to see him thrashing out *Wang Wang Blues* or *Hot Lips* through the 1920s. The building, after they left when their lease ran out in 1929, would be converted into the famous EMI recording studios, so Gregory was by no means the most accomplished drummer the building ever heard.

From 1910, Gregory leased a summer chalet on an island in the middle of the river at Thames Ditton, a dozen miles upstream from London. It was one of a number of wooden bungalows built on the island in the early years of the twentieth century, despite the basic lack of drainage, sanitation or electricity, or indeed access apart from by boat. Within a few months, the lease was placed in the name of Edith Rosse, presumably to protect it from his creditors. Gregory called the chalet *Vanity Fair*.

He may even have gone to ground at the Rosses' bungalow in nearby Staines when he disappeared from view after the *Dorothy* fiasco. Gregory clearly loved the island and stayed there regularly during summer for more than twenty years. He particularly enjoyed tootling about up and down the river in what was then a new-fangled electric canoe, essentially a glorified rowing boat with a small motor. He also had a larger motor launch which he called *Vigilate*, apparently after the family motto of his supposed ancestor, John of Gaunt, and there was also a punt and a dinghy to get across the river. He once claimed that his chum Lord Birkenhead, increasingly sozzled and perennially short of money from gambling,[2] had wanted to sell him his yacht: 'But I don't want it – I've got four already.' This seems a rather grandiose description of his actual craft: there is no evidence that he ever had a yacht.[3]

The former Lord Chancellor told his friend Lord Carson: 'I can always make money but I can't keep it.' Gregory must have subsidised him since he called him the 'cheerful giver'. His son told Cullen: 'There was nothing whatsoever venal in his acceptance of presents from Gregory though doing so showed a naivety which is almost incredible. It never occurred to him for a second that it might be said that he had thus placed himself in Maundy Gregory's debt. My father had certain faults but in money matters he was the soul of honesty and honour ... I should think you are pretty safe in your conclusion that Gregory's income derived quite as much from blackmail as from the flogging of honours.'[4]

The villa on the north side of the island seems to have been just big enough for parties for friends and contacts, though whether the Prince of Wales ever attended one, as Gregory liked to imply discreetly, may be more doubtful. The future Edward VIII was an inveterate party goer in the 1920s, but the idea that he would attend an event at a muddy chalet in the middle of the Thames given by a parvenu social climber does seem a bit of a stretch.

Although the Rosses split up in December 1923, Edith herself continued living in the same accommodation as Gregory, following him to 10 Hyde Park Terrace, when he moved there from Abbey Road six years later. They had meals together and met up in the evenings but were not in a sexual relationship. Friends took them to be – and, apparently, they were happy to allow it to be thought – brother and sister or, sometimes, depending on circumstance, husband and wife. He called her 'Milady' and she called him 'Uncle Jim', and they went around together to social events such as Ascot and garden parties at Buckingham Palace. She also sometimes acted as his hostess at receptions and parties. Cullen interviewed an elderly lady called Mrs Mabel Pirie-Gordon in the 1970s, who had known the couple because her husband had worked for Gregory as an editor on one of his side-ventures, *Burke's Landed Gentry*. She told him: 'I heard so much about "Mrs Gregory" that in a neighbourly spirit, I offered to call on her. At the prospect of my visiting his wife Gregory became all flustered and quickly discouraged me from doing so.' Another source, Sir Harry Preston, the owner of the Royal Albion Hotel in Brighton where Gregory and Edith often stayed in separate bedrooms, said: 'They were the perfect platonic couple. They were in complete harmony, yet a long way from married bliss.'[5]

Edith Rosse must have been a rather trying companion, if the later letters and witness statements in the National Archive files about her are any indicator. Large and blowsy, she seems to have been rancorous, argumentative, self-righteous and a drinker. A photograph in the files, taken presumably in the early 1930s on Thames Ditton Island with Gregory, shows a large, heavily built woman in a trouser suit clutching at a long pearl necklace with one hand while the other has caught up a small lapdog. Lounging nonchalantly by her side with an enigmatic smile on his face is Gregory, dressed in a dark blazer, light trousers and deck shoes, a folded-up newspaper in one hand. They look to all intents and purposes like a prosperous middle-aged married couple on a relaxing summer's weekend, perhaps just off to the motor launch, which seems to be bobbing gently on the water against a jetty just behind them.

Gregory was probably gay, though that was not something to admit to in those days when homosexuality was a criminal offence. His camp taste in art and homoerotic literature such as the works of Frederick Rolfe, known as Baron Corvo, speak to that. When they did not stay at the Royal Albion, he and Edith also had an apartment in Brighton over the Imperial Restaurant.

Whatever happened to Gregory in the year or more that he was lying low to avoid his creditors – he even claimed at one stage much later that he had been visiting the Far East, which seems unlikely – he re-emerged in 1910 calling himself a journalist. He teamed up with three somewhat dodgy, or at least self-invented, brothers called Keen-Hargreaves, who may even have been among the investors in his disastrous show. Jack, who liked to be known as Baron, Harry and Arthur (who soon bailed out) were the sons of a Liverpudlian merchant seaman, himself known as Jack, who claimed to have joined Giuseppe Garibaldi, who, with a volunteer army of so-called Red Shirts, had liberated southern Italy in 1860 during the country's period of unification. If he was indeed part of the British contingent of adventurers who had joined the campaign, their part in the liberation struggle appears to have been limited to getting drunk and fighting among themselves in the bars and cafes of Naples. They were eventually shipped home at the Sicilian government's expense, and the old boy would eventually die in an East End sick asylum in 1905.

That did not stop him and his eldest son from claiming a greater role in the campaign than he was perhaps entitled to, however. He alleged that he had been a lieutenant-colonel and one of Garibaldi's principal advisers, not that anyone has found reference to a twenty-year-old British colonel in the annals of the story. Similarly, Jack Junior seems to have decided to claim the title of baron as having been awarded to his father by Victor Emmanuel II, the King of Piedmont-Sardinia and first monarch of the reunited country. He even travelled to Rome with a delegation of British survivors in 1911 to celebrate the fiftieth anniversary of the struggle and was introduced to Victor Emmanuel III, the late king's grandson and current head of state. Not content with the fake barony, the brothers tacked on Hargreaves to their surname in tribute to their mother's maiden name to make themselves seem even grander. By the time Gregory knew them, the Keen-Hargreaveses were men of fluctuating financial fortunes and claimed to be running a press agency and dealing in art.

The journalist Gregory was never going to be some penny-a-line hack. He had something rather more entrepreneurial in mind and suggested to them the launch of a new society magazine called *Mayfair and Town Topics* in September 1910. It was a glossy affair on shiny paper with the title superimposed on a drawing of Hyde Park Corner, announcing itself as *the* society journal (it even carried a Latin motto). Below the masthead each week was a line drawing of a gentleman in morning suit, striped trousers, spats on his shoes, a cane and a top hat in one hand, paying court to a glamorous young woman dressed in furs and wearing a fashionably large, feathered hat. The inside of the magazine was copiously illustrated with full page photographs of starlets ('Mademoiselle Lantelme of the Vaudeville Theatre, Paris', depicted reclining artlessly *en negligée* against her bed). It was not short of advertisements, either ('Primset Ear Appliances: if they show the least tendency to protrude just slip a primset behind each ear and the disfigurement is instantly corrected: 3/6d').

The main feature was a colour portrait of some worthy accompanied in glowing prose by Junius Junior, who from the style in which the profiles were written must have been Gregory himself. This, typically, in December 1910, was about the ninth Duke of Devonshire: 'Those who know him best will assure you that this quiet, reticent man might, if he cared to put forward his strength, leave an indelible mark upon the age.' The Man of the Day profile was not a new idea: there was already the magazine *Vanity Fair* which had been published for nearly 50 years, featuring a full page cartoon of a figure in the news together with a witty caption about them. It took in a whole gamut of people, including British and foreign politicians, academics, clergymen and bishops, sportsmen of all varieties, scientists, actors and opera singers, depicted by a team of cartoonists of whom the most famous was Leslie Ward, later knighted, who lurked under the pseudonym Spy.

Vanity Fair called itself 'A Weekly Show of Political, Social and Literary Wares' and covered news and comment, fashion and reviews, gossip and even word games and short stories, and among the contributors were Lewis Carroll and P. G. Wodehouse. This was the exalted model Gregory was aiming to emulate, with the subtle twist that the men of the day who were featured would usually be expected to pay handsomely for the privilege. Obscure businessmen, wannabes and society hopefuls would metaphorically rub shoulders with real aristocrats and celebrities and so become known, one week the Duke of Devonshire, the next Mr Charles E. Charlesworth JP. They would receive entirely positive write-ups to accompany their depictions by an artist called Pip, which unlike Spy's drawings, would not be witty and satirical cartoons but rather full-length, straight portraits, head to toe, set against a plain background. Since most were of men in grey suits, their characters were scarcely delineated, but of course that was not the object. They might become better known, but only for a discreet price.[6] It was probably Gregory who suggested the title: *Mayfair and Town Topics*.

Where did Gregory get the idea of charging his subjects for their inclusion from? Andrew Cook suggests it may well have been that other great fraud of the period, Horatio Bottomley,[7] editor, MP, bankruptcy survivor and ultimately jailbird when he finally went down after the First World War for fraudulently selling war bonds. Accustomed to living far above his income, Bottomley launched a newspaper of his own in 1906. *John Bull* was a raucous scandal sheet, shamelessly promoting its owner/editor and brashly pioneering early tabloid techniques: sensation, gossip and right-wing commentary. It was not above hypocrisy either: its masthead proclaimed that it was 'without fear or favour, rancour or rant' to uphold the interests of the common man, and its slogan was: 'If you read it in *John Bull*, it is so', none of which was strictly true. But at the time, Gregory was trying to set up his *Mayfair* magazine, Bottomley was hugely successful, making a lot of money and was newly elected as a Conservative Unionist MP for Hackney South in the January 1910 general election.

Whether Bottomley advised him or not, Gregory's planned weekly was taken up by the Keen-Hargreaveses, and the first issue was published in September 1910. The 'Man of the Day' feature later became 'Men of the 20th Century', and that enabled the paper to run several profiles each week, increasing its revenue. Editorially, it was somewhat more moderate than *John Bull* and certainly more up-market, consciously so, not to appeal to the common man but, as it proclaimed in an issue in January 1913, 'to provide sound, reliable and exclusive society news … [and] make no bow to sensationalism and free from scandal in any shape or form'. Its regular features, mostly self-explanatory, included 'The Court and its Train', 'Gossip in Mayfair', 'Cupid's Diary', which was about aristocratic engagements and marriages (Felicitations were also offered for aristocratic birthdays), 'Turf Jottings', 'With Hook and Cartridge', 'Throgmorton Street' (former home of the London Stock Exchange, so financial news) and 'On the Blue Coast', gossip about the South of France. There was even a feature called 'Mainly about Women by A Man'.

It circulated for preference at Westminster and Whitehall and around the gentlemen's clubs and grand hotels of central London for free, hence its only income came from advertising and the fees paid. What mattered to Gregory as its editor, though, was making contacts, among them the crowned heads of Europe and senior politicians. Rather like an early day *Hello* magazine, when the recently deposed King Manuel II of Portugal married Augusta-Victoria of Hohenzollern in Germany in September 1913, *Mayfair* devoted its whole issue to the exciting event.

Throughout his career, Gregory would always go out of his way to sidle up alongside such personages. Victor Emmanuel was always known as Il Re Galantuomo – the gentleman king – in the pages of the magazine, particularly after his meeting with Jack Keen-Hargreaves, while Alfonso XIII of Spain was ceremonially presented with a string of polo ponies, which featured in a large spread in the magazine. The activities of the Keen-Hargreaveses naturally figured regularly as though they were prominent celebrities. Gregory would later claim also that he had helped to fund the Grand Duke Nicholas of Russia after the Revolution (in strict confidentiality of course, shared only with his clients) and his widow following his death and that he had been awarded the grand cordon of the Order of Danilo by the Prince of Montenegro for his services after his country was overrun by Serbian forces in 1921. The pictures of all these grand figures featured in silver frames and sat like trophies on the walls of Gregory's office in Whitehall Place. None was closer to him than George II, the King of the Hellenes, who retreated to Brown's Hotel in London after being deposed in Greece in 1924. The King, who could not afford a limousine but had to rely on taxis to get about, was often wheeled out by Gregory when he wanted to impress guests at lunch.

Some of the 'Men of the Day' and 'Men of the Century' were important figures or had interesting stories to tell, men like Sir Fitzroy Maclean, a clan chief who had fought in the Crimean War and was still going strong in his seventies, or the young Maharajah of Cooch Behar who was about to get married in London to an Indian princess, but others were obscure provincial businessmen who were buying the cachet of appearing in a metropolitan society magazine next to princes and duchesses.

There were occasional rogues included, such as Arthur Newton, the crooked solicitor, who represented several of the most notorious defendants of the period and was not above lying on his clients' behalf. He sold a bogus letter purporting to have been written by his client Dr Crippen before his execution in 1910, in which the murderer supposedly claimed to be covering up the crime on behalf of someone else. Newton sold the letter naturally enough to his friend Horatio Bottomley for *John Bull*. Gregory was not averse to misleading either: in Newton's profile in 1911, he described the solicitor as 'three and thirty years of age' when he was actually 51 – otherwise he could scarcely have represented Lord Arthur Somerset, accused of buggery with telegraph boys at a brothel in Cleveland Street in 1889 when, by Gregory's count, he could only have been eleven.[8]

It may have been about this time that Gregory paid a visit to the Loraines back in Lyndhurst, apparently to show off his new-found prosperity. He took a taxi from Southampton, itself a flamboyant expense, and exclaimed to Mrs Loraine, who could no doubt remember his borrowings, 'Money's no object now. Clean shirt every day!'[9]

Mayfair magazine moved into progressively grander offices. It started in Oxford Street, then moved to Albemarle Street in Mayfair in 1913, and on to New Bond Street two years later, but it was not the financial cash cow that *John Bull*, with its much greater circulation, was. At best, *Mayfair* had a circulation of 2,000 copies, selling at six pence a time by 1914, double its starting price, for those that were bought not given away, whereas *John Bull's* circulation reached 750,000 by 1914 and brought in £1,000 a week in advertising alone. Neither Gregory himself nor the Keen-Hargreaves brothers were exactly prudent with money. Harry Keen-Hargreaves spent much of his time on the Cote d'Azure and gambling at Monte Carlo ('Uncle Harry would give you anything he had, the trouble being that he never had anything,' one of his nephews told Cullen) and the brothers' other business ventures flopped. They launched the Albemarle Investment Syndicate in November 1914 – admittedly not a great time to do it – planning for it to be capitalised with one hundred £1 shares but managed to sell only three. In 1917, Scotland Yard sent Inspector Herbert Fitch to make 'very quiet and discreet inquiries' into Gregory and the Keen-Hargreaves for the Yard's commissioner, Basil Thomson, and Fitch spoke to the tailors who occupied the ground floor premises below the magazine's office. They wanted nothing to do with the people upstairs, Fitch reported, because they 'looked on their mode of doing business with considerable suspicion, owing to the number of process servers and collectors calling for money'.[10]

Fortunately, Gregory had added another string to his bow in the shape of his own intelligence gathering detective agency. This had arisen out of a feature in the magazine starting in April 1912 called 'At the Hotels', which simply listed the arrivals and departures of guests at the big central London hotels: the Ritz, Claridges, Savoy and Hyde Park and a few select others.[11] Later, the feature would spread to include the grand hotels on the French Riviera. The feature itself does not sound very interesting, but that was not its purpose. Gregory was making contacts among the managers and was passing on intelligence from them and their staffs: who was in town, who was dodgy, who was staying with their latest mistress, who was a bad payer. All was potentially valuable for the hotels' managements to know, and they paid him a retainer for the tips he passed on. He could also let the police know. Among his small army of contacts was a man called Francesco Mazzina, who owned the Royal Trocadero in New Oxford Street, and it would have been through him that he met Peter Mazzina, aged fifteen, who was at that time a pageboy at the Queen's

Hotel in Leicester Square.[12] The hotel was run by a Madam Colletta, whose daughter would marry Peter in 1921. Gregory set up an office in a suite at the hotel during the First World War while working undercover. Peter Mazzina was to become his business partner in years to come, running the Ambassador Club and the Deepdene Hotel near Dorking, in both of which Gregory had an interest.

The outbreak of the First World War in August 1914 caught Gregory and *Mayfair* magazine by surprise. They were not alone in that: the British cabinet did not discuss the international situation caused by the assassination of the Austrian archduke Franz Ferdinand in Sarajevo on 28 June and the resultant chain of diplomatic ultimatums until the end of July, less than a week before Britain declared war on Germany. As late as 17 July, David Lloyd George, the Chancellor of the Exchequer, was telling City men at a speech at the Mansion House that the international situation had seldom seemed to be so blue: 'You never get a perfectly blue sky in foreign affairs. There are clouds even now, but ... we feel confident that common sense, patience, forbearance ... will enable us to pull through these problems at the present moment.'[13]

While the international tensions were building up, *Mayfair* was unconcernedly concentrating on the society season. When it carried an article entitled: 'An Unbiased Review of the Crisis' on 25 July, it was referring to the Home Rule crisis in Ireland. 'If we have not all taken as deep an interest in the political situation as our morning papers would have us believe we should, it is obviously because we have been better employed,' it brightly informed its readers. 'Now for the country and the moors. France and the continent will call a number of us, while others will journey north in search of sport.' The grouse moors still beckoned. A week later, the magazine reported the grave news that King George V had abandoned his annual plans to visit Glorious Goodwood races and, startlingly, its mind still on grouse: 'it will take particularly big bags and real shooting weather to bring us all back to normal spirits.' More shock news followed: the annual Cowes regatta was cancelled. *Mayfair* soon also had to revise its previously benign opinion of the Kaiser, Wilhelm II. On 8 August, it was still referring to him as a peacemaker: 'another of the most powerful influences working for peace has been the German Emperor,' but by the following week he had become labelled as an assassin and depicted in a full-page cartoon with blood streaming out of his mouth and a collar made of bullets. By 5 September, the courtly gentleman and his lady on the cover had been replaced by the stark, page-filling headline in black and red under the Royal crest: 'Do Not Hesitate! To Arms for King and Country.'

And the magazine now noted a new danger abroad in the land: the German spy peril. 'German spies have been arrested wholesale. We know that one was discovered with a supply of bacilli of typhoid germs, enough to incapacitate a whole Army Corps. In Paris, German waiters have poisoned the food of the customers they are attending.'[14]

Fortunately, Arthur Maundy Gregory was ready to do his patriotic duty. With his network of contacts across the dining rooms and hotels of London, he was prepared to take them on. He would spy for Britain!

4. THE CHIEF AT WAR

At the outbreak of war in 1914, it is estimated that there were 50,000 German citizens living in Britain, working in many trades and professions as businessmen, barbers, butchers, bakers, waiters and managers across the country. Generally speaking, they got on well with the British, who still tended to like them more than the French – they spoke better English for a start – and this was in contrast to official fears of Germany's growing belligerence in international affairs. As Charles Hardinge, the permanent undersecretary at the Foreign Office, warned in 1909: 'Public opinion in England has not as yet grasped the danger to Europe of Germany's ambitious designs.'[1]

This was despite quite a long history of invasion literature and newspaper warnings about an enemy – always assumed to be Germany – invading and conquering the country because Britain was woefully unprepared for the threat. The first of these was *The Battle of Dorking* in 1871, not coincidentally the year of the defeat of France in the Franco-Prussian

War and the reunification of Germany. But they came thick and fast after that in a line which took in science fiction – H. G. Wells' *The War of the Worlds* (1897), with aliens from space this time landing in another part of Surrey, and *The War in the Air* (1907), which was aimed at frightening the Americans with a German airborne landing there. Even Bram Stoker's *Dracula* (1897) illuminated the threat of a surreptitious, hidden invasion, but the dean of invasion literature was undoubtedly William Le Queux, whose *The Great War in England in 1897* was published in 1894 and his *The Invasion of 1910* was serialised in the *Daily Mail* when it came out in 1906 and became a bestseller. A series of novels also explicitly predicted an undercover German threat: Erskine Childers' *The Riddle of the Sands* (1903), Saki's *When William Came: A Story of London under the Hohenzollerns* (1913) and John Buchan's *The Thirty-Nine Steps,* written just before the war and published in 1915.

So, when war did break out the public was at least vividly primed about what to expect with undercover German spies, the enemy in their midst, widely suspected of plotting an invasion, or at least subversion and effectively terrorism. As many Germans were heading for the boat trains to go home, the British newspapers combined paranoia and hysteria about the enemy that remained amid the population. Gregory's *Mayfair* prediction of Germans infecting the army with plague was positively mild compared to Bottomley's *John Bull* frenziedly suggesting a boycott of German businesses, especially restaurants. It was written in capitals to emphasise the threat: 'REFUSE TO BE SERVED BY A GERMAN WAITER. IF YOUR WAITER SAYS HE IS SWISS, ASK TO SEE HIS PASSPORT. THE NATURALISATION FORM IS JUST A SCRAP OF PAPER. ONCE A GERMAN ALWAYS A GERMAN.' Bottomley wrote: 'I call for a vendetta against every German in Britain – whether naturalised or not ... you cannot naturalise an unnatural abortion, a hellish freak. But you can exterminate it. And now the time has come.'[2]

Such incitement led crowds in the East End of London and elsewhere to burn and loot about 2,000 shops and businesses with German-sounding names over the door and beat up people they suspected of being Germans. No wonder one barber in Kentish Town displayed a sign in his window: 'This is a Ingelische Schopp', which may not have assuaged the anger. Even Ralph Blumenfeld, the American-born editor of the *Daily Express,* whose father had indeed fled Germany after the revolutions of 1848, felt it necessary to add a note not entirely unlike the barber's, if rather more literate, on the paper's front page on two successive days: 'The chairman and editor of the *Daily Express* is not and never has been a German. The paper on which the *Daily Express* is printed is not and to our certain knowledge has never been made in Germany. There is not one German on the staff of the *Daily Express*.'[3]

Bottomley and others also targeted senior politicians and other suspected of having German sympathies, men like the First Sea Lord, Prince Louis of Battenberg, who was hounded out of office and anglicised his surname to Mountbatten, or Viscount Haldane, the Lord Chancellor, who earlier as the Secretary of State for War had initiated reforms which made the British army better prepared for the coming battle. Despite that, Haldane was known to be an enthusiast for German culture and philosophy, had studied at Gottingen University and spoke fluent German, so was obviously and erroneously viewed suspiciously. His friend Asquith dropped him from the government on the insistence of the Conservatives when the coalition government was formed in 1915, but the Asquiths themselves who employed a German governess for their youngest children in Downing Street only dispensed with her services reluctantly.

In the autumn of 1914, when the German army encountered unexpected opposition from the Belgians as they swept through Belgium, there were indeed atrocities which rather went to confirm the British press' propaganda and certainly gave them plenty of evidence of brutality. But, as usual, the troops at the Front saw things rather differently. When they fraternised, most famously at the Christmas Day truce in 1914, they discovered just how much they did have in common. 'Watcha cock,' one German soldier said to Graham Williams of the London Rifles, "ow's London?" It turned out that the man had lived most of his life in the capital, had gone to school there and had been a porter at Victoria Station before the war. Another Brit came across a man who had been his regular barber in Holborn. And a third German soldier, looking for 'Brummagem lads', wanted a message passed to his wife and five children left back in Birmingham.[4]

In such circumstances, so closely intertwined were the two nations and so relatively easily some Germans could pass for Englishmen, it was perhaps inevitable that spies should be suspected around every corner and that men like Maundy Gregory could set themselves up as intelligence operatives in London to root them out.

There were in fact very few German spies in England. MI5, the newly established domestic intelligence service, had been set up in 1909 under a 36-year-old army captain called Vernon Kell with a staff of sixteen, including the office caretaker. But it managed to stop most of them with the aid of the police, who were generally sent round to arrest those suspected of espionage as the agents didn't have the warrants to do so. The service claimed to have caught 65 of the 120 foreign agents it suspected of working in Britain during the war, and the first dozen of those were court-martialled and shot at the Tower of London, which may have had some deterrent effect.

What the authorities discovered was that German training of potential spies was more amateurish and rudimentary than they had expected: Georg Breeckow, who was a German-American, was caught because his German handlers had not even forged the right size of an American passport and had got the bald eagle crest wrong. The first undercover agent, Carl Hans Lody, a junior Naval officer who spoke fluent American-accented English, having lived in the United States before the war, was sent to Scotland in the first days in August 1914 posing as an American businessman to observe the movements of the British fleet in the Firth of Forth. From a boarding house in Edinburgh, he sent back information in letters and telegrams, some of them not even in code, to a known intelligence officer in Sweden. It was Lody who told the German High Command that Russian troops were being landed in Scotland so quickly that they were arriving still with snow on their boots.[5] His post was opened, and he was caught within six weeks while taking a break in Ireland and quickly admitted to spying. Lody was put on public trial at the Middlesex Guildhall (now home of the Supreme Court, opposite the Houses of Parliament). In a sign of what a chivalrous fashion the war was supposedly conducted in at that stage, Lody said to Lord Athlumney, the officer escorting him to his execution: 'I suppose you will not care to shake hands with a German spy?' to which Athlumney replied: 'No, but I will shake hands with a brave man.'[6]

The other spies who were caught in the first two years of the war were equally amateurish. They were mostly businessmen from Scandinavia, neutral Holland or Latin America, and had little idea of what they were doing, anxious only to get home. At least one was found in possession of a bottle of lemon juice, the favoured liquid for invisible ink, and several were caught when their letters to the same Stockholm address were opened by the Postal Censorship department. The authorities had learned a couple of lessons from the Lody case. In future, court martials would be held in secret to avoid arousing sympathy, giving the accused platforms to speak publicly or revealing to the Germans that their spies had been rumbled. The law had to be tightened since the maximum penalty for espionage under the Defence of the Realm Act was penal servitude. In effect, Lody had been tried and executed illegally.

There was very little evidence that any of the spies who were arrested had given any useful information to the German intelligence unit. The only one who may have done so was a woman called Louise Wertheim, a naturalised British citizen, who was caught after submitting extravagant expenses, and rather too obviously seeking information from British naval officers in Edinburgh. She was given penal servitude because she was a woman, rather than being executed like her male companion, Ludovico Hurwitz-y-Zender, who was a Peruvian businessman. He was the last spy for Germany to be executed in the spring of 1916 as the authorities realised that the executions were counter-productive, handing a propaganda weapon both to the Germans and the countries where the spies had originated.[7]

Maundy Gregory had no hand in any of these captures, though he evidently continually supplied snippets of information from the London hotel circuit to both Basil Thomson, the assistant commissioner of the Metropolitan Police and head of the CID responsible for rooting out subversion, and to Vernon Kell at MI5.

Thomson was an extraordinary figure to be a policeman. His background, after Eton and New College Oxford, was as a colonial administrator in Fiji and Tonga. After returning to Britain, he became a prison governor (he had a particular aversion to the suffragettes, and he was not at all keen on Jews either) and then was appointed to the Metropolitan Police as head of the CID detective bureau. As such, when the war broke out, his officers were in charge of arresting suspected spies and his job was to interrogate them. Thomson enjoyed the role of spy catcher, though how successful he was may have been more doubtful: of twenty-one arrests, only one went on to trial. It was he who interrogated a Dutch woman called Margarethe Zelle and decided she was not a spy so let her go, only for her later arrest and subsequent execution by the French in 1917. She is better known as Mata Hari, a former exotic dancer, and it now seems likely that Thomson was right, and she was not a spy after all, but a scapegoat for French military failures.

Notoriously, Thomson was also the man who disseminated the diaries of the former colonial civil servant Sir Roger Casement, who was accused in 1916 of gun-running to arm the Irish Easter Rising. These showed Casement's homosexual liaisons and were used, successfully, to blacken his character especially with the Americans prior to his execution. It may well be that one of Gregory's services was to help circulate the incriminating material.

As a man obsessed with spies and surveillance of subversives and union activists, it seems very likely that Thomson was only too happy to use Gregory and his network of informants in the London hotels. What is much less certain is how many spies actually stayed at the Ritz and the Dorchester and how useful Gregory's information would have been.[8]

Nevertheless, Thomson seems to have pulled some strings to delay Gregory's call up in April 1917 on the grounds that he was conducting a special operation. He wrote to a Major Carter at the War Office asking for him to be put on the 'not to be called up' list for a short time 'as he is completing some enquiries on which he is furnishing me with reports ... He has from time to time furnished useful information'. Carter agreed to an extension of a month. Later that April, it seems Gregory lobbied the War Office in person. A Captain Cooke of the Intelligence Service noted: 'I was very unfavourably impressed by him, but promised to let him know ... He is not a "sahib" and he is evidently talkative, boastful etc. I think he had much better be called up. Note: I spoke to Mr Thomson about him. He said he could well do without him, though he is doing a particular job for S (cotland) Y (ard), at the moment.'

The Intelligence Agency was clearly less impressed than Thomson was. During the First World War and subsequently, they consistently downplayed Gregory's efforts. It seems he may have been used to carry out trivial inquiries deemed not important enough to take up the time of the public school educated and well-connected young gentlemen of MI5. Gregory would later claim that he had gone undercover, using his acting skills to impersonate a butler at an unnamed stately home in Scotland for some secret purpose. He even asserted that he had impersonated Winston Churchill when the then First Lord of the Admiralty, in the early months of the war, was thought to be under threat of assassination. It is true that they were similar in age and height, and superficially, perhaps, in features, but the idea that he had made a speech as Churchill at a banquet, as he claimed, must surely have been far-fetched. Churchill was well capable of making his own speeches and scarcely hid away from the public.

First person descriptions of Gregory and his manner are relatively rare. In the early 1970s, Tom Cullen found and interviewed a former secretary at the War Office named Phyllis Barnes who claimed to have known that Gregory was employed to spy on an Australian inventor suspected of working for the Germans. Her recollection was that Gregory ostentatiously asked her to keep a note of all telephone calls to and from the Australian's nearby office and any visitors he received. Miss Barnes told Cullen that Gregory was 'very well dressed but wore too much jewellery. His hair was brown, he was not bald then and he did not wear glasses but used a monocle. He was always courteous although he had a pompous and grand manner. There was an air of mystery about him.' She could not recall what, if anything, happened to the inventor, but did remember that Gregory tried to recruit her to be his secretary after the war: 'He said he was going to publish an important periodical and he wanted to engage a confidential secretary and receptionist who was capable of receiving well-known and famous people, including royalty. I thought it was rather amusing.'[9] But she turned the offer down.

The intelligence service's attitude towards Gregory was bluntly expressed in a memorandum prepared for the Cabinet

Secretary Sir Maurice Hankey by an operative called E. Holt Wilson in March 1926, by which time Gregory's work as an honours tout had become well-known in Whitehall. Wilson wrote: 'We don't like him and we don't trust him. We have often refused to employ him because of his character. Has run a private inquiry agency for many years and tries to market volumes of general news of which a small percentage turns out to have an interesting foundation.

'He is difficult to shake off as he is an indefatigable "nosey parker" perpetually on the prowl for something saleable. He succeeded in selling a good deal of rubbish during the war to Basil Thomson who responded by manipulating his exemption from military service in order to employ him further.

'To sum up, his personal quality is not that of a high grade independent agent of nice discrimination but rather that of the wholesale purveyor of likely fables, some of which may prove to be true when tested. He has all the skill and failings of the professing agent and nowadays tries to make himself useful to as many anti-something societies as possible. Independent verification is essential of any information offered by him … it was the opportunity for "German hunting" in the war that switched him over to his more recent activities.'

At the bottom of the report there was a handwritten note from Hankey: 'Most grateful, exactly what I wanted.'[10]

5. SQUIFFY AND THE GOAT

He is an underbred swine.
FIELD MARSHAL SIR WILLIAM ROBERTSON,
CHIEF OF THE IMPERIAL GENERAL STAFF,
ON LLOYD GEORGE IN 1917

By the autumn of 1916, two years into the war, Herbert Asquith, Britain's prime minister since 1908, was exhausted and demoralised. Before the war, he had governed the country with seeming imperturbability through a series of huge domestic crises. His government had introduced pensions for the elderly poor (five shillings a week for the over seventies), in the face of fierce opposition from the Tory-controlled House of Lords, and the first national health insurance scheme which incurred resistance from employers, doctors and even trade unions. This was followed by a protracted constitutional battle with the Lords to rein in their powers to block legislation. Then there was an attempt to implement Home Rule for Ireland, partly to pacify the Irish nationalist MPs on whom the government by then relied for support to remain in power. This in turn led to a threatened insurrection by Ulster's Protestants, opposed to being subsumed as they saw it into a Roman Catholic Irish state, in which they were aided and abetted by the Tories at

Westminster and some of the British Army's officer corps serving on the Curragh west of Dublin.

All this and a background of low-level, genteel violence by militant suffragettes campaigning for female emancipation, was shocking in an era when women were expected to be submissive. There had also been waves of strikes on the docks, on the railways and in the Welsh coalmines, some put down with violence. And all this took place against a mounting international crisis and arms race with Germany. These had all been more or less contained: Asquith's Liberal Party had lost its majority in two general elections in 1910 but remained in government sustained by the Irish nationalist MPs. During these momentous and debstabilising events, *Mayfair and Town Topics* sailed serenely on, recording society weddings and the annual round of hunt balls and fishing seasons or extolling the virtues of places such as the Grand Hotel, Broadstairs ('beautifully situated in the finest position on the cliffs'). As late as the edition of 1 August, four days before the declaration of war, the magazine's cover was illustrated by a photograph of a decorative antique sculpture at the Albani Palace in Rome. A fortnight later, amid its sudden belligerence, the magazine's editorial was still striking a reassuring tone: 'Many people believe that the magnitude of the new Armageddon will heave Europe into war for a year or perhaps longer. For our part we do not think it will last as long as this.'

Maundy Gregory was far from alone in believing that the war would be over quickly. For nearly a hundred years, continental conflicts had ended within weeks or months and it took some time for the grinding power of modern weapons technology to be appreciated and tactics developed to attempt to counter it. Nevertheless, for all the full-throated jingoism and belligerence that *Mayfair and Town Topics* displayed in the opening weeks of the war, Gregory was not inclined to join the rush to volunteer.

By the time he was called up Gregory was aged 39, unfit, overweight and scarcely in the first flush of youth, so was unlikely to be sent to the Front, but even so he was able to delay nearly eighteen months before being called to the colours. If his excuse of his important national service rooting out spies was novel, it was not an uncommon practice for middle-aged men who could prove some civilian need to have their call up delayed, especially if they had a helpful patron like Thomson or could prove their value at work.

Once war was declared, Gregory, through the editorial pages of the magazine, was not slow to urge others to volunteer. The iron walls of Britain's Navy would ensure victory: 'Britannia Rules the Waves', readers were assured. 'Great men tremble when the Lion roars. Britain's Navy, officered by scions of the greatest families of England and manned by the finest manhood in the country is now called upon to maintain the honour of the greatest Empire the world has ever seen.'[1] Gregory could not resist the tang of snobbery: it was at the scions and their families that the magazine was aimed or at least at those who aspired to join them.

But as the war dragged on, Gregory's enlistment could not be delayed indefinitely. He attended the recruitment office at St. James's Vestry Hall on Piccadilly in response to a summons on the 21 February 1916, but the delaying tactics over his alleged spy catching work meant that he was not actually posted to a unit until 10 July the following year. Gregory's medical and military service record remains in the National Archives: height five feet seven-and-a-half inches, weight 153 pounds, but passed A1. The posting was as a trooper to the Household Battalion Reserve at Windsor Castle. He was subsequently posted to the Irish Guards as a private at Caterham barracks on 29 January 1918, despite being very short to be a guardsman. The normal height requirement was six-feet tall, but that had been relaxed by that stage of the war. In any event, his unit was classified as class Z in the army reserve, which does not sound very close to combat readiness. He was demobilised and transferred to the reserve in February 1919 and discharged finally in March 1920 with his character marked as very good. It was scarcely a heroic war record, but he had at least served.

Gregory would have been called up under the Derby Scheme introduced in October 1915, named after Lord Derby, the government's director of recruiting, by which all men between the ages of 18 and 41, who had not yet joined up, were encouraged to attest their willingness to volunteer: the youngest and unmarried to be recruited first. Of 2.2 million civilians, 840,000 attested, 300,000 were rejected on medical grounds and approximately a million ignored the appeal.

From the start of his military service, Gregory was still angling to become an officer in the Intelligence department, and his application is in the National Archives, too. Against the question of his occupation in civilian life, he wrote: 'Investigation work of a diplomatic and political character: literary work.' He added, with a touch of hubris: 'From August 1914 to July 1917, conducted a large organization of informants and regularly supplied intelligence information to the authorities and also received a small government grant.' He claimed he had a thousand spies working for him which, if true, would have made his team exponentially larger than MI5's.

His good moral character was attested by the Rev. Plymouth, who was confusingly the Lord Lieutenant of Glamorgan, but sent a supportive letter from Dalchreichart, deep in the Scottish Highlands, north of Invergarry. He appended an apologetic covering note: 'There is only one post here every other day and one cannot always catch the return.' A further supportive note came from Dr. R. Pope, the censor (administrator) of non-collegiate students at Oxford: 'He passed Mods so he is amply qualified for commission by standard of education.'[2]

The endorsements were clearly a tribute to Gregory's networking skills, but it made no difference. His application was considered by an officer named Page on 21 September 1917: 'As this candidate is A1, but has had no active service overseas we have no opportunity of offering him a commission.' A few days later there was a further inquiry to the intelligence corps: 'Do you know anything of this applicant and are his services likely to be required?' The answer was that he was not required and so a brief note was added to his application from Captain A. J. Finny for the director of special intelligence to the general officer commanding, London district: 'I am directed to inform you that there is no suitable vacancy for which this man can be considered at present.'

On the wider front, Asquith's government stumbled on, lacking both direction and energy. The Prime Minister himself, now 64, continued to dominate the Commons with fluent authority. In peace his insouciance and procrastination soothed crises – 'Wait and see', became a watchword – but that did not work in the urgent imperatives of wartime. The military hero Lord Kitchener, in charge of war production, insisted that weapons and shells could not be manufactured any quicker and were adequate for the Army's needs – battalions only needed four machine guns, he decided.[3] There was drift and indecision, not helped by every military decision being discussed endlessly by the nine-man civilian war cabinet.

Asquith's confidence and drive were exhausted as the casualties mounted and public criticism of the conduct of the war, and particularly the slow provision of arms for the Front, mounted. The press asserted from its contacts in the general staff that the Battle of Loos had been lost through want of munitions. In May 1915, Asquith was forced to accept the Tories into a coalition cabinet, the very men whose pre-war parliamentary conduct in obstructing the government's pensions reform and Irish policy he had disdained. The Prime Minister was already drinking heavily – hence his Westminster nickname Squiff or Squiffy – and had suffered two personal blows which demoralised him.

Winston Churchill, who knew a thing or two about drink, described Asquith as 'sodden'. A Tory MP named Arthur Lee reported watching Asquith return to the Commons chamber for a 10pm vote 'very flushed and unsteady in gait, plump(ing) himself down on the bench and promptly (going) to sleep'. David Lindsay, the agriculture minister, paints a vivid picture of Asquith in the last few months of his premiership: eyes watery, hands shaking, nervous twitching, yet still, just, in command, especially in the Commons: 'He wakes up always when he has to speak in the HofC – of course the two hours before lunch are those in which his spirits and his stock of spirit are at their lowest measurement.'[4]

The Army's Commander in Chief, General Douglas Haig, wrote to his wife in September 1916, shortly after Asquith had visited him at the Front: 'The PM seemed to like our old brandy. He had a couple of glasses (large sherry glass size!) before I left the table at 9.30 and apparently had several more before I saw him again. By that time his legs were unsteady, but his head was quite clear and he was able to read a map and discuss the situation with me. Indeed he was most charming and quite alert in mind.'[5]

Asquith was shocked to discover that Venetia Stanley, 35 years his junior, with whom he had pursued a passionate, though almost certainly chaste, secret relationship for three years, had decided to marry his parliamentary private secretary Edwin Montagu[6] without telling him. It left him feeling bereft and abandoned. 'This breaks my heart,' he wrote to her. 'I can only pray God to bless you – and help me.' There would be no more discreet exchanges of gossip or the conduct of the war, sometimes written in letters, up to 3,000 words a day, during cabinet meetings or from his desk, no more afternoon drives or dinner parties, no one with whom he felt he could chat and discuss the war in a way which he could not with his domineering and voluble wife Margot.

Then, as the disastrous battle of the Somme unfolded, Asquith had lost his brilliant oldest son, Raymond, killed while leading a charge, going over the top with the Grenadier Guards in September 1916: 'Oh! The awful waste of a man like Raymond – the best brain of his age in our time – any career he liked lying in front of him. Whatever hope I had for the far future, by much the largest part, was invested in him. Now all that is gone', Asquith lamented. Occasionally, the Prime Minister would retreat across St. James's Park to the Athenaeum Club in the afternoons to read novels. In October, he suffered a breakdown and was laid low for several weeks.

By now, the catchphrase which he had deployed in allowing events to take their course, 'Wait and See', was being widely ridiculed, speaking as it did of inertia and drift in the conduct of the war. Even the music hall comedians were mocking him, as George Robey sang: 'Just stem this tide of innocent conjecture/Remain inert and dormant just like me/ And cultivate spontaneous quiescence/In other words: Wait and See!' As the Tory MP Leo Amery noted: 'The supreme power of the state has fallen into the hands of a man who combines unrivalled gifts of parliamentary leadership with a complete incapacity to face facts or to come to any decision on them. For twenty years he has held a season ticket on the line of least resistance and gone wherever the train of events has carried him, lucidly justifying his position at whatever point he has happened to find himself.'[7] The metaphor was unfair about Asquith's pre-war conduct but seemed increasingly to hit the mark in war.

The cabinet drift could not continue, and Asquith's colleagues' loyalty was increasingly strained. As Lloyd George wrote in his self-justifying *War Memoirs* later: '[Asquith] gave the impression of a man who was overwhelmed, distracted and enfeebled, not merely by the weight and complexity of his burdens, Whether he was ever fitted for the position of a war minister in the greatest struggle in the history of the world may be open to doubt, but that he was quite unfitted at this juncture to undertake so supreme a task was not open to question or challenge. Asquith's will became visibly flabbier, tardier and more flaccid under the strain of war.'[8]

David Lloyd George, the 'Welsh Wizard' to his followers who admired him for his oratory, energy and drive, 'the Goat' to his political opponents who loathed him for his serial infidelities, untrustworthiness and willingness to ditch colleagues and friends in pursuit of his own ambition, had been one of Asquith's closest government colleagues. He was a fluent and gifted orator who exuded charm and dynamism, serving first as President of the Board of Trade, then Chancellor of the Exchequer in the pre-war Liberal government. By 1916, he, too, had been in office for eight years but was chafing with frustration at the way the government was drifting under Asquith. A supremely capable and self-confident politician, Lloyd George was the obvious man to replace the Prime Minister, as he himself realised, but his coup would not only split the Liberal Party, it would also reinforce his reputation for slipperiness. As the diplomat and author Harold Nicholson said of him: 'The good fairies gave him everything at his Christening, but the bad fairy said: "People won't trust you."'[9]

Lloyd George's rise had been remarkable for the period. He was the first senior minister to have arisen from a working class and nonconformist religious background and, despite the high offices he held, was always seen – and saw himself – as an outsider. He was widely patronised, especially by Tories, but also some senior Liberals as 'the little Welsh attorney'. Although he had been born in Manchester, he had grown up in the small, remote, predominantly Welsh-speaking North Wales village of Llanystumdwy on the Llyn peninsula near Criccieth, where his mother's family came from (now in Gwynedd but then part of Caernarfonshire).

He learned his politics from his mother's brother Richard Lloyd, 'Uncle Lloyd', the local shoemaker, and his oratorical skills came originally from the local debating society and the Baptist chapel where his uncle preached. Although he soon drifted away from religious observance – he said he had a religious temperament but could not accept divine authority – Welsh religious issues, temperance and the long-running struggle for the disestablishment of the Anglican Church in Wales (an early example of the country's urge for an independent identity, though the process took 70 years to achieve), were the ones which first seized his imagination. He became a solicitor in Criccieth, married a local girl, Margaret Owen, despite her parents' opposition, and entered parliament at a by-election for Caernavon Boroughs in 1890, the seat he would represent for the next 55 years until shortly before his death. He made his name through his energy and ebullience and his adherence to radical causes: his opposition to the Boer War in 1901 nearly led to him being lynched by a mob at Birmingham Town Hall, and his peacetime ministerial career saw him not only drive through social reforms, such as pensions and national insurance, but also goad and ridicule his opponents. When the Tory majority in the then entirely hereditary House of Lords blocked the People's Budget, including the pensions reform that he had introduced as Chancellor of the Exchequer in 1909, he cheerfully referred to them as 'no more than five hundred ordinary men chosen at random from among the unemployed'.

In retaliation for the impertinence of introducing a radical measure and marginally increasing their taxation, the Lords blocked a money bill for the first time in 250 years, and some of its more reactionary members responded with a mixture of outrage and obtuseness. The Duke of Beaufort said he would like to see Lloyd George and his then Liberal ally Winston Churchill 'in the middle of 20 couple of dog hounds', and the Duke of Buccleuch felt so hard done by that he refused to make his annual guinea donation to the Dumfriesshire football club. The Duke of Somerset warned that he would have to sack and evict his estate workers and Lord Anglesey, who had just bought himself a new yacht costing £1,500 a month to run, announced that he would reduce his subscription to the London Hospital from £5 to £3 a month. Understandably in view of the way it had treated the Liberal government's policies before the war, it was not a chamber to which Lloyd George gave much respect

The constitutional stand-off over whether the elected government could get its way against the hereditary, unelected chamber was only resolved after two general elections in 1910, when Asquith threatened to nominate enough Liberal-supporting peers to swamp the Tory majority. The public figures who agreed to be put forward (the question of payment was left in abeyance at that stage), about 250 names, mainly of worthy but dull time servers, also included General Robert Baden-Powell, the hero of the siege of Mafeking in the Boer War and founder of the Boy Scout movement, Gilbert Murray, the Regius Professor of Greek at Oxford, the novelist and poet Thomas Hardy and *Peter Pan's* playwright J. M. Barrie. In the end, their nominations were not required, and they did not get their titles. In view of what was to come a decade later, there was a growing willingness to tamper with the membership of the Upper Chamber. If Lloyd George later regarded peerages as something to sell in order to enhance political advantage, there was already a precedent.

Such high profile brinkmanship against a visible and entitled enemy did not worry Lloyd George at all, but already in the years before the First World War he was getting into scrapes which led to questions about his judgement. All was subsumed to his political ambition and, secondarily, his quest for money. As he told Margaret in a letter early in their courtship: 'My supreme idea is to get on. To this idea I shall sacrifice everything – except I trust honesty. I am prepared to thrust even love itself under the wheels of my juggernaut if it obstructs the way ... do you not really desire my success? My love for you is sincere and strong ... But I must not forget I have a purpose in life and however painful the sacrifices I may have to make to attain this ambition I must not flinch.'[10]

Ambition and success bred recklessness and perhaps the aphrodisiac of danger. Although he knew that what he called 'the fast life' was dangerous for his career, he engaged in a series of sexual affairs – 'love is alright if you lose no time', he once said – even almost from the start of his marriage. Margaret bore five children with him and the couple remained married and affectionate until her death in 1941, but she preferred to stay in Wales and his career was centred in London with only occasional (and fewer and fewer) trips back as the years passed. There were a series of affairs both in Wales and London: Mrs Lizzie Jones in a local choir, Mrs Timothy Davies, his landlady in London, Mrs Catherine Edwards, who claimed he had fathered her child, and, perhaps finally, Frances Stevenson, whom he hired as a governess for his youngest daughter Megan in 1912 and who was to live more or less openly with him for 30 years before they married after Margaret's death. Frances was 25 years younger than he was and their liaison was an open secret, known to all at Westminster and to Margaret and the couple's children, who hated her for it, but never revealed in the press. Frances Stevenson's diary indicates that they first became lovers – their 'marriage' – on 21 January 1913, three days before the Lloyd Georges celebrated their silver wedding anniversary amid much public celebration.

In her memoir long after his death, Frances wrote about what first attracted her to him: '[I] instantly fell under the sway of his electric personality. I listened to his silver voice, observed his mastery over his audience. He seemed to establish a personal relationship immediately with every member of it and … I felt myself in some mysterious way drawn into the orbit of his influence … when [his eyes] scrutinized yours, convinced you they understood all the workings of your heart and mind. But what distinguished him from all other men was a magnetism that made my heart leap, swept aside my judgment, producing an excitement which seemed to permeate my whole being.'[11] Lloyd George's adultery was widely known at

Westminster – hence his nickname – he was fortunate that the press, or more likely the proprietors, did not choose to focus on such indiscretions.

But it was a financial scandal, which was widely reported and dragged on for nearly eighteen months, that came closest to toppling Lloyd George's career in 1912. It was money that nearly did for him just as receipts from the sale of honours a decade later played its part in ousting him. The Marconi affair arose after he, as Chancellor of the Exchequer, Alexander Murray, the Chief Whip, and Sir Rufus Isaacs, the Attorney General, agreed to buy shares in the American Marconi telegraph company from Isaacs's brother Godfrey, days before the British Marconi company was publicly announced to be entering a major deal with the British government to build six long-range radio stations across the Empire.

The deal for Lloyd George was to be a thousand shares at £2 each, for which he could pay later, arranged by Godfrey Isaacs who was a director of the American company. Two days later, when the deal went through and when the American company's shares then became publicly available on the British stock exchange, they quickly reached £4. Some of the money went to Liberal Party funds and some of the profits allowed the men to buy more shares (on which they soon lost money as the market dropped), but the story soon leaked to the press and the ministers floundered desperately as they tried to cover up or excuse what they had done.

If the insider trading arrangement was not strictly illegal at the time – the American and British companies were separate entities – it certainly looked disreputable. Murray, who had bought shares for the Liberal Party as well as some for himself, resigned and went abroad to Bogota in South America, well beyond the reach of any inquisition. Before going he was given the quaint Scottish title of Master of Elibank. The shares he had bought for himself, largely to replenish depleted family finances, actually lost money, so his good name was besmirched without gaining financial reward. His telegrams from Colombia apologising for being unable to return to face the music led to raucous Tory jeers of 'Bogota' when Lloyd George and Isaacs rose to speak in the chamber. Elibank did return, however, and he was to play a pivotal role in the Gregory saga in 1919.

A select committee analysed the affair and divided on party lines, which meant that Lloyd George and Isaacs were cleared. Even so, the Chancellor had to give an abject apology to the Commons when the report was debated: 'I acted thoughtlessly. I acted carelessly. I acted mistakenly. But I acted innocently. I acted openly and I acted honestly.'[12] The only people he had let down, he claimed, were his political friends and supporters. So, Lloyd George got away with it. But the whole episode left a stain on his reputation: to adultery and sexual liaisons, financial chicanery was added. He had not acted openly or honestly. His behaviour had been lamentable, Asquith told the King and it was yet more evidence that 'the little Welsh attorney' was both shifty and untrustworthy.

Lloyd George's biographer John Grigg pointed out that it was not his first financial imbroglio: in the 1890s he had lost money investing in Patagonian gold mining shares. He was always desperate to bolster his resources. In the days before MPs were first paid in 1911, he had had to rely on income from his Welsh solicitors' office in Criccieth and on whatever commission he could earn from elsewhere, such as £1,000 for helping arrange the purchase of the *Daily News* for George Cadbury[13] in 1901, a sum off which Lloyd George and his family lived for five years. He lacked the inherited, landed or commercial wealth that he saw all around him in the Commons.

By 1912, however, Lloyd George's finances were less perilous: he earned a salary of £5,000 a year as Chancellor of the Exchequer, but it was not enough. Grigg, who was generally sympathetic to his subject, wrote: 'Lloyd George is open to special reproach for his part in the business. It cannot be seemly for a Chancellor of the Exchequer to gamble in shares, as he did, even when the dealings are completely above board as in this case they were not. The minister with chief responsibility for the nation's finances is expected to maintain certain standards and playing the market is obviously not a proper form of activity.'

Roy Hattersley, Lloyd George's most recent biographer, a former minister himself, of course, wrote: 'He had escaped the consequences of behaviour which was disreputable though not dishonest as he had so often escaped the consequences of personal folly. He was not an introspective man, but Marconi – and the risk of disgrace – must have made him wonder no matter how briefly if the time had come to act with greater circumspection. If he seriously considered treading the straight and narrow path, he quickly discarded the idea. Conformity was not in his character. The rules were for ordinary mortals.'[14]

It was just as well that he escaped formal censure because four years later Lloyd George was the government's indispensable man – and he knew it as he deplored Asquith's woeful inactivity, the war's drift and the consequent loss of British lives. His discontent with the conduct of the war started early in 1915 as he clashed repeatedly with Kitchener over the field marshal's inflexibility and complacency. There was a whole range of sparks including, ludicrously, over the admission of nonconformist chaplains to the army as well as Anglican ones, which the deeply conservative Kitchener opposed. Lloyd George prevailed there as a Welsh division was now created composed of troops who wanted to attend chapel and be ministered to by chaplains of their own denominations. He backed Churchill in searching for a strategic way to end the stalemate on the Western Front, which ultimately resulted in the disastrous Gallipoli campaign at the other end of Europe on the Dardanelles in 1915 – for which Churchill rather than Lloyd George carried the can after its failure.

In May 1915, the Tories announced that they would no longer support the Liberal government over the conduct of the war, and, to maintain a common purpose, Asquith reluctantly conceded the creation of a coalition government with the opposition taking some of the more junior ministries in the still Liberal-led cabinet. Asquith clearly hated taking in the Tories, who had formed such a baleful opposition to his government in peacetime: 'To seem to welcome into the intimacy of the political household, strange, alien, hitherto hostile figures,' he wrote privately, 'is a most intolerable task.'[15] But it had to be done.

Lloyd George became Minister of Munitions, a seemingly junior post compared to the chancellorship, but clearly a vital one in the context of the war. It was an opportunity to demonstrate his energy and organisational skills and to prove that he was right to argue for a more dynamic approach to the conduct of the war. Industry was mobilised and reset, trade unions were squared to accept new working practices, and unskilled workers such as women were to staff the munitions factories. Production was immediately ramped up. Supplies which took a year to produce in 1914 were soon being turned out in three weeks, shells and ammunition were pouring out of factories: 70,000 shells a month in May 1915 became 120,000 by September and 238,000 by January 1916. The department also expanded from one room in Whitehall Gardens with a table and two chairs (one occupied by Frances Stevenson) to a staff of 12,000 by 1916. Lloyd George recruited the ablest civil servants he could find to organise the department: 'men with push and go', ready to cut corners and work long hours to direct and organise the war effort.

It still was not enough. Military disasters continued and even got worse, culminating in the Battle of the Somme in the summer and autumn of 1916 – 450,000 British killed and wounded for seven miles gained over four months of attrition, among them many of the enthusiastic young volunteers of 1914. Ever more men were needed, and the armed forces were running out of willing recruits. Lloyd George's frustration and exasperation were on open display in a speech in the Commons in December 1915: 'Too late moving here, too late moving there, too late in coming to this decision, too late in starting with enterprises, too late in preparing! In this war the footsteps of the Allied forces have been dogged by the mocking spectre of "too late" and unless we quicken our movements, damnation will fall on the sacred cause for which so much gallant blood has flowed.'[16]

The Liberal Party was divided over the introduction of conscription – Lloyd George was pushing for it from late 1915 – but eventually, in May 1916, Asquith conceded that it had to be done: how many of these pressed men would be marching to their deaths? Such losses deeply worried Lloyd George and led him into prolonged arguments with the generals on the Western Front throughout the course of the war. Haig disliked and distrusted Lloyd George ('shifty and unreliable'), and Sir William Robertson, the Chief of the Imperial General Staff (head of the army), described Lloyd George as 'an underbred swine' in 1917 in a letter to General Launcelot Kiggell, Haig's chief of staff.[17] The hostility was mutual, though Lloyd George waited until his war memoirs after Haig's death to express it fully: 'he was intellectually and temperamentally unequal to the command of an army of millions'.[18] Yet, much as he tried, Lloyd George was unable to get rid of either man.

In June 1916, Lord Kitchener was drowned at sea after the ship he was travelling on for a secret mission to Russia hit a mine off the Orkney Islands, and thus Lloyd George took his place as Minister of War. At much the same time, Asquith commissioned him to negotiate with the parties in Ireland ways to resolve the Home Rule issue. It was a sign of his growing indispensability across the government, but it did not reconcile him to the way the war was being conducted. He spoke frequently of resigning, but in late November, following talks with Andrew Bonar Law, the Conservative leader now a fellow minister, and Edward Carson, the Irish Unionist member of the government, the three of them sent a draft memorandum to Asquith proposing that a supreme war cabinet should be set up. It would comprise just three people taking the decisions on the conduct of the war, of whom Lloyd George would be one, but not the Prime Minister, though Asquith would continue in post. It was pretty clear, at least to Bonar Law, what the purpose was: '(it) boiled down to one simple proposal to put Asquith out and himself in'.

Asquith was bound to reject the proposal of being in office but not in power, but he did not initially do so. Then he had second thoughts. He wrote to Lloyd George: 'In my opinion, whatever changes are made ... the Prime Minister must be its chairman. He cannot be relegated to the position of an arbiter in the background, or a referee in Cabinet.'[19]

After a weekend's cogitation down on the Kent coast at Walmer Castle, Asquith once more thought again and suggested that Lloyd George could head the war cabinet so long as he himself retained 'supreme and effective control' as prime minister. He thought he had Lloyd George's agreement, but the following morning a full account of the negotiations appeared in *The Times*, much to Asquith's fury. He blamed the fact that Lloyd George had returned to his office and met Lord Northcliffe, the newspaper's proprietor. Lloyd George was a leaker but may have been blameless on this particular occasion. The words in the newspaper that Asquith was disqualified from leading the new cabinet on grounds of temperament stung and the Prime Minister demanded an apology from his errant minister, who insisted the story was just a misrepresentation.

Asquith then met his Liberal cabinet colleagues who pledged him their support, and a similar delegation of Conservative ministers who also gave him their loyalty. Overnight, Lloyd George and Bonar Law met in a taxi outside the Berkeley Hotel, where Lloyd George had been dining, with the governor of the Bank of England and drove to a meeting with Max Aitken, an influential Tory backbencher – like Bonar Law, a Canadian – and budding newspaper proprietor, to discuss the crisis. The following morning, Lloyd George sought to stiffen the wavering Tory leader's spine and precipitate the downfall of the Prime Minister: 'The life of the country depends on resolute action by you now!'[20]

Asquith dug his heels in and insisted that he must chair the war cabinet and would decide who its members would be: 'any other arrangement ... would be in my experience impractical and incompatible with the Prime Minister's final and supreme control'. That morning, Lloyd George and Bonar Law told him that they would resign, and then the Liberal and Tory ministers who had pledged their support the previous day reversed their positions and said they would not serve in a government without the two ministers. Cornered and abandoned, Asquith had no alternative but to resign. 'It is a great blow to me and will I fear buck up the Germans,' the King wrote in his diary.

Asquith refused to serve under either Bonar Law or Lloyd George: 'What is the proposal? That I who have held first place for eight years should be asked to take a secondary position?' he expostulated. And, with Bonar Law as leader of the Conservatives declining to take the role himself, Lloyd George became prime minister. He had effectively engineered a governmental palace coup in the middle of a war. As his colleague and friend Winston Churchill would write in an article for *Nash's Magazine* in 1928: 'Speedy victory was demanded and the statesman was judged by the merciless test of results. The vehement, contriving, resourceful, nimble-leaping Lloyd George seemed to offer a brighter hope or at any rate a more passionate effort.'[21]

The question of Lloyd George's motives in engineering the ousting of Asquith has remained controversial and has been debated by historians ever since. His supporters claim, as he did, that Asquith was acting disinterestedly to save the war, which was drifting to defeat. Opponents allege he was motivated by opportunism and personal ambition against a weakened but honourable prime minister who had supported him over the People's Budget before the war, defended him during the Marconi scandal and promoted him selflessly to accelerate the war effort.

The consequences of the coup, however, were far-reaching, and it split the Liberal Party irretrievably between Asquithians and Lloyd Georgeites, contributing to the fact that Lloyd George himself was the last Liberal prime minister. It cemented his reputation for deviousness and underhand dealing. And Lloyd George's need to raise money to keep his faction going led directly to the employment of Arthur Maundy Gregory and his novel fundraising techniques.

The economist John Maynard Keynes left an indelible portrait of the Asquiths two nights after the Prime Minister's resignation when he went to dinner with them. He told Virginia Woolf: 'though Asquith himself was quite unmoved, Margot started crying into the soup'.

Meanwhile, Frances Stevenson faithfully recorded the new prime minister's inner thoughts: 'It was in fact owing to the action of the Conservatives that LG was made Prime Minister. History will confirm that he did not desire this office. He had not indeed that confidence … of his power to do all that was needed of him. "I wonder if I can do it?" he said, half to himself, as we sat in a gloomy War Office after his return from Buckingham Palace from the ceremony of kissing hands.'[22]

This maneuvering would surely have been of interest to Maundy Gregory, a man without power and with very little influence, derided and dismissed by those with whom he was dealing at the intelligence service as if he was of no importance and little use. Yet within four years he would suddenly have become very useful indeed to the Prime Minister, arguably one of the most influential men in the country.

6. THE MAN WHO WON THE WAR

He is a blatant intriguer and every word he says is in the nature of an offer to 'do a deal'. He neither likes you nor dislikes you. You are a mere instrument, one among many, sometimes of value, sometimes not worth picking up.
BEATRICE WEBB ON LLOYD GEORGE

The process by which Maundy Gregory went from square bashing in the Guards Depot at Caterham to selling honours for the Prime Minister remains somewhat obscure. He was demobilised at the start of February 1919, just short of three months after the end of the war, and must have been scouting around for something to do. His association with the Keen-Hargreaveses seems to have ended and *Mayfair and Town Topics* had expired early in the war. It is not known when a new publishing venture occurred to him. It would be very different in appearance but very similar in style, with added partisan politics and a similar way of funding. Set up in August 1919, six months after he was demobbed, it was launching at a very febrile political time. The seeds of the instability to come were sown by the way Lloyd George came to power as head of a wartime coalition. In many ways it was surprising the Liberal

Party lasted as long as it did, but it brought in its wake a reputation of corruption and sleaze. And Maundy Gregory would come to typify that sleaze.

As a wartime prime minister, Lloyd George was isolated in Downing Street and in need of advisers and sympathisers. Most of his Liberal colleagues in the Commons had been shocked by the coup and its suddenness, and a majority of them remained loyal to the ousted Asquith. As such, Lloyd George was dependent on the Tories, who he had spent much of the previous decade fighting against, to stay in power. His wife Margaret, who did not like London and felt isolated living in the dark and gloom of Downing Street, chose to remain at home in north Wales and so he was reliant on Frances Stevenson and a small coterie of friends, more acquaintances, mainly from outside politics for companionship.

Lloyd George himself was drawing away from Wales. His mentor, Uncle Richard Lloyd, died from bowel cancer in February 1917, only two months after he had become prime minister, and he had little time to spare for grief. Even so, Uncle Lloyd was one of the few people to capture his attention away from himself. As Frances wrote in her diary: 'D is very upset and will be until after the funeral takes place. It is a great strain for him coming at this time. He will miss the old man very much and he says I am his only devoted friend now; that I shall have to fill the old man's place. God knows I shall try. D needs so much someone who will not hesitate to give him everything and if necessary give up everything and whose sole thought and occupation is for him. Without that it is hopeless to try and serve him.'[1]

As a measure of Lloyd George's neediness, Stevenson noted a few weeks later that he had asked her to die with him if he should be killed, though he tried to avoid physical danger and left London during at least one threatened Zeppelin air raid. 'He begged me not to stay behind but for both of us to go together and I promised to do so unless I had any children of his to claim me … I shall go too and his end will be my end.'[2]

The imperative to win the war may have curbed Lloyd George's previous pugnacious radicalism and he was increasingly reliant on friends from a very different world to his own, men who could get things done, with successful business backgrounds such as Sir Eric Geddes, a Tory businessman recruited to improve rail transport links to the Western Front, Sir Joseph Maclay, a Scottish shipping magnate called in to supervise merchant shipping during the war, and Lord Rhondda, a collieries owner brought in as minister for food control as the government's president of the local government board. All these and others, such as Sir Albert Stanley, brought in from running the London Underground Electric Railways Company to head the Board of Trade, were not party politicians – indeed were often impatient with them – and were of course unelected and not answerable to parliament.

There was now a five-man supreme war cabinet (not three as Lloyd George had proposed to Asquith) headed by the new prime minister: Bonar Law, the Tory leader, was chancellor and Lord Curzon, the high Tory former Viceroy of India, who was leader of the House of Lords and would become air minister. Arthur Henderson, the leader of the Labour Party (and first-ever Labour cabinet minister) and Lord Milner, who had spent much of his life as an influential colonial administrator, were both named as ministers without portfolio, able, in cabinet secretary Hankey's words, to devote all their time and energy to the central direction of the war effort, freed from departmental responsibilities. The composition of the group amounted to two Tories, one Labour, one Liberal and one Liberal Unionist (Milner, an opponent of Lloyd George's People's Budget and Irish Home Rule as it happened and contemptuous of party politics), two of whom were in the House of Lords. They would be joined later by Winston Churchill (still then a Liberal) and General Jan Smuts of South Africa, who had fought against the British in the Boer War and whose role was supposed to be as a voice from the colonies.

Equally important to the administration was the creation of the cabinet office under Sir Maurice Hankey and his deputy Thomas Jones who served to extend Lloyd George's grip across the government. The combined effect of this secretariat and the businessmen appointed to oversee specific tasks was to diminish the influence of the House of Commons while creating a stream-lined decision-making body, many of whose members were not directly answerable to parliament. They were, in Jones's words: 'fluid persons moving among people who matter'. Hankey and Jones would later serve governments of all political complexions throughout the inter-war years for twenty-two and nineteen years respectively.

There was also effectively a think-tank in huts in the garden of 10 Downing Street (hence popularly known as the 'Garden Suburb') made up of various specialists and experts, an Oxford professor, MPs occasionally, the statistician Joseph Davies, and Philip Kerr, an imperialist and foreign affairs specialist and protégé of Milner. Others in the coterie around Lloyd George included Waldorf Astor, the fabulously wealthy American Tory Unionist MP who owned *The Observer* newspaper and was sometimes mockingly described as a 'sentimental socialist'.[3] Some of their advisors were men of integrity, others less so: they came to be regarded as cronies of Lloyd George. Mrs Astor complained to Jones in December 1917 that 'men of moral worth' like her husband were being used by the Prime Minister as 'virtuous window-dressers while in the background he works through Sutherland, Northcliffe and Co'. Jones responded that Lloyd George could not be changed and that he was the one man possible to lead the country.[4] Lord Northcliffe, the owner of the *Daily Mail* and *The Times*, had done much to destabilise Asquith's government over the shells shortages issue in 1915, and was placed in charge of propaganda by Lloyd George, but soon fell out with him after allegedly being denied a cabinet post and subsequently became a bitter enemy, denounced by the Prime Minister in 1919 as having 'diseased vanity'. Controlling 40 per cent of the national press as he did, Northcliffe was not a good enemy to make.

Max Aitken, who was Canadian, another Tory and owner of the *Daily Express,* and had also advised Lloyd George during the coup, was ennobled as Lord Beaverbrook two days afterwards. Then there was Captain Freddie Guest, the Liberal Chief Whip in the Commons, and Basil Zaharoff, the mysterious millionaire arms dealer, Turkish by birth, French by citizenship, English by imitation and inclination. He was a friend of Lloyd George, and would eventually, remarkably, end up being awarded the Grand Cross Order of the Bath, normally a military honour, for whatever services he rendered the Prime Minister.

And then, possibly, there was Maundy Gregory, desperate to prove himself helpful, who, ironically, would end up without any British honour himself.

His role, probably self-devised, was to make himself useful in whatever way his masters wished. One of the ways in which he may have done this was in the curious case of Victor Grayson, whose story remains murky more than a century on because he completely and sensationally disappeared in 1920. He remains the only British politician, certainly in modern times, to vanish, apparently forever, leaving not a trace behind.

Grayson, a fiery young Independent Labour politician before the First World War, had been elected briefly at a by-election aged 25 as the MP for Colne Valley in West Yorkshire, serving between 1907 and 1910. Some even saw him as a potential future leader but his lively rhetoric and refusal to toe the party line had made him enemies, and after his defeat at the next general election, he had drifted into alcoholism and, ultimately, poverty.

He had emigrated to Australia and then New Zealand, and during the war volunteered enthusiastically for the New Zealand army, briefly serving on the Western Front. But it was quickly recognised that his real usefulness was as a propagandist, speaking forcefully, unlike many of his former Labour colleagues, whom he denounced as traitors, in favour of the war at meetings across Britain during its latter stages. He appears to have been sponsored by a body called the National War Aims Committee, which in March 1918, writing from 12 Downing Street, asked him to address a meeting in Huddersfield, near his old constituency.

That oratory, together with his pro-war journalism, brought him to the attention of the government's propagandists and to Basil Thomson, who may well have put Gregory on Grayson's trail to keep an eye on him, get to know him and help him out. This is all conjectural since no publicly available records exist. But Grayson certainly knew people such as Winston Churchill, who by then was minister for munitions and had been friendly towards him in Churchill's radical pre-war phase. He had even written an article headlined 'Why I think Winston Churchill is Great' for the *Sydney Mirror* in 1915 at a time when Churchill was scarcely a popular figure in Australia as the mastermind of the Gallipoli disaster in which so many Australians had been killed.

The government paid at least Grayson's expenses for his propaganda efforts. A letter exists in which he wrote of 'my original grant and financial arrangements ... you know what our verbal agreement was for'. Certainly, somehow, he acquired a degree of wealth and was set up in a comfortable fourth floor apartment in an exclusive block called Georgian House in Bury Street, behind Fortnum and Mason, between St. James's and Piccadilly in central London. Hilda Porter, the manager of the apartments, told David Clark, Grayson's biographer, in the 1980s that two men in uniform brought him a package every fortnight and that Gregory was a frequent visitor. The uniform the visitors wore, which she took to be official, may have been the one that Gregory had designed for his employees to mirror those of parliamentary officials.

It was from the apartment that Grayson would disappear suddenly in the autumn of 1920 in the company of two unidentified men, apparently never to be seen again. Did Gregory, whom Porter said Grayson did not like, provide him with funds from the government, to subsidise his lifestyle and maybe disappearance, in return for his efforts during the war?

One of the theories about his disappearance has long been that he was lured from his apartment by the men and subsequently murdered. This theory gained some credence because an artist named George Flemwell, who knew Grayson a little, subsequently said that he had seen him being rowed up river at Thames Ditton just after his disappearance, towards the island where Gregory had his villa. Was Gregory therefore somehow involved in his abduction and murder?

The former Labour MP David Clark, who has made a lifetime's research into Grayson, believes the answer may be more prosaic: that he simply disappeared from public view to take a new identity and start a new life, perhaps set up with a job and a house in Kent. One or two former colleagues who knew him better than Flemwell attested to having caught brief glimpses of Grayson in London during the 1920s and 30s. Clark believes that he was probably killed during an air raid in 1941, not murdered twenty years earlier.

Disappearance to start his life again would seem a likelier, if less dramatic, outcome. Grayson's political career was over, his bridges burned with the Labour Party and his usefulness to the government likely ended after the war. He had lost his wife, who had died in childbirth in 1918, and he was a heavy drinker, but there was no reason to kill him. He was certainly not a Bolshevik. A fresh start with a reduced or one-off subsidy perhaps appealed to both sides.

Whatever the truth of what happened to Grayson, Gregory seems to have had some involvement with him, probably passing on funds to enable him to disappear after his wartime help. Maybe it was one of Gregory's useful chores – it sounds rather more likely and that would have been more in keeping with his fastidious and secretive reputation as one of the government's unofficial helpers.

Among the others more officially hovering around the Prime Minister, who would be implicated in the honours touting, was a smooth-faced Scottish civil servant called William Sutherland, who had been an advisor at the Board of Trade early in Lloyd George's ministerial career and had helped the drafting of the original pensions legislation before the People's Budget. His career had shadowed Lloyd George's, and the two men were close so that when the Prime Minister had gone to Number 10, Sutherland followed him as policy adviser and private secretary and, most crucially, as a nascent official press officer: probably the first ever. His role was to liaise with the journalists of the Parliamentary Lobby system and to build up relations with their newspaper editors as a genuine, though anonymous 'source' to influence their coverage in his master's favour and, of course, to feed back what they were saying to the Prime Minister. As such, he became known to the correspondents as 'Bronco Bill' after the rumbustious cowboy character in contemporary early silent film westerns because of his role in rounding up and subduing the press.[5]

This was shown damagingly in the summer of 1917 when Christopher Addison, the loyalist Liberal minister then in charge of Lloyd George's former portfolio as munitions minister, negotiated the end of a damaging strike in munitions factories involving 200,000 men across the country.[6] Somehow, the version that was released to the press was that Lloyd George himself had personally negotiated the settlement without mention of Addison at all. That would not be the last time such a thing happened, of course: a prime minister taking credit for a colleague's actions. The minister was so furious that the Prime Minister had to appear in the Commons to correct the record. He told Addison privately that Sutherland would have to go, but he never did and continued in his role.

The following year he would smear General Maurice, who exposed troop shortages on the Western Front.

Today, Sutherland might be called a spin doctor, and, like some later practitioners, he was clearly not above manipulation, bluster and bullying to put his boss in a better light and denigrate and spread false stories about his enemies or even his colleagues. Shades of Malcolm Tucker from *The Thick of It* 90 years later, right down to the Glaswegian accent. He was, said Lord Riddell, the proprietor of the *News of the World* and friend of Lloyd George, 'an amusing, cynical dog'. Others were less complimentary: 'an odious fellow … some sort of political parasite of Ll.G's', said Hankey, the cabinet secretary. 'Really filthy' wrote the poet Hilaire Belloc in a satiric verse. Tom Cullen described him as 'noted for his foul mouth, uncouth manners and outsize cigars'.[7] Like Gregory, Sutherland was shameless in touting honours: he was said to be regularly seen touring the gentlemen's clubs of London offering knighthoods for sale.

Sutherland was knighted in 1918, elected to parliament as a Lloyd George-supporting Liberal for Argyllshire in 1919 and served briefly in cabinet under the Prime Minister as Chancellor of the Duchy of Lancaster in 1922. After his defeat in the 1924 election, he took up interests in the south Yorkshire coalfields, owning the Woolley collieries near Barnsley and, philanthropically, donating the Sir William Sutherland Cup for the Scottish junior shinty championships (a team sport similar to field hockey, now played mainly in the Highlands).

The combined effect of this new way of government was increasingly to move Lloyd George away from parliamentary scrutiny. His focus and his chief battles were against the military hierarchy, in particular Douglas Haig and William Robertson. The dislike and distrust were mutual: Lloyd George worried increasingly about the mounting number of deaths in the war, caused, he believed, by the generals' reckless and ill-conceived strategy; Haig and Robertson were aggravated by civilian interference in their campaign. Haig was particularly aggrieved by the new prime minister asking the French Marshal Foch privately what he thought of his British counterparts. They resented his forceful suggestion that there should be a unified Allied command on the Western Front, led by the French, and both generals themselves were adept at waging political warfare against the Prime Minister.

Instead of improved morale under a vigorous new prime minister, however, 1917 became a year of defeats. Lloyd George backed a French plan by General Robert Nivelle (perhaps helped by the fact that Nivelle spoke English) which culminated in a costly disaster and led to mutinies throughout the French army. The Prime Minister was far less enthusiastic about Haig's plan that summer to punch a way through the German lines in Flanders and capture the Belgian coast, but he was overruled in cabinet and the offensive became bogged down in the course of an unusually wet autumn which turned the already battered ground around the flat lands of Ypres into a quagmire. Far from reaching the coast, the army struggled to capture the village of Passchendaele on a hillside just four miles outside Ypres and that only at enormous cost. For much of the rest of his life, Lloyd George struggled to escape any of the responsibility he had for the disaster and to place the blame on Haig.

1918 at last saw the tide turning as American troops arrived in strength in France and began to fight. A German spring offensive to forestall the increase in Allied troops burst through the British lines but petered out in April. It was fortunate that it did, for had it succeeded the government would probably have fallen. Even so, it led to an accusation by General Frederick Maurice, the previous director of military operations and an ally of the recently deposed Robertson, in a letter to *The Times* and other newspapers to allege that Lloyd George had deliberately lied in the Commons about the strength of the army, and ministers had blocked reinforcements from reaching the front after Passchendaele. Asquith and his Liberal supporters called a censure debate amid a crisis which seemed likely to bring the government down, but in the event, Lloyd George made a storming speech to refute the Maurice allegations. He claimed that ministerial statements had been based on Maurice's own figures, previously given to the government, and, in any event, there were more men at the Front than there had been a year earlier. The crisis was seen off, but it could only have increased Lloyd George's paranoia that influential forces were out to get him. Even though he won the vote, 98 Liberals voted with Asquith. The Liberal split was becoming irreparable, but Lloyd George's position at the head of government was now unassailable.

In 1918, despite the war, the government carried through several major domestic reforms. The Representation of the People Act nearly tripled the size of the electorate, from 8 million to 21 million out of a population just short of 40 million. The vote was extended to all men above the age of 21 and to women aged over 30 with a property qualification (the age anomaly would be abolished in 1928) which substantially changed the franchise and gave more than 8 million women a vote in national elections for the first time. At the same time, the Education Act, pioneered by the academic H. A. L. Fisher, raised the school leaving age from twelve to fourteen and prohibited fees being charged for state primary school pupils. More crucially, the act transferred the majority of educational funding from local sources to the central government as a means of equalising national payment and pension rates for teachers. There were also reforms in housing, agriculture and health provision: all measures to produce the much-promised land fit for heroes to live in, though several were only slowly and partially implemented because of post-war economic conditions. The long-running sore of Ireland, however, remained impervious to solution.

Following the Maurice debate, Lloyd George and his associates' thoughts turned to how to win a general election without having a party powerbase. It was increasingly likely that the Prime Minister would have to negotiate a continuation of the wartime coalition with his Tory supporters. In late August 1918, a meeting was convened by Lloyd George with a range of advisers back at Criccieth. Some remembered it as a bathing expedition since the Prime Minister, clad in his pink trunks, led the group swimming in the River Dwyfor on one of the days. Present were Lord Milner, Leo Amery, who was now a Tory MP in Birmingham, Hankey and a number of the garden suburb group. They decided there would need to be a coalition based on a programme of social reform, including public health.

The war was still expected to last for at least another year, maybe two, for no one foresaw the speed of the German collapse in 1918, but the Conservatives proved surprisingly receptive to the idea of continuing the coalition into an election and beyond. This was partly due to the leadership's fears of the Prime Minister's popularity and charisma once the war was won and partly as a pragmatic way of keeping the Tories together even though they still disapproved of some of Lloyd George's policy agenda. The war had changed a lot and there was a sense that a more activist social programme, including more intervention in the post-war economy, would be necessary: problems would be better solved by a united government with a strong majority in which the Tory Party would have a large say. As Bonar Law, the Tory leader, told his colleague Arthur Balfour in a letter: 'That would ... I am inclined to think be not a bad thing for our party and a good thing for the Nation ... Our party on the old lines will never have any future in this country.'[8]

By the late summer, the German army was in retreat until resistance finally collapsed and the high command sued for peace, agreed at an armistice on 11 November. In the last few months, as victory became assured, Lloyd George's rhetoric became increasingly pugnacious against the Germans: 'He is out for blood and wants to give Germany a thorough hiding', Hankey wrote in his diary in late August 1918. 'In fact he actually used the term "destroy Germany" as punishment for the atrocities by land and sea.'[9] He would be the man to secure the peace. And 'the Man who Won the War'.

The coalition scheme proved relatively easy to negotiate with the Tories, although there was some friction over the allocation of seats. Among the candidates who pledged to support the post-war coalition were 150 Liberals who would not be opposed by Tory candidates. The pro-coalition candidates were issued with signed letters of approval, derisively described as 'coupons' by Asquith – a name which stuck – and they all signed up to a manifesto which included modified Liberal policies, including free trade, Welsh disestablishment of the Anglican church in Wales (the policy Lloyd George had first come to local prominence supporting thirty years earlier) and even Irish Home Rule, which the Tories had so bitterly opposed before the war. There was a half-hearted attempt to entice Asquith himself back with the offer of the future Lord Chancellorship, but the coalitionists probably knew he would refuse, and he did.

The coalition was formally agreed on 12 November, the day after the Armistice was signed, and the general election was held a month later – an extraordinarily quick time following the war. Lloyd George was the campaign's greatest asset as 'the Man who Won the War', promising to build homes and make the country fit for heroes in a raft of social reforms. It was what the country wanted to hear. The outcome was a huge majority for the coalition whose candidates won 520 seats, including 136 Liberals and a few Labour men – all elected on a low turnout of only 57 per cent.

Asquith's Liberal supporters won just 26 seats, and the former prime minister himself was defeated by 2,000 votes after a rough campaign in his East Fife constituency, which he had scarcely bothered to visit for years. Placards there claimed: 'Asquith nearly lost you the war. Are you going to let him spoil the peace?' and he was baited at a public meeting by a gang of former soldiers.

It seemed a personal triumph. Bonar Law told Lord Beaverbrook: 'He can be prime minister for life if he likes.' Lloyd George was, however, now a premier without a party.

7. THE HONOURS TOUT

*It keeps politics far cleaner than any other
method of raising funds.*
LLOYD GEORGE

Lloyd George might have been unassailable as a result of the coupon election victory, but he was not in charge of his own majority. His administration was supported by three times as many Conservatives as Liberals, and the Tories had their own separate identity with their own leadership in place in cabinet. However charming and charismatic he could naturally be when he tried, many of them did not like him. They rightly thought him slippery and many of them had moral reservations about him. In the words of Stanley Baldwin, a rising star of the Tory Party and Lloyd George's future nemesis: he had a 'morally disintegrating effect on all whom he had to deal with'.[1] Moreover, the Prime Minister was constrained in what he could do: his opponents in the coalition could dethrone him whenever they wished to do so. Lloyd George was in government but not entirely in power.

He reacted defiantly: 'I have been told by some of my friends: "you are in favour of progressive legislation but you are surrounded by a reactionary bodyguard."

If reactionaries make it impossible to carry out a progressive policy I shall come back to the people and ask them to decide.' But the Commons seemed an isolated place: the main opposition was formed by the Labour Party which now had 63 MPs and they wanted nothing to do with him. The party had pulled out of the wartime coalition as soon as the Armistice was signed and formally rebuffed approaches by Lloyd George's supporters to continue in alliance. As George Bernard Shaw definitively declared at a party meeting to discuss it: 'Nothing doing!' Anyway, the Prime Minister concluded, they were just Bolsheviks and extreme pacifists. Standing at the dispatch box: 'I felt as I looked in front of me that I was addressing the Trades Union Congress. Then when I turned round I felt I was speaking to a Chamber of Commerce.'[2] He still saw himself as a Liberal, but so did the Asquithian Liberals, and they wanted nothing to do with him either.

Lloyd George was going to spend the first six months of 1919 out of the country at the Versailles Peace Conference, treading the world stage in a way that national politicians had rarely done before and carving up the continent with other leaders of the victorious allies, the US President Woodrow Wilson,[3] Georges Clemenceau of France and Vittorio Orlando of Italy. It was a novel experience, even for colonial powers ('Who are the Slovaks? I can't seem to place them,' the Prime Minister was heard muttering at one point). But it meant that all his energies were spent negotiating, debating and schmoozing with the other victorious men of power – 'Mr Lloyd George was certain to be at the top of his form, full of chaff intermingled with shrewd comments,' noted one British Tory. And, as it happened, he was playing down all the pre-election speeches he and others had made about putting the Kaiser on trial or executing him out of hand. In the end, Wilhelm II would be exiled to live out his days in the Netherlands.

Back home, the job of raising money as a fighting fund for a new party after the coalition was given to the party whips. It was calculated that, ideally, the Lloyd George Fund, as it came to be called, would need to raise £3–4million in order to set up a party organisation and loyal candidates to fight and win an election. And the man they contracted to do it was Arthur Maundy Gregory.

It is not known precisely how and why Gregory was chosen since he was neither a prominent public figure nor a party stalwart. His name was apparently originally suggested by Alick Murray, the Master of Elibank, who was the man who had disappeared to Colombia at the height of the Marconi scandal in 1912. Murray had been a genial and well-liked parliamentary fixer as the Liberals' chief whip for Asquith's government until he was forced to resign because of the scandal. According to one journalist contemporary: 'His ample figure and full-moon face, with its fringe of curls, were always a pleasant vision, and he had a persuasive manner that was hard to resist … his chronic good humour soothed many savage breasts.'[4]

Known to all sides as 'the Master', Murray was now back at Westminster, a backstage figure on the lookout to raise party funds, and he must have known or heard of Gregory because of his undercover war work, editorship of *Mayfair* or probably through his parliamentary sources. But Gregory was ideally placed to tap up his contacts or those he had written about, and they, in turn, having already paid to appear in the magazine's pages, must have been thought ripe for plucking again for an honour. That would have been Murray's reasoning. He himself, having raised money for the Liberals during the Constitutional crisis ten years earlier and the two general elections in 1910, knew how to play on people's weakness for knighthoods and also the technique of dangling the prospect in front of them.

The euphemism which got them opening their cheque books was 'anticipating the favours of the Crown'. It was an ideal process: they paid the money up front in return for a promise that Gregory, and through him the party, would do its best – though there were no guarantees, of course – to see that their name was put forward for the next announcement. Sometimes cautious donors backdated their cheques until after publication of the next honours list just to make sure that their name did appear. One such was G. S. Marple, a Sheffield manufacturer, who had been approached on a freelance basis by a local Liberal Party worker named Mrs Parish in November 1918. His cheque for £5,000, for a knighthood, was postdated to 7 January, a week after the new year's list was due to appear. It was made out to the chief whip, Captain Guest. And it was accepted without too much scrutiny at the time, though apparently later paid back.

Murray seems to have invited Gregory to visit his family estate in the Scottish Lowlands at Christmas 1918, and the invitation would undoubtedly have been rapidly taken up by the arch crawler, who was always impressed by wealth and power – though the wealth may have been more illusory than real since the reason the Master had decamped to South America was to work for Lord Cowdray's business interests there in order to restore the depleted Murray family's fortunes and preserve their Scottish estate in Selkirkshire. He must have found Gregory to be an ideal candidate: ingratiating, personable in a rather pompous way, venal – and apolitical at least so far as the honours business was concerned. He would be an equal opportunities tout, selling baronetcies and knighthoods for Lloyd George as easily as for the Tories, with whom he had a closer political affinity.

Gregory even had the ideal vehicle for the job: he was setting up a new newspaper. The new publication would now be called *The Whitehall Gazette and St. James's Review*, and it would appear first monthly, then latterly every second month, eventually for the next thirteen years, until December 1932, after which Gregory would be otherwise engaged.

The first edition came out in August 1919, and it looked as much as possible like an official publication and as little as possible like the previous magazine. For a start, it was printed on expensively thick paper between plain, unchanging buff-coloured covers. Unlike *Mayfair* it carried almost no photographs, at least to start with, and virtually no commercial advertising, and its pages had unadorned slabs of words in double columns. Such advertisements as there were looked official: they were for National Savings Certificates (enticingly suggesting a £40 investment would yield £60 in ten years), and appeals for King George's Fund for Sailors (president the Duke of York, the future George VI; contributions to be received by HRH the Duke of Connaught). Others were for Earl Haig's Officers' Association and how to apply to buy land in East Africa through the government. There was also a court and social page consisting entirely of official circulars couched in the traditional formularies ('The Queen has graciously consented to perform the opening ceremony at the New Nurses' Home at Lower Sydenham,' January 1926). The back page was similarly mundane, consisting of a list of the telephone numbers of government departments.

Each issue had a page-sized line drawing cartoon of the sort of ponderousness that looked dated and was going out of fashion in *Punch* magazine even then. Drawn by a cartoonist called Tabard, it usually consisted of a comment on current events couched in mythological or legendary terms – Lloyd George steering the Ship of State, a thundercloud of demons entitled 'Spirit of Bolshevism', each accompanied by a Biblical, Shakespearean or other quotation.

The *Gazette* did regularly carry portraits of the King or other members of the Royal Family. Sometimes these were in colour, and naturally the dashing and eligible Prince of Wales was a particular favourite (for the September–October 1932 issue he was on horseback in uniform as Colonel of the 12th Lancers). The cover price was half a crown,[5] but the paper was mostly circulated around Westminster, to government departments, MPs and ministers, embassies, clubs and hotels, for free. Its income really came, as before, from those who paid to be favourably profiled in what was now called the 'Officials I have Met' slot and for advertising supplements such as those extolling the virtues of Sweden or Spain. In the magazine's first edition, the first celebrity official, naturally enough, was Basil Thomson. These at least followed the style of the *Mayfair* profiles with full-length colour portraits and orotund Gregorian prose ('The chairman of the London and North-Eastern Railway is one of the really busy men in Great Britain ... and it is to be hoped that the day of his retirement may be yet far to seek', April 1926).

Tom Cullen analysed 140 of the profiles and discovered that the largest number, over a third, were businessmen and industrialists, many of whom had done well out of the war and just the sort, perhaps, who might like an honour to enhance their status. Nearly the same percentage were members of parliament, civil servants and civic dignitaries, and the remainder he termed exotics, some of them Indian princes who paid especially well to be included in the *Gazette*.[6]

Other features in the first issue included 'Unpopular Celebrities', a series extolling those Gregory and his editorial line did not like: first, the former King Ferdinand of Bulgaria, who had sided with Germany in the war. Later figures included Eugene V. Debs, the US trade union leader and five-time presidential candidate for the Socialist Party, the Turkish leader Mustapha Kemal, Charles Ponzi of the US-originating fraudulent money raising scheme (though the magazine still described him as 'America's Modern Midas') and Noel Ablett, the Welsh miners' leader.

The first edition had an article by Captain Colin Coote DSO, MP, on the battle of Caporetto on the Italian Front two years earlier (this was presumably the piece for which he was paid £50); Sir Herbert Austin the Birmingham motor manufacturer on the need to standardise car parts and an article on the revolutionary movement in Britain. The magazine also included articles on the Treasury, the London clubs, 'The Auditorium', which was a sort of theatrical round-up and was soon dropped, as was 'The Sportsman', neither of which really lived up to their billing. Many of the articles were too obviously fillers, such as the 'Pithy Sayings' column; 'the Treasury' column, for instance, turned out to be a history of bank notes, and 'The Whitehall Almanack' was a diary of forthcoming events. In the words of Gerald Macmillan: 'It was well-calculated to make the uninitiated believe that here was a publication of wide scope which had official blessing, that the Editor was well and confidentially informed and that he moved in high official and social circles.'[7]

Basil Thomson and Gregory remained close after the war, and it seems that the assistant Metropolitan Police commissioner wrote occasional articles for *The Whitehall Gazette* using the suitably classical pseudonym Gellius after the Roman author Aulus Gellius. It certainly looks like they were the same person. Thomson, like the Gellius who wrote for Gregory, was obsessed by Bolshevism and international Jewry: a not uncommon trope of the day. He wrote in a work called *Queer People*: 'It is inevitable in a country like Russia when the dregs of the population had boiled to the top, a preponderance of Jews would be found among the scum.' Such antisemitism fitted right in with Gregory's editorial line in *The Whitehall Gazette*, which claimed it was fighting 'a consistent and insidious campaign on behalf of monarchy and against the growth of Bolshevism and Communism and their ramifications'. In an early issue in October 1919, it alleged there was a 'conspiracy of the unsuccessful Jews throughout the world ... A confused rabble is pouring into Whitehall from the East End led by Russian Jew tailors ... armed to the teeth with any weapon that comes handy'.[8] They had pockets full of looted diamonds, their hands were suspiciously clean as if they had never done a proper day's work and they became angry if they were asked what were the sources of their income or what they had done in the war.

The original source of funding to set up the magazine was equally obscure, including the finding of an office in close proximity to parliament. Colin Coote, who by then was working in the coalition whips' office and who might have been expected to take an interest in where the money that was paid to him to write articles came from, wrote in his newspaper many years later: 'Gregory was no fool. He never by a word or a look hinted to me where the money came from. That was psychologically quite acute because he knew I had a connection with the whips' office but perceived it would be fatal to try to recruit me as a tout or even as a confidant.'[9]

It probably would not have been Northcliffe, who had fallen out with Lloyd George in a big way, having been denied a place in cabinet that he thought he deserved during the war (he had rather fancied the Air Ministry, the *Daily Mail* having sponsored pioneering pre-war flying races) and whose newspapers, both the *Mail* and *The Times* were henceforth unremittingly hostile to the Prime Minister. It would not have been Horatio Bottomley either since he, too, had fallen out with Lloyd George and had been elected as an Independent MP for Hackney South in the Coupon Election, announcing that he intended to be the unofficial prime minister 'to run the show'. Anyway, he was also busy with his own fraudulent Victory bonds Ponzi scheme which would eventually land him in jail. Maybe it was Beaverbrook, though he too was moving away from Lloyd George towards the Tories. Probably senior Liberals put money into the new project. Gregory hinted as much, although, as with many of his hints and insinuations, it is hard to be sure. If Beaverbrook and Northcliffe had been involved, *The Whitehall Gazette* would surely never have been so deadly dull.

The paper took a robustly reactionary line. It was anti-semitic, anti-Labour and anti-trade unions. They were all in the editor's view linked together in subversion as Socialists, Marxists and Bolsheviks. When the police broke up a demonstration by workers, many of whom would have been war veterans, the *Gazette*, in which case almost certainly Gregory, noted approvingly that mounted constables laid about them with truncheons in a sportsmanlike spirit 'more like polo players'.

On the other hand, the *Gazette* was fulsome in its praise of Italy's Fascist dictator Benito Mussolini and carried his portrait several times. Even as late as 1931, an article head-lined: 'Fascist Efficiency: A Factor in International Goodwill' appeared, and later still, in September 1932, the magazine carried a full supplement entitled: 'The Tenth Festival of Fascism'. That indeed did carry large photographs of the ministers in Mussolini's government and a facsimile of a signed photograph of Il Duce himself on horseback. It was accompanied by glowing prose: 'Fascism is without doubt already compelling Europe to a completely new social and political outlook. The Duce who is most justly admired and honoured throughout the world after ten years of intensive hard work combined with titanic efforts (which) seems to have assured his final victory ... the whole of Europe must accept the fascist system or perish in utter confusion.'

The writing style is evidently entirely and characteristically Gregory's. Fortunately, the magazine closed shortly before Hitler came to power in Germany in January 1933, but it still had warm words to say about him as a defender against Bolshevism in Germany.

The magazine was robustly royalist. Spain's King Alfonso XIII and the Montenegrin royal family received a great deal of coverage, including, in June 1930, a 38-page supplement detailing the Montenegro government's submission to the Versailles peace conference eleven years earlier (as Gerald Macmillan says, Gregory must have been very short of copy that month). The magazine was littered with near-adulatory pages about European princes, grand dukes and kings, many of whom would shortly be driven out, with their royal highnesses memorialised only in the silver picture frames of Gregory's office. Who now remembers Prince Wolkonsky of Ukraine or Grand Duke Nicholas of Russia? In 1930, Gregory would even purchase *Burke's Landed Gentry*, though his interest in it was only fleeting.

Rolling throughout the pages of every edition was Gregory's sycophantic prose shamelessly extolling the highest ranking of officials, members of the aristocracy and those supplicating for honours. Of course, he was not above praising organisations in which he had a pecuniary interest, such as the Ambassador Club, and he did it quite shamelessly, in the club's case over two pages in September 1927 shortly after it opened. It was: 'an organization with the amenities and conveniences of a club, but with the luxury and finish of a first class hotel in addition to the gaiety and exquisite music of a very exclusive ballroom: in other words, a rendezvous for those who wish to entertain in the best surroundings and the most exclusive company'.[10]

If that did not impress the supplicants, nothing would. Gregory lunched and dined there every week, sometimes every day, and in addition the club housed formal dinners, notably for an Eve of Derby gathering for several years before the annual race each June, 'where, for one night in the year, celebrities in the world of politics, sport, art and finance meet in strict impartiality'. Winston Churchill was a regular, as was Lord Birkenhead, former prime ministers Balfour, Rosebery and Asquith, and even the Labour Party's J. R. Clynes. Their host, the dinner's organiser, would modestly remain in the background, though write the event up for next month's magazine.

If there was a club, Gregory wanted to join it. He could be seen at the Henley Regatta with the Rosses, at the Annual Metropolitan Police Horse Show, he got himself invited onto one of the launches which followed the Oxford and Cambridge boat race, there were endless City dinners. Being an usher at the Duke of York's wedding to Elizabeth Bowes-Lyon at Westminster Abbey in 1923 was, presumably, a reward for all his boosterism for the Sailors' Fund.

The one dining circle he would have relished but was never invited to was called the Other Club, which was too exclusive to be broken into. It had been founded by Churchill and F. E. Smith in 1911, and it was a political club limited to 50 members drawn from each party and meeting every other Thursday for informal private chats and debates. There were politicians including Freddie Guest, Alick Murray and Lloyd George, but also actors such as Herbert Beerbohm Tree and newspaper proprietors (but not journalists) including the *News of the World's* Lord Riddell and eventually Lord Rothermere of the *Daily Mail*. Coote, who was introduced to the club by Guest despite being a lowly backbencher and, as he said in his memoirs, a person of the utmost insignificance, described it as a forum in which Liberals and Tories could indulge in reciprocal rancour and asperity certain that their exchanges would not be publicised: 'Its fifty members comprised the liveliest characters in politics, journalism, industry, literature and the arts. There were even some overseas members such as Smuts and Lew Douglas, a former American ambassador. It was and continued to be … Winston's favourite milieu and I am quite sure the enemies of Britain would have given their eyes to be under the table.'[11] But Maundy Gregory was too brown hat – lower class – for such a gathering.

Alick Murray, the Master of Elibank, was ailing – he would die at the age of 50 the following year – so he introduced Gregory to his successor as chief whip. Captain Freddie Guest, who would be tasked with raising the money, immediately saw advantages in having the fund diverted through a middleman. Gregory would be ideal. He did not have a direct party allegiance, so he could be kept at a distance and, if he got into trouble, could be disavowed. He was also discreet, he had contacts, he was close at hand, and he would work on commission, channeling funds through the whips' office. Much better to keep things simple, dealing with one man rather than a pack of chaps wandering the clubs selling knighthoods to all and sundry. The magazine would be an excellent cover for drumming up business: the marks could pay for their promotional articles, donate to the party for the eventual favours of the Crown – and then get mentioned again in the pages of *The Whitehall Gazette* when the honour was awarded. Like a rolling stone, the cycle of publicity, payment and promotion could continue gathering dosh almost perpetually. What could go wrong? It was all perfectly legal.

Even so, discretion was needed because it did not look quite right if the public got wind of what went on. Guest himself, a cousin of Winston Churchill and a former Life Guards officer – hence his military title – was a terrific snob, so handling the frightful people who wanted to pay for the privilege of receiving an honour from the King was not something he wished to do himself. That could be left, in his own words, to the 'grubby little men in brown bowler hats' who touted honours.[12] Colin Coote, who knew both men, compared the relationship between Gregory and Guest as like that of 'a sportsman who employs a retriever to bring the game into the bag'.

Guest's entry in the Dictionary of National Biography (DNB) portrays a sort of 'Hooray Henry' figure, a Liberal only because he supported the policy of Free Trade, which the Tories had dropped earlier in the century, and a man who was a bit of a cad. He had been unseated at his first attempt to enter the Commons for East Dorset in 1910, a constituency where his father owned property, because he had exceeded expenditure limits and was accused of intimidating the tenantry into voting for him. Nevertheless, he eventually won election there and, later, in 1922, after being beaten by a candidate favoured by Beaverbrook, with whom he had fallen out, he then became the MP for Stroud, then Bristol North, then finally, as a Conservative, for Plymouth Drake. He was keen on polo and big game hunting, and the party's intelligentsia regarded him as a halfwit. The DNB says he regularly bombarded Lloyd George with banal political advice. Like most chief whips, however, despite outward appearances, he collected secrets about his colleagues and was prepared to deploy the intelligence when the time was right. Some knew him as Lloyd George's manipulator-in-chief, but he may even have made the Prime Minister himself uneasy: he would mutter later: 'Guest knew too much.' Guest was effective as a backstage negotiator and, in Maundy Gregory, found someone who would happily do the fundraising business.

At this time, while it was Liberal Party practice to leave fundraising to the chief whip and his office, the expenditure of the funds raised was also left to his discretion. It was notionally intended for the upkeep of the party office and staff as well as for fighting elections, but the way the money was disbursed was up to the whip. Guest does not seem to have had to answer to anyone for how the money was spent, least of all the party leader and other senior figures who generally did not want to know, and any records were informal and unsystematic. The Liberals needed money more than the Conservatives because they had fewer wealthy backers from the great landowning aristocracy; those they did have were largely from northern industrialists, or, it was said as late as 1935, 'very rich Quakers and Jews'.[13]

In those circumstances, it is easy to see how the sale of honours came to be seen as a vital source of income. It had been done over many years, at least since the 1890s, and there had long been scouting around for potential honorands. Winston Churchill's suggestion in 1912 that they should be awarded to Liberal-supporting journalists was turned down by Asquith on the grounds that it would be awarding radical newspapers' attacks on the party's patronage system. In any event, the party could not function just on membership fees. As the Liberal-supporting *Manchester Guardian* argued in 1910: 'What would be the state of the Liberal Party chest if it depended on the voluntary subscriptions of the rank and file?'

What became different in the aftermath of the Great War and a prime minister without a party (or scruples) was that the touting for honours became much more systematised, organised and ruthless.

What was in it for Gregory? Money on commission for coming up with powerful and influential names. He was the gatekeeper with privileged access to what they wanted, a broker of influence and celebrity. Perhaps he might even gain social acceptance in the homes and clubs of the wealthy and privileged. He would be a spider at the heart of government, knowing everyone, bestowing favours, manipulating supplicants. He had come a long way from treading the boards in third rate plays at provincial theatres. Clean shirt now indeed. The only thing he lacked was political nous.

Gregory was not the only honours tout in the business. He had several sidekicks who seem to have worked as his agents. There was a Captain Wells and a man called J. Douglas Moffatt, who had once been a Tory candidate but had to stand down after being found out writing threatening letters. Now, and for at least the next decade, he worked with and for Gregory, writing speculative letters to sound out possible honours clients and entice them to lunch.

Apart from occasional freelancers like Bronco Bill Sutherland informally tapping up donors, for the other side there was a portly chap called Harry Shaw, who worked mainly for the Conservatives. Shaw was a businessman, a property dealer and horse breeder, who owned three houses in Belgravia, had a stud farm near Newbury and farmed extensively on a 2,000-acre estate in Leicestershire. He also, very briefly, for just a year in 1921, owned the great neo-classical Stowe House mansion in Buckinghamshire and its extensive grounds, though he was not able to afford the place and sold it to the founders of what was to become Stowe public school. John Temple, of the family that built Stowe House, bought both his knighthood and later his baronetcy directly from King James I in the early seventeenth century.

Shaw's method appears to have been similar to Gregory's, according to a Whitby ship owner called Walter Pyman, who said he was approached by him out of the blue 'on a social matter of a very confidential nature'. They agreed to meet at the Reform Club, where Shaw told him that he had been suggested as a suitable candidate for a baronetcy by a former lord mayor of Newcastle upon Tyne and, if he agreed, Shaw could have it done in an hour. Pyman said: 'I told him that if it was a question of finding £2,000 or £3,000 to turn this government out and dipping Lloyd George into the Thames I would subscribe with pleasure, but as far as paying anything for a baronetcy, I would not give three ha'pence.'[14]

Similarly, Shaw did not have any luck when he approached a man called Ernest Doxford, who was a shipbuilder from Sunderland, though he did at least on that occasion manage to tell Doxford what the price of a baronetcy was: £40,000, which seems to have been more or less the standard tariff since that is what Gregory charged, too, a rarified sort of cartel. It was this case that prompted the Duke of Northumberland to complain about the sale of honours, first in a letter to the *Morning Post* and then by initiating a debate in the House of Lords in 1922.

A reporter from that deeply Conservative newspaper which had been following the honours scandal for some time secured an interview with Shaw at his flat in Knightsbridge in August 1922. Observing the photographs of his prize pigs on the walls, none of which seemed to have received peerages recently, the reporter noted tartly, he asked Shaw about who his particular friend was in government. 'Oh, I know quite a lot of them,' said Shaw. 'On both sides.' He was, he said, a coalitionist so did not have favourites. 'I suppose these transactions are with the Whips?' the reporter asked. 'You seem to know more about it than I do,' retorted Shaw, rather giving the game away.[15]

Perhaps Gregory was more subtle in his choice of victims, or luckier. Although both he and Shaw were aiming for the same goal: the Tories after all were in coalition with the Lloyd George Liberals. If Gregory sensed that one of his marks like Pyman was robustly a Tory and unlikely to be convinced to support the Welsh wizard, he would try a different tack. The money was needed to fight Bolshevism: the Russian Revolution had started with strikes and demonstrations, just like those that had been going on in Britain, and it was time for all good and patriotic men to come to the aid of the government, he would apparently tell them.

Lloyd George claimed to know nothing whatsoever about what was going on. Many years later he told the *Daily Mail* that Guest and the other chief whip, Leslie Wilson from the Conservative side of the coalition, went through the lists of names between them before forwarding them to him and to the Tory leader, first Bonar Law and then, after his retirement, to Austen Chamberlain. They made decisions as to which names to submit purely on public grounds: 'For my part I had no information as to who had, or had not, subscribed towards the party funds.' Chamberlain responded furiously: he had never taken part in such a joint enterprise: 'I have never considered myself in any way responsible for the selection which you made.'[16]

Lloyd George was being disingenuous. Bereft of a party machine, he needed money to set one up and fight a campaign leading his Liberal Coalitionists. Of course, he knew who was making donations and why, even if not necessarily how much each was paying. The truth was, he did not care. One anonymous figure, who had been approached, told the *Morning Post* that the tout (presumably Gregory or one of his associates) 'had told him that the Government would not last very long, and when the prime minister went to the country he wanted funds for contesting certain seats'.[17] Some Tory peers believed there was a deliberate political element to his strategy, too. Lord Selborne wrote to his wife: 'We are being simply sold' and that the manoeuvre was a move to discredit and undermine the second chamber every time another reprobate was added to the peerage.

Lloyd George had held a contempt for peers and peerages; as a Welsh nonconformist, they offended his democratic principles. In any case, how else was he to fund his planned political organisation? Colin Coote, who was one of his MPs and served in the whips' office under Guest's grumpy successor Charles McCurdy, wrote in his memoirs: 'The methods [of raising money] were really very thinly disguised. Lloyd George was genuinely indifferent to all that sort of flummery and did not mind how money was raised provided he was not told. Freddie Guest … was completely cynical about it. His side of the Coalition had to have the sinews of war and this was the only way to get them quickly.'[18]

As Lloyd George frankly admitted to the Tory insider John Davidson in 1927, making an enthusiastic defence of raising money through the sale of honours: 'You and I know perfectly well it is a far cleaner method of filling the Party chest than the methods used in the United States or the Socialist Party. In America the steel trusts supported one political party and the cotton people supported another. This placed political parties under the domination of great financial interests and trusts. Here a man gives £40,000 to the party and gets a baronetcy. If he comes to the Leader of the Party and says I subscribe largely to the party funds, you must do this or that, we can tell him to go to the devil. The attachment of the brewers to the Conservative Party was the closest approach to political corruption in this country.

'The worst of it is, you cannot defend it in public, but it keeps politics far cleaner than any other method of raising funds.'[19]

Lloyd George was again being disingenuous: the payments were made more or less secretly without the public being informed. He could hardly have been unaware how weighted the honours lists were. This was long before the days of life peerages or gongs for ordinary people, though some awards such as the Order of the British Empire had been introduced during the First World War to recognise public service. But these latter were of no interest to touts like Gregory because they did not bring any special privileges with them. The majority in the few years after the First World War when Gregory was most active went to newspapermen and businessmen: all wealthy individuals. Freddie Guest tried to point this out privately to Lloyd George in a memo as early as February 1919. It was a time of unrest and privation, and Guest wanted to indicate that people who were suffering in the harsh winter weather would notice. He wrote: 'I do not suggest that there is a single improper recommendation, on merits, if these had been ordinary times, but I point out the whole burden will be on you.' Bronco Bill Sutherland added separately: 'the appearance of any honours list at the moment with a lot of wealthy men in it will act as a red rag to the Labour extremists'.[20]

But it was not that which caused the trouble. It was that Gregory was too successful in shovelling names through and, even worse from the Tories' point of view, he was hijacking donors who should be giving to them instead.

8. HONOURS ABOUNDING

It is quite hard to assess how many names obtained honours and therefore how much money Gregory secured for the Lloyd George Fund in the four and a half years of his peak practice. Between 1917 and 1922, 82 new peers were nominated: 50 by Lloyd George and 32 by Andrew Bonar Law and his successor Austen Chamberlain from the Conservative side. This, however, does not give a full picture of the honours that were awarded, still less whether they were paid for. In the 1930s, the journalist Patrick Balfour, whose hereditary title was 3rd Baron Kinross, reckoned there would have been about 34,000 wealthy war profiteers and nouveau riches who could have been tapped up for an honour.[1] Who knows? But if so, Gregory barely touched the surface.

The generally accepted estimate is that the King created four marquessates, eight earldoms, twenty-two viscountcies and sixty-four barons in the first five years of Lloyd George's premiership, though not all were down to him.

Some, awarded in 1917, were peerages nominated by Herbert Asquith in his resignation honours list. Some were peerages awarded uncontroversially as a matter of course: to the First World War generals Haig, Plumer, Allenby, Rawlinson and admirals Jellicoe and Beatty. Some were for those taking particular judicial posts, such as Gordon Hewart, who was made Lord Chief Justice, and F. E. Smith, the Conservative politician and lawyer who became Lord Chancellor, the head of the English and Welsh judiciary for the coalition, after the Coupon Election. Highly unusually, Smith was actually promoted three times through the peerage in three years, having become a baron when he was made Lord Chancellor in 1919, a viscount in 1921 and an earl in 1922 after the fall of the government, each time taking his title from his hometown and original constituency, Birkenhead.

Clearly such men had no need to buy their peerages (though Smith's escalating honours were widely criticised because his arrogance, sharp tongue and vehemently partisan politics had made many political enemies). Andrew Cook, the historian, who made a detailed study of the Lloyd George awards for his book *Cash for Honours*, estimates that only fourteen of the eighty-six barons and viscounts may have involved some form of payment: and eight of those were nominated by the Conservative coalition leaders, Bonar Law and Chamberlain. As all were hereditary titles in those days, forty-nine of the eighty-two are now extinct having run out of heirs.

It appears that only five hereditary peers currently able to sit in the Lords (though for how much longer is unclear given the Starmer government's intention to remove those with honorary titles) owe their places to appointments made during the Lloyd George administration: Baron Glenarthur (Conservative, ancestor originally nominated by Bonar Law), Baron Meston (Crossbencher, ancestor originally nominated by Lloyd George), Baron Trevethin (Crossbencher, ancestor originally nominated by Lloyd George), Baron Borwick

(Conservative, ancestor originally nominated by Austen Chamberlain) and Baron Bethell (Conservative, ancestor originally nominated by Lloyd George).

There were twenty-six baronetcies created during the period between 1917 and 1924, of which twelve are still extant, now in their third or fourth generations. Baronetcies are hereditary and so were more expensive than knighthoods, but they do not carry a seat in the House of Lords. Holders are Sirs or Dames, so carry some prestige for those who value it, such as, it would seem, the manufacturers and businessman who were given their titles which they could pass on to their heirs during the coalition government period. All had commercial backgrounds in shipbuilding, brewing, iron and steel, steamships, or finance with two exceptions: Sir William Ackroyd of Lightcliffe was a carpet manufacturer and Sir Alexander Grant of Forres was the chairman of McVitie and Price, the biscuit manufacturers. Sir Alexander was finally awarded his baronetcy by Ramsay Macdonald during the first Labour administration in 1924, though the title seems to have been discussed during the preceding coalition government. Grant probably did his chances no harm by lending Macdonald the use of a Daimler limousine and £40,000 in securities. Thereafter, Macdonald tended to be greeted with mocking shouts of 'Biscuits!' by Tories in the Commons.

Perhaps the best-known of the current generation is Princess Margaret's former friend, the garden designer Roddy Llewellyn, whose great grandfather, Sir David Llewellyn of Bwllfa near Aberdare in the Rhondda, was granted the title in 1922 when he was chairman of the local steam collieries company.

The real inflation in honours was in the number of knighthoods that were awarded during Lloyd George's premiership. There were 294 newly-minted knights in the eighteen months after the First World War, but these were of lower consequence and status than the higher awards. A new medal, the Order of the British Empire, was instituted at King George V's initiative in 1917 to honour civilians who had given exceptional public service as well as members of the military. It was distributed wholesale in the years after the war: 22,000 by the end of 1919 and a further 3,000 by 1922. Its ubiquity making it of little use to honours touts. As one wrote in a letter dangling a knighthood for sale: 'not of the British Empire, no nonsense of that kind, but the real thing'.[2]

Not everyone obtained the honours that they had paid for. Cook lists eighteen names who had given Gregory money but didn't receive their knighthoods. Among them, it seems, was William Whitelaw, the grandfather of the home secretary of the Thatcher era of the same name, who was chairman of the London and North Eastern Railway. At least one of the non-recipients, Walter Kent, was subsequently awarded a knighthood in 1929, Cook suggests. Kent appears to have been the victim of bad timing in that his honour was in the works in 1922 at the time when Bonar Law retired through ill health and was ultimately succeeded by Stanley Baldwin, who made little secret of the fact that he did not like the idea of paying for honours. Kent had received the Gregory treatment, being praised in *The Whitehall Gazette* for 'his prominent place in the engineering world'. He seems to have got his money back, and when he did eventually receive his knighthood it was posted as 'for political services', although, as his local paper, the *Luton News*, pointed out, he had only joined the Conservative Party in late 1923, which would have been some months after Gregory first put his name forward.[3]

Some of these undoubtedly bought their titles. Sir Thomas Watson, whose reward came in 1918, was a director of Pyman Watson and Co., the ship owning company, and a colleague of the Walter Pyman, who objected so strongly to being approached by Harry Shaw. Sir Rowland Hodge, granted his baronetcy in 1921, was one of those whose transparent dodginess inadvertenly helped to drag the scandal of honours for sale into the open.

Peerages and baronetcies were at the upper end of the charging scales, if indeed they were bought. Much more common were the lesser awards of knighthoods, which carried a title but nothing more than prestige, though of course there was no bar to knights sitting as MPs if they got themselves elected. Cook estimates that more than two thousand knighthoods were granted through the course of the Asquith, Lloyd George, Bonar Law and Chamberlain leaderships of their respective parties. It must have been quite a busy trading period for Gregory and his fellow touts, though none of his rivals seem to have been as systematic and as diligent as him in spotting opportunities and moving in for the hard sell.

The sale of honours had been the subject of concern for some years before Maundy Gregory came on the scene. It was customary for the whips of both parties to shake down supporters for donations in return for honours. George Whiteley, the Liberals' chief whip during the premiership of Sir Henry Campbell-Bannerman, Asquith's predecessor, between December 1905 and April 1908, appeared to be particularly adept: as Arthur Ponsonby, 'C-B's' private secretary noted in his diary in 1906: '[he] enjoyed the money squeezing part of it which I think is particularly disagreeable'. He was nevertheless successful: inheriting a Liberal political fund of £20,000 when he became patronage secretary on being made chief whip in 1905, when he left the post three years later the balance was £514,000.

Asquith himself was squeamish about the practice and asked Jack Pease, Whiteley's successor, to tone it down, but it seems that what happened was that fund raising was farmed out to touts in the years before the First World War, perhaps by Alick Murray, the man who later recruited Gregory. Douglas Moffat, who later worked with Gregory, was one of these, but the pre-war cadgers as they were sometimes known worked on a freelance basis, offering possible nominees piecemeal rather than systematically as Gregory would after the war.

Murray nominated large numbers of peers: fifteen in 1910, twenty-two in 1911 and ten in 1912. This must have been partly a response to the constitutional crisis as the Conservative-controlled House of Lords blocked the Liberal People's Budget, a start to evening up numbers, even if ultimately the Tory peers caved in and Asquith never had to resort to flooding the upper house with 249 new peers as he had warned he would if the legislation was further obstructed. The number of baronetcies increased, too: thirteen in 1910, thirty-five in 1911, twenty in 1912. Asquith did not go so far as approving those with criminal records as Lloyd George would do, but he certainly seems – if Jack Pease's diary in June 1908 is reliable – to have suggested to him that trying to seduce a young woman or marrying because one's girlfriend was pregnant should not necessarily bar one from nomination for an honour.[4]

Certainly, by 1913, there was political concern about the sale of honours and the suitability of some recipients. In that year, the cross-party National League for Clean Government was set up by, among others, the writer Hilaire Belloc, James Bar of the Eugenics Education Society, Fred Jowett, a future minister in the first Labour government, and a number of Conservative MPs and peers. The league's utopian object was 'to demand purity of government and to expose and punish political corruption'. They affected the result in several by-elections, too, by asking pointed questions to candidates. The campaigners against the honours scandal in the 1920s were largely drawn from the Tory Right, known as the Die Hards, the men who had bitterly opposed Irish Home Rule, the People's Budget and reform of the House of Lords a decade earlier before the war. Their hostility to Lloyd George was deeply personal, as was his towards them.

From the upper house, the Conservative peers, the Marquess of Salisbury (the son of the Victorian prime minister) and his brother-in-law, the Earl of Selborne, both attempted to persuade the party leadership to have nothing to do with selling honours – 'I do not want to be prudish but I do want to be more particular than Lloyd George,' Selborne had told the party chairman Lord Lansdowne in 1913 – but they got nowhere then with their campaign. Bonar Law told Selborne that 'the present time is ill-chosen for raising the subject'. When a debate was held in the House of Lords in February 1914, they were suavely told by Lord Crewe, the Liberal leader, that there was no corruption and anyway things had been much worse before the passing of the Great Reform Act in 1832. There was even a bill entitled Traffic in Titles introduced in the Commons, but that was dropped because of the onset of the war. Selborne would still be around after the war when the honours scandal bubbled up once more.

That occurred in early 1919, even before Gregory set up shop in Whitehall, and the first to raise the issue in the Commons was a backbencher called Sir Henry Page Croft, the MP for Bournemouth. He was a doughty right-winger and tariff protectionist, one of several who had actually left the Tory Party in 1917 to form the breakaway National Party, partly in disgust at the sight of war profiteers buying their way into the peerage. He spoke in a debate in the Commons in May 1919. Croft's views and those of his fellow Tory dissidents at the time would probably, in some respects, place him further to the right than Reform today. He did not like foreigners, especially Jews who he regarded as Bolsheviks, he was concerned about immigrants undermining the country and he was scandalised by the possibility that the sale of honours would enable such people to buy their way into British society and so undermine it. He was also a trade protectionist, in favour of erecting barriers to imports and to immigration, and, although he had led a territorial battalion at the Western Front, his vehement criticism of his political allies about the military commanders had led to him being recalled in 1916, back into Parliament where he was known as General Croft.

There were only a handful of National Party MPs, and they tended to be dismissed, rather like David Cameron's early description of Ukippers as 'nutters and fruitcakes'. One Tory MP in the Honours debate, William Lane-Mitchell, whose constituency was Streatham, described them as 'the most stupid set of men that ever walked'. They drifted back into the Tory Party later in the 1920s, and Croft himself, by then ennobled, served as a junior minister in the war department during the Second World War. He caused some bemusement in the House of Lords during a debate in 1942, suggesting that troops might be issued with pikes for close range fighting: cold steel being most effective in taking on any invading Germans.

The purpose of his debate in late May 1919 was to make political parties divulge the sources of their funding, to make the auditing of their accounts compulsory and to set up an independent committee to scrutinise the awarding of honours. Croft's concern, however, seemed to be that Bolsheviks were infiltrating the country to buy honours, though he did not produce any evidence of this unlikely occurrence. He told the House: 'I say it is desirable – to put it mildly – that we should know what are the sources of the funds of these various political movements in this country. Foreign money can at this present moment, unknown to the public, be used to influence the commercial or financial policy of this country.

'I think it is generally recognised, that in the recent Honours List gentlemen received titles whom no decent man would allow to enter his house. several of them would have been blackballed by any respectable social London club. If you want to create Bolshevism and revolution in this country you will continue this practice and allow these scandals to go on.'

Almost as bad as the Marxists were the numbers of honours awarded to journalists: 'They had a fair proportion – amongst the viscounts 100 percent, and of the baronetcies 20 percent. These are hopeful proportions, which encourage us to think that the future is indeed rosy for the few remaining journalists in this country who have not been honoured.'[5] This was a little unfair as it was the owners rather than reporters who were gaining peerages.

Croft said: 'Let the House declare that all party funds shall in future be audited by a chartered accountant, and that such accountant should vouch for the substantial subscribers – those over £500 – and see that a list of them is lodged where anyone who desires to know where these funds come from can ascertain the facts. If you adopt that policy you destroy at one blow the germ of corruption.'

The party leaders must be ignorant of the character of some of those receiving honours, he said, 'otherwise they would have been deliberately polluting the fountain of honour by presenting such names to the Sovereign. We should have an examining body, preferably a committee of the Privy Council and not of Members of this House who are deeply connected with political headquarters. They should inquire into the character of those proposed to be recommended and should be informed of the real reasons why the recommendations are made.'

Croft was perhaps a little unfortunate in having his motion seconded by none other than Horatio Bottomley, who at that stage was busily defrauding innocent subscribers to his war bonds scheme. He, of course, was proud to proclaim that he was untainted by the lure of honours: 'So much do I regard it as one of the privileges of which the British can now be proud that I emphasise it by printing the word "Mr." on my visiting card in red ink, to indicate that I am still uncorrupted.'

Bonar Law, the rectitudinous Scots-Canadian Presbyterian Tory Coalition leader, was put up to answer the debate in Lloyd George's absence, and he had little difficulty in doing so, along much the same lines as he had deployed six years earlier. 'It has been asserted tonight that there has been a widespread belief that honours are in effect bought and sold. I say that if it were true that the party Whips either go to individuals and say to them, "If you will give such and such a sum to the party fund, you will get an honour," or if when a man is selected as suitable for the honour, he is then told by the party whips that he must pay a certain sum of money – I say if that is true it ought to be put an end to by the House of Commons. I do not believe that it is true, and on this point I think I can speak with more knowledge than probably anyone else in the House at this moment.

'The Prime Minister has made, and will make, no recommendation to His Majesty as a reward for contributions to party funds. I have asked the Whips, and they have told me there has been, and there will be, no such bargain.'[6]

Croft would no doubt be pleased to know that there is now an independent honours scrutiny committee, with nine specialist sub-committees reviewing nominations in various public spheres such as arts and sport, science and political services. But it took quite a while to come about, and not before another cash for honours scandal in 2006–7. It does not have the power to nominate peerages.

Croft's motion was easily seen off, defeated by 112 votes to 50, but the ayes included 20 Labour MPs, some Asquithian Liberals and even five supporters of the coalition government. Nevertheless, privately, both Freddie Guest and Bonar Law both wrote to Lloyd George, who was still in Paris engaged with the Versailles negotiations, urging him to lay off announcing any political honours for the time being.

Guest wrote to him two days after the debate: 'There is no doubt that there is still considerable restlessness in the public mind on this subject, more particularly on the grounds that soldiers and sailors have so far failed to achieve recognition ... we are all of the opinion that the ordinary political list should be deferred until Peace is declared and the soldiers and sailors recognised.' Bonar Law chipped in the following day, evidently having received some assurances from Paris: 'I am thankful that you have agreed not to have a political honours list just now. I was frightened of it after my speech the other night.' Perhaps his speech had given him a guilty conscience.

So it was that the peerages for the generals and admirals followed later in the year. Meanwhile, Arthur Maundy Gregory was setting up his office opposite Downing Street, ready to be open for business.

The embargo was short-lived. There were only six peerages in 1920: they went to two government ministers, one governor-general of Australia, the king's doctor,[7] the governor of the Bank of England and George Riddell, the managing director of the *News of the World*, who was one of Lloyd George's closest media confidants. Even so, Riddell's peerage was nearly scuppered because he had been divorced twenty years earlier, a social solecism in the King's mind that could have disbarred him. In the end it did go ahead, though the award probably only served to increase George V's concern about the type of person who was getting a peerage.

One baronetcy, which was put forward in 1920, was for Sir William Stewart, a whisky distiller from Dundee, who was nominated for unspecified public services. He had apparently paid £50,000 to Gregory but fell into such financial straits that the money had to be refunded to stave off his bankruptcy. He shot himself three years later, leaving debts of more than £500,000. Cullen quotes from a *Daily Telegraph* report of a subsequent creditors' meeting at which the solicitor representing Stewart's largest creditor suggested that he might have paid £150,000 for his award at which the chairman of the hearing responded equably: '£50,000 may have been sufficient at the time.' Stewart was denounced as a whisky baronet, 'a bootlegging pal of Mr Lloyd George'. The solicitor asked whether those handling the Prime Minister's political fund could be produced for the meeting, but apparently not and Gregory's name was kept out of the papers.[8] Lloyd George's government seems to have had something of a penchant for whisky distillers: Sir Thomas Dewar received his peerage in 1919 and Douglas Haig (though of course for different reasons) later the same year.

In 1921, the number of peerages was back up to 15 and, meanwhile, the number of baronetcies created in the two years 1920–21 was 85. People were noticing that many of the awards went to businessmen and journalists who had no particular record of public service, but it took an egregious nomination for the honours issue to swim back into public attention.

This was Rowland Hodge, listed for a baronetcy in the New Year Honours of 1921 to add to his earlier knighthood. Hodge was a Newcastle-based ship builder and owner, and he had been angling for a further award for several years, going from contact to contact and party to party in search of a helping hand. Eddy Marsh, Winston Churchill's secretary, had written to J. T. Davies, Lloyd George's secretary, as early as December 1918 with a warning: 'Mr Churchill thinks he ought to let you know that he was approached on Saturday, to his great surprise, by an acquaintance who should have known better, with a suggestion that he should procure a baronetcy for a certain Hodge ... and receive £5,000 on delivery of the goods. Naturally the intermediary received short shrift – and Mr Churchill thinks you may wish to make a note to be borne in mind if the idea of any honour for Mr Hodge is mooted again.'[9]

Hodge did not give up the idea and later also tried the Conservatives, as George Younger, the party chairman, told Bonar Law in January 1921, he had made 'offers so brutally frank that I made up my mind to have nothing to do with him and showed him the cold shoulder'.

The trouble with his application was that Hodge was not quite the upright figure he seemed. He had been convicted of food hoarding in April 1918: a ton's worth, apparently, a crime at a time of national shortages almost as outrageous in the public mind then as to the partying that Boris Johnson's staff indulged in during lockdown a century later. Hodge had done it on such a large scale that Sir Henry Page-Croft, still keeping a beady out for honours finagling, alleged in the Commons that he had built a special hiding place in his house to conceal his ill-gotten food supplies. In any event, Hodge had been fined the enormous amount of £700 (equivalent to nearly £33,000 in modern values) and had effectively been driven out of town by local hostility, settling at the other end of the country in Kent instead. Gregory had once profiled Hodge in *Mayfair* magazine in 1912 before the war, extolling him as 'one of those all-round good men of whom no country can have too many' and as a keen politician 'without arousing any animosity'.

Such a crime might have been expected to be held against him when it came to honours, but apparently not. Did he go to Gregory for help? However he managed it, he was listed for a baronetcy in Freddie Guest's list for 1921, and within weeks Croft was on his feet in the Commons asking the Prime Minister whether he was going to take any action about the appointment. Lloyd George blustered in reply: apparently the offence had been merely inadvertent, as if Hodge had not noticed the stockpile. 'Although he accepted technical responsibility for the offence, it was committed entirely without his knowledge. Since then he has been chosen to represent the diocese in which he lives on the Central Board of Finance of the Church of England ... I do not propose to take any action as the recipient rendered conspicuous public services to the country during the war.'[10]

The Prime Minister must have realised it was a poor excuse for he met Croft privately to tell him that he was 'much worried' about the Hodge award, saying it had been urged on him by the Admiralty because of his service to the shipbuilding industry during the war. The MP was not persuaded and told a colleague that he would press for the honour to be dropped as a powerful blow for public honesty, and, anyway, Hodge had made very substantial profits on the barges he had sold to the government.

Croft probably did not know it, but he had an influential ally in King George V, who was also concerned about the inflation of honours and particularly the baronetcy for Hodge. His memory of meeting the man on a tour of the Tyne dockyards in June 1917 had been triggered by a letter of complaint from someone in the northeast, and the King's private secretary, Lord Stamfordham, wrote to the Prime Minister expressing his concern. Hodge had clearly made an unfavourable impression: 'His appearance, dress and manner left an indelible mark on His Majesty's mind. Such appointments react upon the Sovereign and the king has expressed to me his feelings of annoyance and indeed disgust that this man should have received any honour, let alone a baronetcy.' It is a mark of Lloyd George's insouciance that even such a clear indication of the King's displeasure at the award did not prevent it from going ahead.[11]

This all fed into an atmosphere that the Tories could exploit as the coalition government began to creak under the pressure to dissolve what had always been a temporary alliance, even though Lloyd George hoped that it might become a permanent arrangement – under himself, naturally. His old Liberal allies noted he was growing closer to the Conservatives and their views.

One of the main internal reasons for Tory annoyance at this stage was that Gregory was too successful. He was hawking honours even to potential Conservative donors, snatching them from under the noses of the Tory whips. It prompted a letter from George Younger, the party chairman, to Bonar Law on 2 January 1921, blaming Freddie Guest who was the recipient of the names that Gregory was forwarding: 'There must be a stop to Freddie poaching our men,' he wrote. 'These damned rascals come to me demanding to be made knights and when I refuse go straight to Lloyd George's whips office and get what they want from him.' Younger had evidently not heard of Gregory at that stage.

The immediate cause of his aggravation was a baronetcy awarded to a man called Frederick Mills, the chairman of the Ebbw Vale Steel and Iron Company, who was known to be a

Conservative, so much so that he had been looking for a Tory constituency with Younger's help in order to become an MP. 'I haven't a doubt that if I had got Mills a seat and got him into the House he would have proved a generous annual subscriber & it was for us & not for Freddie to give him something more later on.'[12]

And some of those Liberal-nominated men were not the sort who should have been receiving honours anyway – perhaps, like Hodge, they had turned to an alternative source who offered better prospects of getting what they wanted. The worst of it, to Younger's mind, was that the Tories got implicated when unsuitable names were put forward: they were being 'blamed for giving honours which it never would have occurred to us to bestow'. There was a clear danger that they would bring the whole system down and the Tories would share the public opprobrium that rightly belonged to Lloyd George and his cronies alone.

There was of course some hypocrisy involved. The Conservatives were not raising money from honours in such a systematic and indiscriminate way as Gregory and Lloyd George, but they were doing it quite successfully on their own account. Younger had more than doubled the party's funds between 1919 and 1922 from £600,000 to £1.25 million partly by similar means, though there was a certain degree of denial. Younger wrote to Stanley Baldwin six years later to admit: 'I never, so to speak, sold an honour, nor did I ever make any bargains [but] superintended the collection of ... the contributions occasionally made by the medium of the honours list.'[13]

In the spring of 1921, Bonar Law's ill health had led to his stepping down and he was succeeded by the man who was the party's obvious successor, Austen Chamberlain, the chancellor of the exchequer in the coalition government. Chamberlain was the image of his famous father, Joseph, the Birmingham screw manufacturer, former mayor and MP for the city who had split first the Gladstonian Liberal Party in the 1880s about

Irish Home Rule and then, after he had switched sides, he had split the Tories in the early 1900s over the imposition of tariffs on imports. But Austen, who bore a remarkable resemblance to his late father, right down to his monocle and the orchid in his buttonhole, was no splitter. Perhaps he was even too honourable for his own good – poor Austen, Winston Churchill said, he always played the game and never won it. He would stick by the coalition and Lloyd George even as the party sitting on the green benches behind him was beginning to chafe for change.

He believed it was the honourable thing to do for the country, so he desperately sought to maintain party unity and the continuation of the Coalition. As he wrote to his colleague, the former coalition minister Walter Long who had himself just been made a peer: 'I am most anxious to keep the party together and have very carefully refrained from saying anything to anger or embitter them. I am very disappointed that I see no sign of their responding in the same spirit.' When the right-wing backbencher Sir William Joynson-Hicks (whose baronetcy for political service, which he surely did not pay for, dated from 1919) with colleagues moved a censure motion against him, Chamberlain responded: 'For the sake of narrow party spirit and old party jealousy they are wrecking the great cause for which we are working. They have been unable ... to state the principles of our party to which we have been unfaithful.'[14] A number of Tory leaders more recently might have echoed that sentiment.

If it had been just one controversial award, the scandal might well have blown over, but it was not. And a general election was looming in the distance. It must be held before the end of 1923, and many Tories did not want to fight it under the banner of Lloyd George. The Prime Minister's need for cash quickly was growing.

9. AN INSULT TO THE CROWN

By the spring of 1922, Lloyd George, like many a prime minister after him, was spending increasing amounts of time abroad as an international statesman. It was a refuge from the government's domestic troubles: coal strikes, rising unemployment and a faltering economy exacerbated by spending cutbacks – the so-called Geddes Axe[1] – and an equally faltering Coalition. Lloyd George's post-war pledges: homes for heroes, jobs for servicemen, the golden uplands of peace were progressively being diluted. There had been a series of crises from the Russian Revolution and its aftermath to the Irish war, and the cabinet was increasingly and acrimoniously divided. The most vociferous opponent in meetings was Winston Churchill, still a Liberal, just, but more and more disenchanted with his old friend Lloyd George, especially over whether the government should try to reach an accommodation with the Bolshevik government in Russia, which Churchill fiercely opposed.

Lloyd George struggled, as anyone might, in handling more than one crisis at a time. As the cabinet secretary Hankey noted: 'Lloyd George's erratic, inconsequent and hasty methods are the negation of organisation. Owing to his personal habits (sleeping after lunch for instance) involving late evening meetings and very discursive talks on every question, he exhausts to an extraordinary degree not only his own colleagues and his immediate subordinates, but the whole executive of state.'[2] By this time, Lloyd George had been continuously in high office for nearly sixteen years.

As a prime minister without a party, he had, he said, three options as a general election loomed in a year's time: he could retire, try to set up a new coalition or attempt to achieve a fusion between his supporters and the Conservative leadership. 'I have told Bonar Law I am not going on like this,' he told his friend, the *News of the World's* owner Lord Riddell, as early as 1920. 'We are losing by-election after by-election. There is no proper political organisation in the country.'[3]

All this was hardly conducive to sound administration. Such political imperatives as a shaky party base required a drastic increase in political funds. But at the same time, the Prime Minister was spending large amounts of time abroad. It has been estimated that Lloyd George attended more than twenty international conferences between the end of the war and 1922. Not only were these new developments for heads of government and political leaders – such events had been very rare before the war – but unlike modern summits, where such ministers fly in and out within a day or so, these sometimes involved absences from home of weeks if not months. Lloyd George could be in touch with Downing Street and with colleagues by letter and telegram but was isolated. He did not trust or respect Lord Curzon, the aristocratic and pompous Tory foreign secretary, and so largely ignored him for his latest initiatives and policy choices.

The latest gathering in April and May 1922 was intended to be an ambitious foreign policy coup: no less than an international gathering in Genoa, Italy, to reset Europe's economy after the war, settle the question of German reparations and create a new political and financial framework for the continent. In Hattersley's words: 'It was not just his low opinion of [Curzon] that prompted Lloyd George to be his own foreign secretary. He wanted to be everything because he believed that nothing was beyond him. So he initiated a practice which subsequent prime ministers copied, often with similarly disastrous results. Lloyd George was a pioneer of personal diplomacy ... an independent conference was a forum in which he would be guaranteed to shine.'[4]

It did not work, of course: the French were in no mood to limit or delay reparations from the Germans, and the Americans in their isolationist phase would not attend a political gathering. The Germans and Russians remained locked out of the main body and were involved in secret negotiations of their own without reference to the rest of Europe. For all Lloyd George's fine words launching the conference, very little of substance was achieved. His personal diplomacy amounted to promising the Russians a massive credit boost to stabilise their wrecked economy without troubling to inform the cabinet back home first.

More seriously, the Prime Minister was away in Italy for five weeks, and it was during that time that the most controversial Birthday Honours List yet was devised, a parade of the dubious, the corrupt and the shady that made the King blanch and the Conservatives furious.

The list, when it became known after being published in the official *London Gazette* on 2 June, the day before the King's birthday, contained a number of unsuitable candidates which Gregory, presumably focused on the bottom line, had not checked for potential warning signals, and Charles McCurdy, Freddie Guest's successor as Liberal chief whip, surely did not notice. He soon realised differently when the list provoked a storm of protest. McCurdy was an altogether less emollient figure than Guest, whose charm allowed him to get away with a lot. By contrast, his successor was described by Robert Sanders, one of the Tory coalition whips, as 'a particularly bad-mannered fellow, the reverse of Guest'.

Among the names was Sir John Drughorn of Ifield, a Dutch-born director of the Anglo-Brazilian shipping line, who had been convicted of trading with the enemy in 1915 and yet was still proposed for a baronetcy in 1922. Sir Archibald Williamson, a Scottish Liberal MP, was to be promoted to the peerage as Baron Forres, despite similar accusations that his oil company, Williamson Balfour and Co., had also traded with the Germans – an accusation that he denied.

Then there was Sir Samuel Waring (of the Waring and Gillow furniture company), who was accused of wartime profiteering, overcharging for the sale of aircraft parts to the government after he was proposed for a peerage for his war work. As with Rowland Hodge the previous year, it was pointed out he had made substantial personal profits from helping the war effort. When the accusation was made, Waring was watching from the Strangers Gallery and stood up shouting: 'It's a lie!'

Sir William Vestey, who had moved his £20 million meat packing business to Argentina to escape wartime taxation, was also nominated for a peerage. His citation read that he had 'rendered immense service during the war to the country, and provided gratuitously the cold storage accommodation required for war purposes' as a Blue Star shipping line owner. But the cold storage his company provided was not free. Vestey had applied for tax exemption for supplying the British meat market in 1915, and when he did not get it transferred the business, exploiting a tax loophole.[5] Vestey was however nominated for his peerage by Younger, the Tory party chairman, not Lloyd George.

The birthday honours list on 3 June 1922 contained five peerages: Vestey, Waring, Williamson and Robinson. The only nomination that was uncontroversial was Sir Robert Borwick, whose family fortune was based on the manufacture of custard and baking powders though the award was given to him for providing hospital treatment for sick and wounded colonial officers throughout the war. Lord Borwick, by then in his late seventies, lived on the French Riviera so was unlikely to stir things up.

By far the most controversial nomination in the 1922 list was the proposed peerage to Sir Joseph Robinson, who had lived all his life in South Africa and had become immensely wealthy as a pioneering gold and diamond mining magnate around Kimberley in the northern Cape. Robinson had already obtained his baronetcy by paying for it to the Liberal Henry Campbell-Bannerman's administration in 1908,[6] but now wanted more and was prepared to pay for it again, though he knocked down Gregory's normal asking price to £30,000. The South African gold fields were no place for blushing violets in the late nineteenth and early twentieth centuries, but Robinson was much hated for his ruthlessness, intimidation and arrogance. As Louis Cohen, an unfriendly witness, wrote of him: 'Robinson was never popular with anybody in Kimberley: he had no personality, no magnetism, but resembled a mortal who had a tombstone on his soul.'[7]

The best-known photograph of Robinson shows a sour, red-faced individual glowering suspiciously behind a bristling moustache, under a pith helmet. His unpopularity in the Cape meant he had no friends to speak up for him either there or in Britain. Any business partnerships soon foundered on his irascibility, and his rapacious seductions of other men's wives scarcely produced kindly feelings. It was said that the magnate, who was worth more than £18m, never entered the bar of the Queen's Hotel in Johannnesburg without first checking whether there was anybody in there for whom he might have to buy a drink.

There was very little reason why he should be given a peerage, and this was compounded by the outcome of another court case in 1915 when he sold up his Rand businesses to another magnate, Solly Joel, who rapidly discovered that their value had been greatly exaggerated. Robinson's mines were badly run and in a poor state and he had engaged in insider trading on a large scale, selling a property he had bought for £60,000 to one of his own companies within a month for £275,000 and pocketing the difference. Joel sued and had been awarded the enormous sum of £462,000 in damages. The outcome stood. Robinson was refused permission to appeal by the Judicial Committee of the Privy Council in London in November 1921.

None of this seemed to make Robinson suitable for a peerage seven months later in 1922, especially because the citation was supposedly a reward for his national and imperial services to his own bank, the Robinson South African Banking Corporation Ltd., which had been wound up and liquidated in 1905, nearly twenty years earlier. There was no question of the nomination having been put forward by the South African government, which would have been the normal channel for an honour to be proposed, and members of the Privy Council committee sitting in the House of Lords could scarcely have forgotten the outcome of the case within a few months. If they had decided that he had behaved legally disreputably in November, how could they be expected to accept him willingly into their House the following June?

Understandably, too, King George V, who had already made his displeasure known privately to the government about the number of bad hats on whom he was expected to bestow his honours, now reiterated his criticism. He had certainly not been consulted about them and was aggravated to be expected to wave them through. Lord Stamfordham, his private secretary, wrote to Lord Salisbury, the Conservative peer who had previously criticised the way honours were being traded. 'The whole question of honours grows more and more disagreeable and distasteful to the King whose one object is to reduce the numbers that are submitted to him twice a year and naturally to secure their being conferred upon reputable people,' Stamfordham wrote. 'You will naturally be inclined to reply that His Majesty's efforts are not very successful.'[8] Those peers in the House of Lords who were growing concerned about the rise in the number of dubious honours would know that the King himself was at least privately with them when they raised the matter in a new debate.

It has been unusual for a particular peerage and its nominee to be queried publicly by name in the modern era. The debate might have got more publicity than it obtained because it was held on the afternoon on which Field Marshal Sir Henry Wilson, the former chief of the Imperial General Staff, was assassinated by two Irish republicans in broad daylight on the steps of his home on the corner of Eaton Place just down the road from Parliament. The lords were understandably buzzing with that, but then their attention was drawn to the contrasting worthiness or otherwise of Sir Joseph's peerage. The question posed by Lord Harris, a former business rival of Robinson as chairman of Cecil Rhodes's old Gold Fields company, who was also the former governor of Bombay (Mumbai) and, incidentally, a former England cricket captain, was so simple as to seem innocuous. What exactly were the services that Robinson had rendered to the nation and the Empire since his bank was closed down?

Lord Harris was feline in his questioning: 'I think I can honestly say that no one who knows Sir Joseph Robinson either in the Cape or in this country knows what those services are.' He had the transcript of the Joel trial with him and quoted from the judge's devastating criticism of his behaviour: 'It is wholly inconsistent with the obligation of good faith that the defendant should have made for himself these profits by the method which the evidence discloses.' It was 'a device to camouflage the transaction' and, presumably with a straight face, Harris asked: 'Surely these facts were not before the Prime Minister when he recommended Sir Joseph Robinson for distinction at

His Majesty's hands. Surely the Prime Minister must have been misled, and consequently His Majesty was misled?'

Harris was backed up by Earl Buxton, who had the advantage of having been Governor-General of South Africa between 1914 and 1920 so knew all about Robinson's reputation. His words were devastating to the would-be peer: 'When I saw this grant, this appointment, in the Press I confess I was astonished. I searched my memory in vain to find any legitimate reason why this Peerage had been conferred.

'The war, after all, was a touchstone of public and Imperial services. It gave an opportunity, grasped by many thousands in this country and in the Dominions, of doing real Imperial or local service. But since 1914, when I went out to South Africa, I have never heard Sir Joseph Robinson's name connected with any public service, either by itself or in co-operation with others, and as far as I know – and I am in a position to know – he showed no marked liberality to the various war funds which were inaugurated for the assistance of the dependants of soldiers and sailors.' Clearly no one in South Africa, or Britain, owed him anything.

'No single person in the Union, white or black, considered that either by his services or by his record he deserved this honour. When it was announced in the Press, so far as I can learn, it was received with universal astonishment and mystification; I will not use a stronger or uglier word.'

Lord Selborne, still on the case eight years on from his traffic in titles bill, pounced to say things were getting worse: 'The evil has become much greater. It amounts now to nothing less than a public scandal of the first magnitude. I must say that Parliament and the Press here have been cynically indifferent to what has been going on. It is not an exaggeration to say that immense sums of money continue to flow into the coffers of the political party in power at the moment. The whole world knows that. It is the subject of general discussion in society, in the clubs, wherever you meet men. It is a matter of general notoriety, and yet there is not a single Minister who has any knowledge of a single transaction.

'I do not believe that these immense sums can continue to pass in complete secrecy, with no publicity, no responsibility, and personal corruption not ensue. I think there is a real danger, not of the corruption of Ministers, but of corruption on the part of those who, unknown and in the dark, do this dirty work for the Ministry, and I think it is altogether unconstitutional.'

Selborne, too, had served as High Commissioner for Southern Africa between 1905 and 1910, and he also knew of Robinson only too well: 'He was known everywhere as pro-Boer ... his sympathies were never with this country.' This was true, too. Robinson had kept his head down during the Boer War and retained his friendship with the Boer president Paul Kruger. He had supposedly acted as a go-between negotiator with Kruger and the British, but more likely he had acted in his own interests to protect his investments for when he supposed the Boers would win.

Selborne said: 'Peerages are conferred upon individuals about whom nothing is known except their exceeding wealth, whose services are unknown altogether to their fellow countrymen, and one or two of whom, at least, have been the subject of severe criticism before a public tribunal.

'And who really is responsible? Who really knows why these Peerages were conferred? Nobody here knows; nobody in the country knows. The real responsibility for these recommendations to His Majesty rests with an individual wholly irresponsible, and wholly unknown to any of us. The Prime Minister, I suppose, knows; nobody else knows. The Prime Minister has taken his recommendation from somebody he trusted – I think a little too carelessly. And that person is so cynical that he has taken no trouble to dress up the gazetted reasons with any approach to accuracy or plausibility.'

Selborne did not name him but there was very little doubt that he was fingering Gregory: 'Surely this amounts to something not unlike a farce. If the public, if the Press and Parliament, sit down under this without any further protest or effort to clean this Augean stable, is it any wonder that foreigners accuse us of being hypocritical?'

The Conservative peer given the thankless task of replying for the Coalition was the 27th Earl of Crawford, newly appointed as the government's transport minister and commissioner of works, a genial figure whose wealth came not from his Scottish title but from the family's English collieries ('I am the premier Scottish earl,' he was known to say, 'but in reality I am a Lancashire coal merchant'). He could only mumble in reply that the Robinson citation for his peerage was clearly misleading.[9] The House adjourned to reconvene for further discussion on the issue a week later, evidently, though it was unsaid, once the government had sorted out the mess.

It was obvious after what had been said that the peerage could not proceed. Robinson was waiting in his suite at the Savoy Hotel, but the government belatedly realised that the aggressive and litigious elderly Randlord would have to be talked out of it. But how? The peerage had been posted in the official *London Gazette* so it would be highly tricky to withdraw it and both embarrassing and humiliating for Robinson.

A delegation was sent round to persuade him to back off voluntarily. It is said that Robinson, who was hard of hearing, initially thought that yet more money was being demanded of him and got out his cheque book to sign it over, asking: 'How much more?' Eventually, however, he was persuaded to sign a letter of withdrawal, which, understandably, he did with bad grace. It may even have been dictated for him.

When the Lords convened later that day, 29 June 1922, it fell to the Lord Chancellor, Gregory's friend Lord Birkenhead, to relay the tidings. He did so, his biographer says, unwillingly as he had also been shocked to the calibre of the men on the Birthday Honours List and told Lloyd George he could not defend it. The Prime Minister persuaded him to do so apparently by warning that if he did not, the coalition would fall. Birkenhead was not one to scoff at titles or wish the House of Lords devalued, but neither did he want to see the coalition collapse.

Accordingly, like the skilled lawyer he was, Birkenhead set about defending the award while admitting that it was a subject of the greatest difficulty and the greatest delicacy. This was not because of who Robinson was but because bureaucratically the colonial secretary had not been consulted before it was made. He skated over Robinson's past as, after all, he had earlier been recommended for a baronetcy and he ignored his reputation in favour of sympathy: 'No one, I think, has ever said this against him: that he was not an extraordinarily zealous and able pioneer in the development of the diamond and gold industry.' Birkenhead implied he had read the documents in the Solly Joel case but without admitting they had showed Robinson up as a rogue. And, speciously, that the desire for recognition in the eyes of the public was not a sign of decadence: 'the desire that the deeds and the merits of individual citizens should be marked in the sight of their fellow men by some public sign of distinction is not in the least an evidence of a decadent society; it is an evidence, provided these things are properly and decently done, of a society in which there is still credit accorded for that which is well done.'

Just as their lordships were getting restless at the cant, Birkenhead was able to pull the rabbit out of the hat: Robinson's letter declining the honour. He read it out in full:

'My dear Prime Minister,
I have read with surprise the discussion which took place yesterday in the House of Lords upon the proposed offer of a Peerage to myself. I have not, as you know, in any way sought the suggested honour.

It is now some sixty years since I commenced as a pioneer the task of building up the industries of South

Africa. I am now an old man to whom honours and dignities are no longer matters of much concern. I should be sorry if any honour conferred upon me were the occasion for such ill-feeling as was manifested in the House of Lords yesterday, and while deeply appreciating the honour which has been suggested, I would wish if I may without discourtesy to yourself and without impropriety, to beg His Most Gracious Majesty's permission to decline the proposal.'

The matter of Sir Joseph's peerage was therefore closed, Birkenhead claimed, and surely their Lordships would not wish to pursue an 83-year-old any further. Perhaps, if they wished it, there could be informal discussions with the Prime Minister and the House of Commons about the honours system?[10]

The scandal, however, was not so neatly wrapped up. Four days after the debate, the King wrote directly to Lloyd George, raising his 'profound concern at the very disagreeable situation' which had arisen on the question of Honours. 'You will remember that both in conversation and in written communications I have deprecated the ever increasing number of those submitted for the half yearly *Honours Gazette* and in recent years there have been instances in which honours have been bestowed where subsequent information has betrayed a lack of care in the inquiries made as to the fitness of the persons selected for recognition.

'The case of Sir J. B. Robinson and all that it has evoked … must be regarded as little less than an insult to the Crown and to the House of Lords and may, I fear, work injury to the Prerogative in the public mind at home and even more in South Africa … I do appeal most strongly for the establishment of some efficient and trustworthy procedure in order to protect the Crown and the Government from the possibility of similar painful if not humiliating incidents, the recurrence of which must inevitably constitute an evil, dangerous to the social and political wellbeing of the state.'[11]

The Prime Minister's reply to the King was dismissive, essentially that it had been got up by his political enemies to embarrass the government, and, anyway, the Conservatives were doing much the same fund-raising themselves: there were few nominations which had aroused criticism. Robinson had been objected to because he was independent-minded – a euphemism for being pro-Boer in the war against Britain a quarter century earlier – and that had made him powerful enemies in Africa and on the stock exchange. 'I doubt whether any change of system would result in fewer accidents and errors than have marked the Honours Lists of the last seven years,' Lloyd George brazenly declared, as if to say: errors. What errors? He did not make quite that argument in the Commons where opposition was growing, not just among the Tories who were vital to maintaining the coalition in power but also among his Liberal supporters. When Austen Chamberlain answered questions in the Commons on 21 June, he unconvincingly dead-batted away those from his own colleagues: personally, he did not think a select committee of inquiry into the way honours were nominated, or a joint committee of both houses, was desirable. Allegations about payments for honours 'have, for the most part, been entirely unfounded', Chamberlain insisted. 'I am somewhat doubtful whether there is a general wish for [an inquiry].'

Colonel Wilfred Ashley, the Tory MP for Fylde, asked meaningfully: 'How does it happen that nearly always it is only rich men who are made peers?' Chamberlain was sure that was not so.[12]

Lloyd George was equally dismissive the following day: if MPs wanted an inquiry, how far back did they want to go? But he was having to give ground, especially once five coalition supporting under-secretaries (the equivalent of junior departmental ministers) told Leslie Wilson, the Tory chief whip, that they could not support the government unless a joint committee from both Houses was set up to vet nominations.

The press too was hot on the scent, particularly the Conservative-supporting *Morning Post*, which had been pursuing the story for years and was expressing editorial outrage directed squarely at Lloyd George. Its editorial on 13 June 1922 pronounced: 'If righteousness exalteth a nation, how shall unrighteousness debase it? Political corruption is one cause of the decay ... the sale of honours has become so notorious that names and prices are openly quoted and the profits amount to a handsome fortune. The existence of that secret hoard, available for every device of the unscrupulous politician, is a public danger.'

H. A. 'Taffy' Gwynne, the paper's editor and probable author of the editorial, had long been an opponent of his fellow Welshman, but other newspapers, even those which had been loyal to the coalition, were also beginning to have doubts and were urging the Conservatives to end their pact with Lloyd George and revert to party politics as formerly. Proprietors such as Beaverbrook, Rothermere and Hulton, and editors like Wickham Steed at *The Times*, were beginning to sidle away from the Prime Minister.

The press barons, whose honours had mostly come from Lloyd George, predictably showed little gratitude now the Prime Minister's administration was faltering, and they were not to be brought off by the viscountcies they had been awarded:[13] the political story was too good to miss.

And there was also a new phenomenon, an organisation promoted by the *Post* to counteract National Dishonour and restore clean government which started raising money to field candidates against coalition MPs. It did not get very far, partly because politics moved on, but the newspaper's appeal 'to the old ideals and traditional justice and seemliness of British public life' did raise £22,000 in a few months from public subscriptions – though, as *The Scotsman* newspaper ungraciously pointed out, that would not have been enough to buy a single knighthood.[14]

Lloyd George, believing in his indispensability, still hoped for a political realignment in the form of a permanent coalition, a 'fusion' with himself at its head. With all the great events on the world stage, he felt himself needed more than ever and could not believe anything so mundane as the honours scandal could threaten the government. The trouble was that the Prime Minister by now was spending very little time in the Commons chamber, the committee corridor or the tea rooms, so he had no idea at all about the growing discontent among the Conservative MPs upon whom he relied. He did not know who they were, did not speak to them and certainly did not listen even to his colleagues in cabinet. He rather disdained them. For the most part, the Tories in the government wanted to maintain the coalition, while the Prime Minister listened to his cronies, like Bronco Bill Sutherland, the advisers from the Garden Suburb offices in the Downing Street garden, and those press barons like Riddell who were still speaking to him.

The King meanwhile was egging the government's critics on: 'Far from the king being dissatisfied with what was said ... His Majesty is only glad that the truth should be known "better late than never",' Stamfordham wrote to Salisbury on 26 June.

On 17 July, both Houses debated the Honours system. By now, peers were bandying about how much the tariff was for a knighthood or a baronetcy and reading out the letters contacts had received suggesting they might like to apply for an honour, for a price. The 8th Duke of Northumberland,[15] an able polemicist and Tory Diehard, led the charge in the Lords. He cited both the tariffs being demanded for honours and the methods being used to entice potential nominees, discreet letters asking for meetings, confidential chats, appeals to vanity, requests to help save the government and prevent Bolshevism. It was pretty clear that he knew who was doing it too, because he had letters and descriptions from several of those who had been approached. They bore the handiwork of Harry Shaw and the inveterate letter writer Douglas Moffat, who at some stage had gone to work for Gregory.

Northumberland thought it was strange that Lloyd George and his supporters seemed to be benefitting from such fund-raising measures despite being a minority in the Commons: 'The curious thing is that one of those Parties, numbering little over a hundred members, the Party of the Prime Minister would seem to have profited to an extent out of all proportion to its numbers ...

'It is generally admitted that although the Unionists are by far the most numerous and influential Party whereas the Prime Minister's Party, insignificant in numbers and absolutely penniless four years ago, has apparently amassed an enormous Party chest, variously estimated, at anything from £1,000,000 to £2,000,000. The strange thing about it is that this money has been acquired during a period when there has been a more wholesale distribution of honours than ever before, when less care has been taken with regard to the services and character of the recipients than ever before. It also coincides with a period when touting for honours has become a practice extensively carried on, and, to judge by the numbers engaged in it, is not a wholly unremunerative trade. What conclusion is the public likely to draw from this strange series of coincidences?'

The Duke outlined what he had been told by a personal friend who had been approached, reading out his letter: 'The tout commenced the conversation by saying that he was authorised to ask me whether I would accept a high honour if it was offered me. I replied "Why?" He then said that my "outstanding services to the country" had long been recognised and that the Prime Minister would be very glad if I would accept an honour, but first wished to ascertain through him whether I would accept it. I replied that such services as I had been able to render during the war had been already recognised by the bestowal of an O.B.E., and I think I added that my charwoman had received the same honour.

'I then asked him again why, if the Prime Minister thought I was deserving of some high honour, he should approach me through ... I am sorry to say that at this point I lost my temper ...'

Northumberland ended his remarks with relish: 'If that is the position which the Government are going to elect to stand upon, if they succeed in burking[16] a full inquiry into this matter I shall regret it, but I shall find considerable consolation in the reflection that no course could do them more harm in the country. And, as I regard the continuance of the present Government as an unmitigated evil, I shall not pretend to be sorry if the public forms the only justifiable conclusion that this Government have been responsible for inaugurating a system of corruption such as has not been seen in this country for a hundred years, and that they have deliberately used the Prerogative of the Crown in order to support that system.'[17]

The debate was fraught with danger and potential humiliation for the government, which announced that the division at the end would be treated as a vote of confidence in an attempt to bring any dissenters into line. Defeat in such a motion would lead inevitably to the government's resignation and a general election, but the cabinet decided on a tactical retreat several days in advance. While it would not concede a public inquiry or a joint committee of both Houses to consider the honours system as a whole, it would agree to a Royal Commission to consider the future awarding of honours. A commission had several advantages as far as ministers were concerned as such a body had a more focused and narrower remit. Its personnel would be chosen by the government and their report would be set to a timetable: it would be more controllable than a committee which could look into what it chose. A commission would technically be appointed by the King so could be publicly distanced from the ministers themselves. The commission could be a justified choice as the issues it would be examining covered the Royal Prerogative, the customary executive powers and privileges of the sovereign, in awarding honours. The commission idea was astutely leaked to the press in advance of the debate to defuse any potential explosion or embarrassment.

It was nevertheless to be a major Commons occasion but, like so many over the years, proved to be something of a damp squib, both sides being so keyed up that they floundered. Asquith announced that while some of those he had nominated had been mediocrities, he could not remember 'a single occasion' when one of his nominees had been criticised for unworthiness. Others, too, pronounced on their own integrity. The Liberal MP William Wedgwood Benn (father of Tony) called for all titles to be abolished – this was twenty years before he himself accepted the viscountcy which his son would subsequently resign.

Lloyd George took unusual care over his speech in the debate, for he was evidently highly nervous about it: he told friends he planned to speak for an hour and a quarter, which Lord Riddell told him would be too long. He insisted he would not allow an investigation into what had happened previously but only into how the honours system was to be operated in the future. In the event, the speech was a rambling mess as he tried to prove that he had acted with integrity and had behaved no differently in nominating honours than any of his predecessors. He admitted that selling honours to the highest bidder was a discreditable system, but Lloyd George argued that awarding a party donor who had also done good deeds was not discreditable. He even claimed at one point that Germany had lost the war because it lacked a privately funded party system – a suggestion that produced laughter. But he ended by announcing that the government would set up the proposed Royal Commission, something he had vehemently opposed a few weeks earlier.

The motion itself had called for a joint select committee, so there was confusion, and eventually the debate was talked out, which seems to have been regarded as an honourable solution by allowing the government to survive but seeming to find a way out of the honours quagmire. It was helpful to Lloyd George that a Royal Commission was the outcome because its brief was entirely a forward-looking one, not an attempt – as Arthur Henderson, the Labour leader had wanted – to investigate what had just been going on with the sale of honours under Lloyd George and the coalition government. In that sense he got away scot-free.

The Prime Minister's allies, however, thought his reputation had been irreparably damaged. Winston Churchill wrote to his wife, Clementine: 'Our revered leader is no doubt greatly relieved ... but on the subject of Honours or rather Dishonours he is as timid as a hare ... He has consented to a Royal Commission to see what steps sh[oul]d be taken to prevent a Prime Minister from committing abuses of the Prerogative. An awful humiliation out of wh[ich] he hopes to slide and slither in a fairly cheap way.'[18]

The commission's report, which came out at the end of 1922, less than six months after the debate and only three months since it had started its hearings, was just nine pages long and restricted itself merely to advising on future procedures to assist a prime minister in making recommendations of the names of persons deserving special honours to the king. The commission interviewed former prime ministers (except Lord Rosebery, who was too old and ill, and who had anyway left office nearly thirty years earlier) but not touts or those canvassed to make donations in return for honours. Gregory was not interviewed, and his name did not appear.

The report recommended a committee of three privy councillors independent of the government of the day to vet the names and suggested that it should be a criminal offence to offer money for a title or to act as an intermediary in the business. That outcome was a compromise: Lord Dunedin, the Conservative Scottish lawyer chairing the commission, wanted to close the issue down and understood that was his role from the start. He proposed to hear only from the recent prime ministers and their patronage secretaries, whereas other members wanted also to hear from the honours brokers as well. This was not deemed necessary: there was no wish to compromise anybody. None of the witnesses, including the current chief whips, desired to cause any embarrassment, least of all to interfere in the confidential and personal relationships between prime ministers and the monarch. As is the way of such things, the commission closed down the row. By now, the coalition government had fallen and the Conservatives were in power alone under Andrew Bonar Law. They promised there would be legislation as soon as possible.[19]

Maundy Gregory, as always when in trouble, kept his head down, and, unlike Shaw, avoided mention in the newspapers as the scandal rumbled on. Perhaps as Cullen suggests he was too powerful and knew too much for anyone to risk taking him on. Called in secretly by McCurdy, he was told that Sir Joseph Robinson had demanded his £30,000 back and did he know what had happened to it? 'Of course I know what's happened to it,' he replied. 'I've spent it.'

10. INDISPENSABLE NO MORE

It is curious that historians most sympathetic to Lloyd George tend to regard the honours scandal as essentially trivial (see for instance Kenneth O. Morgan's description[1]), whereas his critics placed it much more centrally in the reasons for the downfall of the coalition government three months after the July debates. While it is true that the Tories' attacks on the way the government was distributing awards was motivated at least partly by aggravation that their party was not getting its fair share of the spoils, the scandal certainly contributed to an atmosphere of sleaze surrounding those in power, not unlike how the awarding of contracts to party donors and cronies during the pandemic a hundred years later affected the standing of Boris Johnson's administration.

Parts of the Conservative press, such as the *Morning Post*, were certainly critical, but the coalition retained the support of other papers, including *The Sunday Times*, the *Daily Chronicle* and, curiously, the *Daily Mail*, which seems to have played down the story. The *Chronicle* even suggested in an editorial on the day after the parliamentary debates that British public life was conspicuously free of corruption because the system of conferring honours enabled governments and political parties to survive without selling out the public interest[2] – a view close to Lloyd George's assertion that ministers could tell influence seekers to get lost if they became importunate.

What was clear was that the coalition was faltering. Lloyd George had been seeking a way to form a new centrist government almost since the Coupon election of 1918, but many of the Tories on the backbenches were not keen about soldiering on under a prime minister they distrusted and who was voicing policies they disliked. The anti-coalition Liberals who had not signed up to the coupon were scarcely likely to reunite behind him. Nor, indeed, was the Labour Party, the beneficiaries of the Liberal split, who Lloyd George regarded as little better than Communists and subversives, even under moderates such as Arthur Henderson and Ramsay MacDonald.

For the time being, while the Conservative leadership in the upper reaches of the government led by Austen Chamberlain remained loyal, further down the party ranks there was growing dissatisfaction. The Prime Minister had wanted to go to the country in a general election in the summer of 1922, but international events and the honours scandal made that impossible, so he clung on hoping for something to turn up, even while by-elections in Liberal seats were being lost to Labour. The coalition did not have a centralised, still less a unified, party machine and organisation – that was something the fund might have been directed towards – but meanwhile the Tories themselves were not anxious for an immediate election until they had found an issue to distinguish themselves from their coalition partners. Eighty declared that they would not stand as candidates for a coalition party when an election came, but meanwhile the leadership did not wish to bring the government's demise about. The surmise – there were no scientific opinion polls yet – was that the coalition would lose at least 100 seats in an election. Lloyd George dangled the possibility of Bonar Law becoming foreign secretary if he resumed the leadership of the Conservatives, which he had relinquished because of his incipient throat cancer, so long as he maintained the coalition, while meanwhile the press barons Northcliffe and Rothermere were privately urging Churchill to resign from the cabinet in order to rejoin and lead the Conservatives: to re-rat, as some Tories had it, back to the party he had left as a young MP nearly twenty years earlier.

The political omens were all bad as far as Lloyd George was concerned. He was tired after seventeen years continuously in office, and he even started talking about leaving politics altogether: he quite fancied becoming editor of *The Times* (where there was no vacancy). Lloyd George was not a rich man and did not have substantial reserves – the honours fund revenues were being earmarked for fighting the election – so he was heartened when an American publisher offered him the enormous sum of £90,000 for the eventual US rights to his memoirs. Unfortunately, when the offer became known through a story in the *Evening Standard*, the Prime Minister had to say the money would go to ex-servicemen's charities: he realised he could not be seen to profit quite so ostentatiously from the war.

As for *The Times*, Lloyd George and a consortium schemed to buy the paper following Lord Northcliffe's death in the summer of 1922, but were easily outbid by the Tory MP and scion of the Anglo-American Astor clan John Jacob Astor V who put up £3m to buy the newspaper (three times what the Prime Minister's friends could manage) and keep it out of his hands.

Instead, the Lloyd George fund was invested heavily via Freddie Guest in the Liberal *Daily Chronicle* after it was sold in October 1918, giving a controlling interest to the extent of getting rid of the editor Sir Robert Donald for being insufficiently supportive (and for his provocation in employing

General Maurice of the troop shortages debate as its defence correspondent). Freddie Guest, effectively representing Lloyd George, was the majority shareholder and acting in his interests. Lloyd George's son Gwilym was also on the board as business manager. Imagine a prime minister today having such an interest in a national newspaper. The *Chronicle* became Lloyd George's chief mouthpiece in the press: 'the official organ, the defender through thick and thin, fair and foul', and in return it became the chief recipient of the government's scoops, leaks and favours.[3] It was part of the United Newspapers group, which also published the *Sunday News,* the *Yorkshire Evening News* and the *Edinburgh Evening News,* and its dividends went into the Lloyd George fund coffers. Lloyd George did not become an editor but his position with the group was more powerful and lucrative: when United Newspapers was sold in 1927, it netted him more than £2m.

Like many long-term executives, Lloyd George could not face quitting the premiership: what would the country do without him? On 22 July 1922, five days after the honours debate, he told his confidante Lord Riddell: 'The atmosphere is bad. It would be impossible to go out now, much as I should like to do so. I am tired and no wonder! But I am not going to lay myself under the charge of deserting my friends when they are in a tight space.'[4]

Instead, the choice would be made for him that October, precipitated over an international crisis that came to be known as the 'Chanak Incident', which placed Lloyd George (and Churchill) in support of Greece against Turkey and threatening war. Their belligerent stance was quixotic, threatening to go to war with Turkey against the advice of most of the cabinet, including Curzon, the foreign secretary, the military top brass, including Sir Charles Harington Harington (sic), the commander on the spot, public opinion in Britain, several of the white dominion governments and Britain's French and Italian allies.

It came about as Turkey under its new leader Mustafa Kemal (later known as Attaturk) pushed Greek occupation forces out of Anatolia, what is now western Turkey. The Turkish army seemed also to threaten a British garrison supposedly keeping the peace in the neutral zone, established after the collapse of the Ottoman Empire at the end of the First World War around the port of Chanak (now Canakkale), on the eastern side of the Bosphorus. Pragmatic opinion suggested that Britain should reach a deal with the Turks, but Churchill and the Prime Minister seemed determined to fight a new war even as the French were compromising, and it appeared evident that everything was against a resumption of hostilities just four years after the end of the Great War. Lloyd George doubled down: making a vehemently anti-Turkish speech in Manchester, which infuriated his opponents and reduced his usual supporters to despair. By contrast, and more realistically, Bonar Law wrote to *The Times* saying Britain could no longer act as the world's policeman.

Lloyd George's bellicosity against the Turks did him little good when a compromise was indeed reached and British troops withdrew in the face of superior forces. The outcome served only to expose national pretensions. Coming on top of the failure of the Genoa conference earlier in the year, the Prime Minister's stance as a supposedly world statesman and arbiter of international affairs rang hollow.

The crisis removed any possibility of calling a general election mid-crisis in the early autumn and ultimately took the initiative out of his hands. The Tories were plotting specifically to unseat Lloyd George, and the international crisis gave them the opportunity to pre-empt the attempt he was hoping to make to appeal to the country. A meeting of Tory backbenchers at the Carlton Club on 19 October saw the MPs refuse to back their party leader Chamberlain, who appealed for the coalition to continue out of loyalty to the Prime Minister.

The mood was swayed by Stanley Baldwin, the president of the Board of Trade, whose assault on Lloyd George crystalised his colleagues' suspicion of what an untrammelled and unscrupulous leader might do after a future election. Baldwin, an Anglican churchgoer, was a genial and steady figure in the Commons, well liked for his courtesy but was apparently not ambitious for high office and was accordingly not seen as a threat by potential rivals of whom the most obvious was the disdainful, aristocratic Curzon. Over the summer, Baldwin had decided he could no longer stand Lloyd George and his corruption, of which the honours scandal was a prime example. He had already come to the conclusion that he could not follow Chamberlain's lead and remain a candidate for the coalition and so would have to resign. In the words of his wife, Lucy, writing to his mother at the time: 'I knew that Stan wasn't happy at the way things were going under the PM's leadership. But just this last peril of war and the way it had been brought about was too much for him. So we decided we must make our protest, knowing that we should probably go under and of course Stan would not get office again as long as the PM was prime minister. But Stan was willing to sacrifice all that and stand out for what he felt was right.'[5]

It was a moral decision, and he made his reasons public to 275 excited and rebellious colleagues at the Carlton Club.[6] They were buoyed by the knowledge that an independent Conservative candidate had unexpectedly won a parliamentary by-election in Newport the previous day, leaving the coalition Liberal in third place, so they had the viable electoral possibility of going it alone without Lloyd George.

Baldwin's speech lasted for only eight minutes, but he captured the growing mood. He politely explained why the Tories ought to break with the Prime Minister. Lloyd George would drag down the Conservatives as he had brought down the Liberals: 'He is a dynamic force and it is from that very fact that our troubles … arise. A dynamic force is a terrible thing: it may crush you but it is not necessarily right. It is owing to that dynamic force and that remarkable personality, that the

Liberal Party to which he formerly belonged has been smashed to pieces and it is my firm conviction that, in time, the same thing will happen to our party.'[7]

The die was cast a few minutes later when Bonar Law, the party's elder statesman and former leader rose to speak. He had apparently been havering about his position with sleepless nights, subjected to intense pressure from colleagues to declare the coalition at an end. It had not even been certain that he would attend the meeting right up until the previous evening, and he was still in his carpet slippers when Sir George Younger, the party chairman, arrived at his house in Onslow Gardens the following morning to collect him. When he did arrive, he was greeted with wild applause. Bonar Law declared that it was more important to keep the party together than to win the next election – but that victory would be best achieved precisely by ending the coalition. The two speeches entirely eclipsed the lengthy attempt by Austen Chamberlain to maintain the status quo and loyalty to the Prime Minister. Bonar Law stated: 'If you agree with Mr Chamberlain in this crisis I will tell you what I think will be the result ... it will take a generation before it gets back to the influence which the party ought to have.'[8]

The motion against carrying on the coalition was won by 187 votes to 87. Within four days, Bonar Law had resumed his leadership of the Conservative Party and, on the same day, became prime minister after the resignation of Lloyd George, who could not continue in power following the resignation of Chamberlain and nine other Conservative ministers. Bonar Law, the 'unknown prime minister' in his biographer's phrase, would serve in Downing Street for just 211 days before the spread of his cancer caused his final resignation, and in just over a year he would be dead.

For himself, Lloyd George believed that he would soon be back in Number 10: 'I can't see Bonar Law lasting too long,' his wife Margaret wrote to their daughter Megan two days after the family's move to a temporarily rented house in Vincent Square. She was right about the new prime minister but wrong about her husband: in his remaining 22 years in the Commons, he would never again hold ministerial office.

Bonar Law called a general election in November 1922 immediately after taking power, standing on a platform of tranquillity and stability. With 344 MPs, the Conservatives lost 35 seats but nevertheless conclusively won a majority of 87 in a Commons which no longer had southern Irish MPs so was reduced by nearly 100 members. The Asquithian Liberals and Lloyd George Liberals formed two separate factions, with some candidates competing against each other, and were beaten for the first time by Labour and would never in the succeeding century take second place again. Labour won 142 seats, up 85, to become the official opposition. The Asquithians, with 62 seats, up 26 from their drubbing in the 1919 Coupon election, actually beat the Lloyd George Coalitionists, with 53, down 74, into fourth place.

The speech at the Carlton Club meeting brought Baldwin himself to a new prominence and appraisal by his colleagues. Bonar Law appointed him Chancellor of the Exchequer in his new cabinet and eight months later he would be propelled into the premiership following Bonar Law's resignation. 'A fellow of the utmost insignificance' in Curzon's anguished phrase when he heard that the King had appointed Baldwin as prime minister instead of himself as he had expected. The truth was, as the King was advised, a prime minister could no longer lead the country from the House of Lords. The arrival of the moral man, robust and ruddy, 'honest to the point of simplicity' it was said, with the carefully cultivated image of a countryman exhibiting all the attributes of sturdy and traditional English common sense, was as different as possible from the preceding sleaziness. This was even though Baldwin had served in the coalition government.

It was an appealing picture. Taffy Gwynne, of the impeccably loyal *Morning Post*, wrote in January 1924: 'We have at last thrown up a man of such conspicuous ability, statesmanship and honesty of purpose that he is bound in the long run to win the suffrages [votes] of his fellow countrymen.'[9] That was not the view of the press barons such as Lords Beaverbrook and Rothermere, the latter of whom loathed the new prime minister for not giving him an even higher-ranking peerage (perhaps an earldom, the next noble rank up), or his son Esmond a ministerial post, and threatened that the *Daily Mail* would back socialist candidates instead (it didn't: Rothermere feared Socialists even more than he loathed Baldwin). For his part, the new prime minister disliked the power and influence the two men wielded, particularly as they sought to overturn his leadership, perhaps in order to restore Lloyd George to the premiership. He understandably didn't like the slant of the stories their newspapers wrote about him or the lies that they told as he saw it. Baldwin incautiously told an interviewer from *People* magazine that he would not have either Beaverbrook or Rothermere in his house and they were the specific targets of a famous speech he gave in the Queen's Hall in 1931: 'What the proprietorship of these papers is aiming at is power, and power without responsibility – the prerogative of the harlot throughout the ages.' The words were probably provided by Rudyard Kipling, Baldwin's cousin, and they certainly stung.

It helped that Baldwin was independently, though not extravagantly, wealthy from the family's Midlands iron and steel manufacturing firm. His arrival would signal the beginning of the end of Maundy Gregory's influence in politics and business touting peerages. Baldwin believed that the sale of honours was 'a system that was poisoning the whole atmosphere of public life'.[10]

11. AN ACT FOR THE PREVENTION OF ABUSES

*The first thing to do was to break him
financially and this involved making
many enemies.*
J. C. C. DAVIDSON, CONSERVATIVE
PARTY CHAIRMAN

What happened to the Lloyd George fund following the fall of
his government? The answer is that it had an elusive and much
contested life through the 1920s and 30s as the divided Liberal
Party sank into a remote third place further and further behind
the Conservatives and Labour parties.

In the wake of their general election humiliation in 1922,
the two Liberal factions somewhat reluctantly decided to
work together once more: grudgingly reunited in defence
of the historic Liberal policy of free trade in the face of
Baldwin's planned introduction of trade tariffs to cut unemployment. Just as urgently, if more pragmatically, the Asquith
Liberals needed Lloyd George's money from the fund and
Lloyd George needed the party machine and organisation if
he was ever to return to power. He decided he could once
more work with Asquith, who was still head of the party.

Unconvincingly, Lloyd George insisted he had never had a quarrel with the former prime minister and had never ceased to admire him. Perhaps best not to mention the coup of December 1916, though Asquith certainly still felt bitterly about it. He decided he would work with him so long as Lloyd George was not readmitted to the heart of the party. Despite the party receiving about £100,000 from the fund to fight the next election, unlike Asquith, some Liberals were queasy about accepting the money. Lord Gladstone (Herbert Gladstone, son of the Victorian prime minister), who was in charge of party organisation, denounced it as the proceeds of corruption and said they would be better off without it.

Reunited in time for a further general election in December 1923, the Liberals gained 43 seats to win 158 MPs. But they still came out third in a hung parliament, 100 seats behind the Tories and 33 behind Labour on 191. The Tories were outvoted in the chamber and Labour formed a minority government with unofficial Liberal support. But ten months later, the third general election in two years[1] saw the Liberals enter into near terminal decline as they lost 118 MPs to end with just 40, in the face of the Tories' 412 and Labour's 151. They have never subsequently come close to achieving 100 MPs.[2]

Throughout the next decade, the near bankrupt Liberals strove desperately to claim possession of Lloyd George's fund, which by then was worth anything between £1m and £3m, while he proved reluctant to give more than small subventions at election times. Who owned the money? The party claimed that, since it had been raised to aid Lloyd George's electoral chances, as he was now effectively leader of the Liberals (for the first time), the money should be turned over to them. Lloyd George insisted that he did not control the money and that it was for the trustees of the fund (whom he himself appointed) to decide what to do with it. He was only interested in policy issues. In August 1929, he wrote to Lord Reading – Rufus Isaacs, with whom he had been embroiled in the Marconi scandal back in 1911 – to say: 'I never interfere in any of their payments unless there is a great question of policy upon which I am consulted.'[3]

The issue was only finally decided in 1938 after the deaths of the fund's last two trustees and Lloyd George and his son Gwilym appointed themselves as successors. After a legal challenge, the courts ruled that as the presumed intentions of the original donors to the fund could no longer be determined or enforced, the money was therefore Lloyd George's to do with as he wished. In the words of Sir Wilfred Greene, the then Master of the Rolls, the former prime minister had the legal right to gamble the fund away at Monte Carlo if he so wished. By the time the determination was made, there was still £470,000 in the fund. After Lloyd George died aged 82 in 1945, his worth was valued at £139,855, eight shillings and two pence.

Despite the scandal of 1922, the political upheavals of the following years meant that a bill to curb the selling of honours was not introduced until the summer of 1924. It might as well have been called the Maundy Gregory bill because it was aimed so precisely at him, and the chief mover, or at least most diligent prosecutor, seems to have been J. C. C. Davidson, who had been Bonar Law's private secretary and served in Baldwin's government as chancellor of the Duchy of Lancaster. It was, and remains, an obscure but senior administrative post, notionally supervising the revenues of the monarch's duchy estates, but usually more importantly advising the prime minister of the day on appointments and policy.

Davidson was well qualified for the post as a close friend of Baldwin, who had been a civil servant but was now a Conservative MP for Hemel Hempstead.[4] He preferred a backstage role as what today would be known as a fixer, and, as a firm Church of Scotland man, had a severe distaste for what men like Gregory were up to. Robert Rhodes James, the editor of Davidson's memoirs, said that his stern and somewhat

Puritan attitudes made him ideal for the task of cleaning up the system and he approached it with firmness and elaborate care.

However much Baldwin and Davidson disliked the sale of honours, it was not as if the Conservatives had not done it themselves. Davidson started by discussing how to tackle the problem with Baldwin: 'I approached my tactics with SB who of course hated this sort of thing. I had the right to take whatever steps I thought best to prevent Gregory getting any of his names on to the Honours list … The first thing to do was to break him financially and this involved making many enemies amongst the people – and some were very well-known people indeed – who were his clients and who expected honours in return for their payments to him.'[5]

The plot began by infiltrating a spy into Gregory's office. This was Albert Bennett, a backbench Tory MP for Nottingham Central and former London magistrate and so likely to be regarded by Gregory as a useful contact and informant.[6] But Bennett's task was to obtain the names of Gregory's contacts and clients so that Davidson could make sure that none of them would receive an honour of any sort. Since Gregory's reputation as a fixer depended on his success in getting what his clients wanted, this was a devastating strategy. Meanwhile, Davidson maintained close and apparently friendly contact with him. Gregory clearly had no idea of what was happening, and meanwhile Davidson continued to be invited to lunch at Gregory's club a few weeks before the next honours list was due to be published.

'There I had to sit, a marked man of course, at his table and consume an excellent lunch washed down by half a bottle of champagne followed by at least one sherry glass of green chartreuse. He would discuss the qualifications of his Honours list candidates and I would depart full of expressions of sympathy and explanation of how difficult these things were and having made arrangements that the list of men and the honours for which they were suitable should be conveyed to me secretly by hand.

'The most distasteful aspect of the distribution of honours was that the Royal Prerogative was being prostituted for sordid reasons ... it became assumed that in the case of a businessman, or even a press proprietor, there was money in it.'

The Ambassador Club did not impress Davidson. 'It was an elaborate and respectable-looking façade for his real activities, designed to impress clients. On the only occasion I went into his room at the club to see what it was like, I noticed a photograph and a cigarette case from the King when he had been Duke of York[7] and a photograph – also personally inscribed – of the then Duke of York, later King George VI. Neither of course had any connection whatever with Gregory.'

Davidson may have been shocked, but in that he was perhaps naïve, since Gregory had acted as an usher at one royal wedding and ostentatiously carried prominent free advertisements for the Naval charity in *The Whitehall Gazette* every month. Signed photographs and even a cigarette case might not have been too difficult to obtain.

The ruthlessness with which Davidson attempted to stamp out Gregory's influence became clear in his papers in a story concerning a City Tory donor who had been recommended by his local Conservative Association for an honour. The man[8] acknowledged to Davidson that he had also paid money to Gregory just to make sure: 'He admitted rather naively that he had paid a large sum on account to Maundy Gregory. I told him that was not a very clever thing to have done, because Baldwin could not possibly recommend to the Sovereign for an honour to a man who was on Gregory's list. I said that it was equivalent to buying an honour through a broker. He said he hadn't looked at it in that light and that he had been told that it was quite a usual thing.'

Davidson told him there was no hope of him being recommended for an honour unless he was able to show proof that he had got the money back, in his 'complete and sole possession', then the nomination might be considered. The man seems to have produced a receipt, but whether the honour then went forward remains unclear from Davidson's memoirs. He remarked only that the man was lucky not to ruin his ambitions through his foolishness: 'it was a grim indication how far matters had progressed when such men were persuaded that the direct purchase of honours was the usual thing'.

Not all quid pro quo proposals came through Gregory, but they had the same result. Another figure, an extremely wealthy industrialist, worth £200,000 a year in 1926, wrote directly to the Prime Minister on 11 January 1927 that: 'the insidious propaganda of Socialism and Bolshevism, nursed by industrial disputes and bad trade has recently had and I am afraid will have in the near future considerable influence in determining who shall govern the country after the next election … I am one of those who firmly believe that a Conservative Government with up-to-date and progressive ideas is the one most fitted to serve the best interests of our country.

'With that in mind therefore I have pleasure in enclosing a contribution of £100,000 – which I trust the Prime Minister will be able to utilise to advantage. Believe me, Yours very truly.'

Baldwin met the man (again unnamed by Rhodes James) and gave him back the cheque before sending him over to see Davidson, who by that time was chairman of the party. The man was persistent. A few months later, in May 1927, he called on Davidson again to ask whether he would be included in the next honours list, due out a fortnight later: 'I told him he was not. He asked whether that meant January. I told him that I did not know but that I was sure his services to the party would not be forgotten. I pointed out that youth was on his side … I think he was disappointed and we must look out for pressure from other quarters.'

Davidson was right. Next, he heard from a peer who called to suggest that a GBE – Knight Grand Cross – might be appropriate for the man, though he did not think he was suitable for a peerage.

Davidson had lunch with the man at Claridge's that July when he said, 'rather naively that he hoped he might receive some recognition for the various public services he had rendered'. Six weeks later, he wrote saying he had given £500 to the Conservative Educational Institute and that 'in the event of a certain promise to me being fulfilled' he would donate the same sum annually for ten years: 'Clearly he had something grander in mind than a GBE.'

The correspondence continued for several more years with the increasingly desperate industrialist becoming more and more importunate and Davidson increasingly brusque in implying he should be satisfied with the knighthood: 'I of course made no promise of any kind except that I should not forget the service he had rendered to the party.'

Eventually, it seems the man threatened to sue for his money back and in settlement Baldwin authorised Davidson to return £100,000 to him. In that he was probably luckier than if he had gone through Gregory, who generally had stickier fingers so far as cash was concerned.

This was all admirable, and Davidson was doubtless sincere in his wish to end the system of honours touting, but the fact was that the Tories, too, had raised money from donors who might expect an honour because of it – and pretty blatantly so if Davidson's industrialist, who thought it was 'quite the usual thing' to pay money to Gregory, was to be believed. There is also evidence that Davidson as party chairman accepted money for honours nominations when it suited and the donor was a Conservative: The historian G.R. Searle in his book *Corruption in British Politics* says the chairman's papers show that an Indian merchant called A. J. David was given a baronetcy after donating £30,000 and that other businessmen who donated money for the Conservative College of Citizenship[9] in 1929 at Ashridge in Hertfordshire also received awards.

In the four and a half years of his second administration (November 1924 to June 1929), the Baldwin administration nominated forty-two new peers, just under ten a year, compared to Lloyd George's annual average of sixteen (a number only partially increased because of honouring the war generals), but the selection was more carefully chosen and the nominees did not cause a scandal – no scoundrels among them. The administration, however, did observe the rule recommended by the Royal Commission that each nomination should be accompanied by a description of why the honour was being made. Such descriptions were (and are) a generalisation, such as 'for public and political services', which, in the case of political awards, is not particularly illuminating.

When George Lloyd, the governor of Bombay, approached Viscount Peel, the Secretary of State for India, in 1923 to ask whether he might be considered for a peerage, he was told that honours 'had been cheapened by too lavish a distribution in the past', and that the number was being deliberately restricted. Lloyd, who already had a knighthood, only had to wait a couple of years, however, before getting his wish and proceeding to the House of Lords. Proof that Baldwin was not entirely ill-disposed towards newspaper owners came in 1929 when he nominated William Berry, the owner of a stable of loyal newspapers including the *Sunday Times, Financial Times* and *Daily Telegraph,* to become Lord Camrose.[10]

Legislation to curb the honours touts was finally brought forward in the summer of 1925 and became law on 7 August. *An Act for the Prevention of Abuses in Connection with the Grant of Honours* was short and laid down that:

'If any person accepts or obtains or agrees to accept or attempts to obtain from any person, for himself or for any other person, or for any purpose, any gift, money or valuable consideration as an inducement or reward for procuring or assisting or endeavouring to procure the grant of a dignity or title of honour to any person or otherwise in connection with such a grant, he shall be guilty of a misdemeanour.'

The penalty for such a misdemeanour was to be imprisonment for two years and/or a fine not exceeding £500. If the accused pleaded guilty and accepted summary judgement, the penalties were reduced to three months and £50. Any money handed over or received in pursuit of an honour would be forfeited to the Crown. The act made no distinction between the person who offered payment for an honour and the tout who trafficked it: both were equally liable to prosecution. It even had the potential to benefit the tout because if the award of an honour did not result from a payment the supplicant had no recourse to recover their money unless they were prepared to be prosecuted themselves: they would have no grounds to complain and had no legal leverage over the tout to get their money back. By making the payee potentially as guilty as the tout, there was every disincentive to complain. The tout could safely pocket the money with impunity and, if threatened with the law for failing to deliver the promised honour, could legitimately deny the whole transaction and quietly keep the cash. He could even blackmail the payee by threatening exposure.

Even at the time, there was no shortage of MPs pointing out the shortcomings of the legislation: what, for instance, would constitute proof of such a misdemeanour and how and where would it be prosecuted? Who would be responsible for investigating and prosecuting it? Would the offence be committed because of an approach, or when money was handed over, or when a person was nominated? Were the penalties a sufficient deterrent, or indeed a sufficient punishment, bearing in mind – although MPs did not know it – that Gregory had allegedly been making £30,000 a year in commission.

The parliamentary proceedings were brief but predictable. Remarkably, Sir Douglas Hogg, the attorney general, began the second reading debate on Friday, 24 July 1925 by admitting that the legislation would not necessarily stop honours trafficking, but making it a penal offence would 'mark the feeling' of the general public and make it less probable that 'persons would engage in a traffic that is dishonourable to themselves and discreditable to the country to which they belonged'.

MPs on all sides felt honour-bound to support the legislation – they could scarcely not – but they had pointed questions about its practicality, none more so than Rhys Hopkin-Morris, a barrister, the Liberal MP for Cardiganshire. All parties agreed that trafficking should be condemned, he said, and the best way to do that would be to pass the bill, but: 'the bill cannot be enforced … it cannot be put into practice. How this bill is going to be enforced when passed puzzles me.'

Jimmy Maxton, the left-wing Labour Glasgow MP, one of the so-called Red Clydesiders, called for much stiffer penalties: 'Two years' imprisonment is a very common sentence given to ignorant and unlettered persons convicted of minor crimes. When a public man of some standing has been guilty of a disgraceful act of this description the penalty seems to me far too small.'

What he really wanted was no honours system at all: 'In this era of so-called civilisation surely we are beyond the stage of these tinselly, baubly honours which have absolutely no significance whatever, and which do not enhance the character or the dignity of the man to whom they are attached. It is a humiliating thing to the men who have rendered great public service during their lives under their old names to be buried under some new title in the declining years of their life. It would be raising the whole dignity of public life in this country if people retained their own names without prefix or affix of any description.'[11]

That was never going to happen. Even life peerages (which no one suggested at the time) were not created for another 33 years until the Life Peerages Act of 1958, but the demand for honours has never gone away and honours are still awarded to party donors for their public services. The Act remains on the statute book, but only one person has ever been prosecuted, and that was Maundy Gregory. Some would say he got off lightly.

12. THE AMBASSADOR CLUB

Mr Gregory is a very busy man indeed.
MRS KATE WELLS, GREGORY'S
HOUSEKEEPER, FEBRUARY 1933

The passing of the Prevention of Abuses Act did not have the outcome its framers intended, but it did cause Maundy Gregory to diversify his business interests. There were still honours that could be sold such as Papal knighthoods and he turned his attention to them. If they did not quite have the cachet of British knighthoods and baronetcies, they did at least carry exotic and historic titles such as the Equestrian Order of the Holy Sepulchre, the Order of the Golden Spur and the Most Noble Order of Pius IX. It turned out that Catholic religious orders were just as interested in raising money as Lloyd George's coterie had been and were similarly not particular about how they did it.

Catholicism in the 1920s and 30s was very much still the denomination of social outsiders in Britain. There were some aristocratic hangers-on, recusants surviving after several centuries of persecution, punishment, exclusion and isolation, but much more numerous were the descendants of the nineteenth-century Irish diaspora. Post-Reformation attitudes still held sway, that Catholicism was an alien religion governed by a foreign autocrat who had designs to rule the secular as well as the Christian world and recapture England for Popery. Although penal restrictions had long been lifted, it would be at least another thirty years before some social attitudes began to change, around the time of the second Vatican Council in the early 1960s under the patronage of the saintly and unthreateningly elderly John XXIII. It would be thirty more before senior Catholic politicians or judges would rise to high office without comment, or the suspicion that they would subvert the country. Some well-known public figures such as Evelyn Waugh or Edith Sitwell, even the Duke of Marlborough, might convert from Anglicanism, but it was usually quite a long and convoluted process requiring sincerity, courage and commitment, an awareness that one might incur (unless you were a duke or a celebrity) a degree of social ostracism or disapproval and most importantly, of course, faith and belief. As late as the 1960s, marrying a Catholic could occasionally mean abandonment by friends and family: in the 1930s it might be social death. The church's rules required mixed-marriage couples to promise to raise any children as Catholics, interpreted by some, not entirely unreasonably, as a rapacious seizure of souls.[1]

Nevertheless, Maundy Gregory applied himself to acquiring such honours, which seemed to skirt the prohibitions of the act, and he converted to Catholicism. The 1925 legislation did not specify that it applied only to the award of political honours, not honours or even foreign honours in general – that was one of the shortcomings of the act – but it clearly was targeted at the domestic market and widely understood as such. A Papal honour by contrast did not have the same social or political clout though it might entitle the holder to call themselves a knight and would give them a ribboned medal to wear, if they were brazen enough to do so. A peerage might be beyond them, but there were enough arcane titles to choose from. Medieval

privileges theoretically followed, such as the power to legiti-
mise bastards, change baptismal names and pardon prisoners
prior to their execution – not that any of these were exactly
feasible propositions for the holders of Papal honours in the
Britain of the early 1930s (or now).

Gregory was the son of a High Anglican vicar and had
read some theology at Oxford so perhaps the stretch towards
conversion was not so far as it might have been for a more
mainstream or firmly evangelical churchman. He did take
instruction from a Jesuit priest, Father Francis Colchester, at
the order's Church of the Immaculate Conception in Farm
Street, Mayfair, and was received into the church in Paris at
the Soeurs de la Retraite du Sacre Coeur in January 1932. Was
this a cynical matter of convenience to help a new business
venture or a case of genuine conversion? It is hard to say now,
but quite probably given his other secular activities the the-
atricality of Catholic worship together with the possibility of
making money attracted him.

He immediately started accumulating Papal honours for
himself at a rapid rate. He was invested as a Knight Commander
of the Equestrian Order of the Holy Sepulchre within six weeks
by Monsignor Luigi Barlassina, the priest who had welcomed
him into the church and was the grand master of the Order.
Another month and he was made a Knight Commander of the
Most Noble Order of Pius IX and then, six months after that,
a promotion to Knight Grand Cross of the Holy Sepulchre
Order and its special representative in England. Conveniently,
the order's headquarters 'for the British Empire' were in
Gregory's offices in Parliament Street (he would certainly have
offered their use for the purpose), and Maundy himself became
chancellor, entitled to call himself His Excellency, which was
probably what pleased him most.

Nor did it take Gregory long to combine business with
reverence. In April 1932, he was approached by a young, fair-
haired Australian named John Villiers Farrow with an urgent

problem. The 28-year-old was starting to make his way as a scriptwriter in Hollywood and was desperate to marry a rising young Irish actress called Maureen O'Sullivan, who had just starred as Jane in *Tarzan the Ape Man* with Johnny Weissmuller. There was just one significant difficulty: O'Sullivan was a devout Catholic and he was a divorcee and she would not consent to marriage unless he could get his first marriage annulled rather than merely ended by divorce, so that in the eyes of the church it had never occurred.[2] There was also some uncertainty about whether he was a properly baptised Catholic or not: he claimed that he had recently discovered that he had been baptised as an infant by his Irish nurserymaid, but he had also gone through an adult baptism in 1929 two years after his divorce. Perhaps he had been doubly blessed.

Farrow was staying in London and was advised by a friend working at the Danish embassy that Gregory was the sort of fixer to get the annulment problem sorted out. Accordingly, he went round to the office in Parliament Street, met Gregory, and was given a tour of the place including a 'sumptuous' private chapel. He was shown Gregory's pristine white robe trimmed with black befitting his role as Chancellor of the Order of the Holy Sepulchre in the British Empire. Farrow presumably did not know that Gregory had only been received into the church himself three months earlier. They went to lunch, naturally at the Ambassador Club, where Farrow was introduced to Gregory's friend General Jack Seely, who had been at different times a Conservative and a Liberal MP and indeed a government minister under Asquith, and two MPs with whom Gregory seemed to be on excellent terms, and the young man was subsequently a guest at the Derby Eve Dinner at the club.

When it came to dealing with his personal problem, Gregory said that 'as a confidential agent of the Vatican' he could obtain the annulment, but it would require a little money, £320, which Gregory would then distribute to Catholic charities.

That would make a good impression on the Catholic authorities. Farrow duly wrote the cheque.

It was not enough apparently as a fortnight later Gregory was demanding a further £1,000 to make an even better impression. When Farrow protested that he did not have that kind of money, Gregory proposed a deal: a £500 bill of exchange which the scriptwriter would redeem to pay Gregory on 30 September 1932, or which would be cancelled if the annulment had not yet been granted by then. Gregory strung Farrow along – the deal was always coming along in just another couple of weeks – and eventually, with no annulment on the horizon, Farrow cancelled the bill shortly before it fell due.

Gregory sued for payment of the £500 and Farrow counter-sued for the £320 he had paid the supposedly confidential Vatican agent in advance. By the time the action was going to proceed to the High Court two years later, Gregory had other problems, and it never went ahead, unlike Farrow's annulment which he eventually obtained elsewhere, and which then allowed him to marry Maureen O'Sullivan in September 1936. Both went on to stellar Hollywood careers: Farrow as a writer, director and eventually Oscar winner for the script of *Around the World in Eighty Days* in 1956, and O'Sullivan for a string of films with the likes of Laurence Olivier, Greta Garbo, Myrna Loy, William Powell and the Marx Brothers. As the eldest of their seven children, Mia Farrow has not done too badly either, but doubtless her father's expensive brush with Gregory was a bitter experience for him.

Another, even more reputable organisation which shared the premises, up on the third floor, was the Venerable Order of the Hospital of St. John of Jerusalem – better known these days as St. John Ambulance – with which Gregory associated himself. He was described as 'factotum' in a police surveillance document in the National Archives, dated February 1933,[3] although that does not seem to be an official post of the modern order. If Gregory did hold such a position, he would doubtless have relished wearing the insignia of the Maltese cross and the long black cloak worn by senior members on official occasions.

Barlassina, an imposing figure with a long, forked beard, was an enthusiastic fundraiser for the Order. He was also Bishop of Capernaum and had been Latin Patriarch[4] of Jerusalem since 1920. This was some way from his Italian homeland, and Gregory could scarcely have risen so swiftly up the medals table without His Beatitude's active involvement. The two had much in common, both were deeply conservative antisemites, and the patriarch was in particular an enthusiastic promoter of the notorious forgery known as *The Protocols of the Elders of Zion*.

Gregory was at least useful to him and must have been doing some Honours broking since his accountant Ben Pengelly subsequently went to prison for six months in 1934 for trying to blackmail Barlassina into giving him money in return for keeping quiet about senior members of the Church's involvement in the honours trade. At his trial at the Old Bailey in March that year, a letter from Pengelly to the patriarch was read out in court: 'If you are prepared to assist me financially ... I will withhold publication of the matter so far as the Order is concerned and stop publication of the cheques.' Evidently, they had been cheques for money for honours that had not been passed on. It is not clear how many Papal honours Gregory actually sold – there was a relatively brief window of time for him to do so – and probably no records were kept or have survived. Cullen says that after Gregory's downfall some of those he sold to decided not to wear their medals again. By the early 1950s in any case there seem only to have been eight members of the Order left in the country.

There were other honours, too, from secular European states and statelets, including Portugal and San Marino, and Gregory's friend the deposed king of Greece George II was always on hand to accept lunch and dispense honours even though his domain stretched no further than Brown's Hotel. Perhaps it was the Order of the Redeemer which admitted foreigners either for past services to Greece, or due to their ability 'to bring honour to the Order, through their outstanding personal virtues and excellence'.

In 1929, when Gregory was at his busiest, he and Mrs Rosse had had to move because the lease on Abbey Road was expiring. They moved into an altogether grander and much more central house, part of a grand terrace on the north side of the Bayswater Road overlooking Hyde Park, just a few yards west of Marble Arch. It had the impressive address of Number 10 Hyde Park Terrace, and Gerald Macmillan suggests that Gregory spent several months looking specifically for a property numbered 10 solely so that he could deceive guests at his office when the telephone rang by saying it was Number Ten on the line. A similar ruse was to get his staff to call Buckingham Palace, tell his contact there, Sir John Hanbury-Williams, an equerry to the King, that Gregory wished to speak to him and then, when Sir John was put through, tell whoever he was seeing that the palace wanted to speak to him.

The house[5] had a large, wood panelled drawing room running the width of the first floor with tall arched windows, but the property itself was two separate apartments: Gregory upstairs, his friend Edith, the former wife of the orchestra leader Fred Rosse, below, just as previously. It was here that Gregory kept his collection of statues of Narcissus and his rare books and manuscripts (including an Italian passport which had once belonged to Mussolini before his famous march on Rome in 1921). He and Edith dined together on the evenings he was not out and about at the Ambassador Club or the Carlton Hotel on Haymarket seeing clients or working late at his office in Parliament Street. What also appealed to him about the address was its secluded rear entrance through which he could scuttle unnoticed, slipping into his taxi without attracting attention. This was the acme of his affluence and apparent success.

A flavour of the two apartments and Maundy and Edith's life together is given in a chatty and artless letter to a potential professional companion she wrote on 15 April 1930. Edith must have been feeling lonely and depressed: 'My brother [Gregory] is in politics etc and well off. He supplies the luxuries and I the necessities. We have three pianos and a wireless etc and a lovely house. I often feel I would like a woman pal about during the day to go out and about with. We live well and simply having all we wish and have a very interesting life.

'I am not frightfully clever but versatile in my tastes. Cheery, broad-minded, travelled etc. We have a wonderful library if you love reading.'[6]

The foreign honours trade did not get into full swing until the early 1930s. In the meantime, there was still *The Whitehall Gazette* with its shameless boosterism and self-serving editorials, and in April 1927, Gregory, unable to resist a bargain and one that would gain him kudos and influence, bought himself a club. He acquired the Ambassador Club in Conduit Street, Mayfair, with the aid of a £20,000 mortgage from Barclays Bank after its original owner had gone bust, somewhat mysteriously, apparently following a loss of trade during the general strike (even though it had only lasted ten days). It was also a Gregory vanity project for it did not make money, largely due to his profligacy, but its whole point was to enhance his reputation. We have already seen how he enticed senior figures to its Derby Eve dinners, the most obvious of its celebrity annual events and one in which Gregory could discreetly bask: the apotheosis of his public career, mingling on 2 June 1931 for instance with 161 guests including peers such as the Duke of Marlborough, senior politicians including Churchill and Chamberlain for the Tories, Sir John Simon of the Liberals, Labour's J. R. Clynes and Jimmy Thomas, the government's dominions secretary, the architect Edwin Lutyens and a battery of generals and admirals.

For the club was a place for Gregory to show off and be seen as a man of influence, mingling with powerbrokers and politicians. It only opened at the start of 1926 and had little expense spared. Its dining room at the centre of the building had a décor of muted pink (or Rose du Barry as Gregory preferred to describe it), marble pillars, a balcony running round three sides and, as its pièce de rèsistance, a glass ceiling. There was a grill room and an American bar, and even a reading room filled with bound copies of *Punch* magazine and *Hansard's Parliamentary Debates*. Forty-eight portraits on vellum of members of the nobility who had attended the coronation of King George IV a century earlier lined the staircases. Upstairs, there were bedrooms, but who slept in them (or *if* they slept in them) was rather obscure. Everything as far as Gregory was concerned spoke of tone.

Gregory's lunch table was in the centre of the dining room, and each weekday he could be seen lunching (at his or rather the club's expense) with the likes of Birkenhead or Austen Chamberlain, gossiping with the King of Greece or agreeing with Sir John Hanbury-Williams, the King's equerry and former head of the British military mission to Russia during the war, about the evils of Bolshevism. Two bottles of champagne would be placed on ice each lunchtime next to the table ready for his arrival. Of course, the chief's domain there was known as the High Table.

Despite its relative distance from Westminster, out of range of division bells or even telephones in that pre-mobile era,[7] MPs enjoyed lunching there, the food was excellent, with produce flown in daily from France, though there was apparently a cheapskate policy of blending unused wine and recorking it in different bottles – certainly Gregory himself stuck to champagne which could not be so treated. He apparently told friends that he had ordered a gross of corks and a corking machine with which to stick newly undrunk wine in old bottles. The staff had a tendency to be surly, though, and as Gregory made them dress in uniforms with velvet knee breeches, perhaps that was understandable. If they were disagreeable that might have been why the dining room was often nearly empty.

Distance from the Commons was part of its charm according to John Baker White, then a director of the Economic League, an anti-communist pressure group, but later a right-wing Conservative MP: 'MPs felt they were far enough away for them to relax.' It was, of course, a gentlemen-only club and, although it reputedly had 11,000 members, many of them seem to have been on reduced subscriptions or given free admission and membership on no subscription at all.

In the evenings, the ambience changed and the Ambassador became a nightclub, not one of the racier (and more successful) sort such as the 43 Club in Gerrard Street run by the likes of Kate Meyrick, the Queen of Soho, imprisoned five times for contravening licensing laws and running what the prosecuting counsel at one of her trials enticingly called a sink of iniquity. At the Ambassador the band was led by Jack Hylton, one of the top British band leaders of the period. It was said (probably by Gregory) that the Prince of Wales was a regular, known discreetly as Number One when he arrived.

In a typical piece of self-serving puffery, Gregory himself penned a eulogistic review of the club in the September 1927 edition of *The Whitehall Gazette* just after he bought the place, so by that stage the convoluted prose must have been more aspirational than actual as a description. Of course, his connection to the club was not made clear. It was 'an organisation with the amenities and convenience of a club but with the luxury and finish of a first-class hotel in addition to the gaiety and exquisite music of a very exclusive ballroom: in other words, a rendezvous for those who wish to entertain in the best surroundings and in exclusive company'.

Other 'institutions specifically termed "Night Clubs"… offered peculiar attractions to those who have been termed "the leisured seekers of the lighter life"', the article trilled on, but 'their undoubted attractions had been marred by an undesirable promiscuity giving the term a decidedly unpleasant significance'. Not so the Ambassador, clearly: it would have all the gaiety without its social disadvantages. As for its cooking: 'Those who have tested the capabilities … in this direction aver that it has nothing to fear from any culinary competition.'

Presiding over this *sans pareil* organisation was 23-year-old Peter Mazzina, who Gregory had originally met as a 15-year-old page boy at the Queen's Hotel on Leicester Square when he was using it as a base at the end of the war. Mazzina was the son of one of Gregory's other clubland contacts, Francesco Mazzina of the Royal Trocadero restaurant in the West End, which had a louche reputation as a pick-up point for prostitutes before the First World War. The Mazzinas seem to have been part of an interrelated Italian diaspora, not to say Mafia, directing several London night spots, hotels and restaurants at the time, all of whom were useful for Gregory to know. Peter himself had also been a waiter at the Queen's Hotel before Gregory poached him. He was personable and darkly handsome in a Rudolph Valentino-ish sort of way, had been privately educated at the Mercers' School in Holborn, and, like his father, was routinely suspected by the police of various nefarious activities including receiving stolen goods. Mazzina probably allowed the premises to be used for the exchange of stolen jewellery between robbers and fences and would have received a rake off from the profits, but the police never acquired enough evidence to prove it.[8]

He must have seemed a likely (even fanciable?) lad when Gregory took over the club, for he would effectively become his manager of choice and was installed on the enormous salary of £3,000 a year, the equivalent to what some government ministers earned, and he indulged himself by buying a

Rolls-Royce. In *The Whitehall Gazette* article, Gregory, perhaps slightly defensively, praised the young man: 'To be young is by no means a bar to success ... Mazzina, known to so many as Peter, will pass many moons before he needs the assistance of Dr Voronoff or any of his cult ... He is a fluent linguist and intimately acquainted with the customs and needs of those who are habituated to regular use of such an institution as that over which he now presides.'[9] Perhaps, one later police note in the file in the National Archives speculates, Mazzina had some sort of hold over Gregory. As a mark of his esteem, Gregory bought him the Equestrian Order of the Republic of San Marino. Mazzina was in exalted company: the two most senior British recipients of the order since then have been Queen Elizabeth II and her father George VI.

The club was not really making that much money to justify such a salary as Mazzina was paid, and it is a little difficult to see who was defrauding whom, for Gregory developed quite a sheaf of outstanding debts from those who left without paying: maybe as much as £2,000 in bounced cheques were kept in his desk from men who knew that he would not take them to court for fear of deeper investigation and further disclosure. He said it was a club rule not to prosecute offenders or absconders. As a police report in the National Archives from March 1932 states, the club had 'everything but clients, an excellent dance floor, one of the best bands in London, waiters, flowers, discreet lighting and even finer discretion in the matter of payments. It was certainly not cheap if one paid, but people of consequence signed their bills and these were seldom presented.'[10]

Gregory was already under suspicion for his activities since the honours scandal and he was under covert surveillance even as he dined at the club. A Colonel Harker of MI5, eating there one lunchtime in 1927, was surprised to see Lord Birkenhead dining and apparently gossiping with Gregory at the High Table. The possibility that they were sharing state secrets as

Birkenhead was still secretary of state for India at that stage prompted an investigation. Cullen quotes Harker as telling a colleague rather over-heatedly: 'I could not believe my eyes when I saw F.E. sitting there with that villain in the middle of the dining room. I felt like rushing up to the Honourable Secretary of State with my coat in order to cover his nakedness.'[11]

Birkenhead still tended to be known by his initials from when he was plain Mr F. E. Smith. Only close friends called him Fred. It seems Birkenhead accepted Gregory's largesse and hospitality: 'the cheerful giver' without being particularly corrupted by it: 'F.E. accepted gifts from all sorts of people, not least Beaverbrook, without any hint of political corruption, just as Lloyd George for instance had a house built for him by Lord Riddell. It was quite normal for politicians of that period to be subsidised by wealthy patrons without any eyebrows being raised.'[12] Birkenhead died aged 58 in 1930 some years before Gregory's fall from grace.

The investigation did not get far. Harker believed he had enough evidence to charge Gregory with selling an honour to a Midlands businessman, then embezzling the money and refusing a refund when the honour did not materialise. He thought he had a watertight case, possibly even involving blackmail, and made an appointment to see General Sir William Horwood, the then commissioner of the Metropolitan Police, who would need to give permission for a prosecution in such a sensitive matter.

He was accompanied by the right-wing Tory John Baker White, who had also been looking into Gregory's contacts. At Scotland Yard, they waited for Sir William's private lift to take them up to his office on the third floor. It turned out to be a prolonged wait as the lift seemed stuck outside the commissioner's office. When it did finally arrive at the ground floor, the door opened to reveal none other than Gregory just leaving. According to White, he was: 'immaculately dressed as usual and with the smug expression on his face of a canary that has just swallowed a cat. Colonel Harker, who had Gregory's dossier under his arm, looked at me, then his shoulders came up to meet his ears in a comic shrug and he said, "That does it – there's no point in going up." With that he tore the dossier into small pieces which he deposited in a rubbish bin as we went out. That was the end of the matter.'[13]

Nevertheless, Gregory was by now losing what highly placed protectors he might have had. Sir Basil Thomson, the former assistant commissioner of the Metropolitan Police and chief spy hunter of the First World War, the contributor of antisemitic articles to *The Whitehall Gazette,* had been forced out of his position as director of intelligence at the Home Office after falling out with Lloyd George. He had been further compromised in 1925 when caught by the police in conversation with a prostitute named Thelma de Lava one December night in Hyde Park and was fined £5 for engaging in an act in violation of public decency. He claimed to have been researching a book.

Sir William Horwood would leave the Met in 1928 under something of a cloud. Appointed by Lloyd George in 1920, General Horwood (the Met being still saddled at that time with commanders who had been army officers without policing experience) proved to be unpopular within the force. He was a distant, humourless figure who kept away from his men and indeed attempted to impose a five per cent salary cut on them as a result of the Geddes axe. Much worse, however, was his refusal to investigate abuses within the force, including widespread corruption, bribery, backhanders and kickbacks, threats, violence and bullying. Just the man then for Gregory, but he retired, with the customary knighthood, in 1928.[14]

The club was not Gregory's only acquisition. In 1931, he obtained the Deepdene Hotel just outside Dorking in Surrey. To its impressive Victorian Italianate architecture, on the roof he added a large flashing neon sign, which could be seen for miles around, and installed tennis courts and a golf course in its extensive grounds. He again chose Peter Mazzina to manage it.

The estate had originally been bought in 1807 by Thomas Hope, a banker, owner of the Hope diamond and one of the richest men in England, who systematically set about rebuilding the Palladian-style house, completed only thirty years earlier, with orangeries, conservatories, a library and picture galleries. He also ornamented the grounds, which stretched at one stage for twelve miles beyond Box Hill, with grottoes, temples, statuary and fountains. After Hope's death in the 1840s, his son Henry rebuilt the house yet again, this time in the fashionable Italian Renaissance style with Romanesque towers, columns and verandas, not unlike and only slightly less grand than Queen Victoria's own Osborne House on the Isle of Wight, which was being built at the same time. Disraeli wrote *Coningsby* while he stayed there.

The house later devolved to a great-grandson, who used the estate for pheasant shooting parties but let the house to the Duchess of Marlborough, whose nephew, Winston Churchill, used to visit regularly. In 1917, the contents of the house were sold: a six-day auction included Greek and Roman statuary, Chippendale furniture from the forty bedrooms, two grand pianos and a billiard table, china, porcelain, 2,000 books, a nine-foot high statue of Napoleon and a slightly smaller one of Jason with the golden fleece, Persian rugs, chandeliers, right down to the coal scuttles.[15]

After the First World War, the estate was broken up, some of it used to build housing, and part of the remaining grounds would later be used to build the Dorking bypass. The house itself became a hotel in 1920, a decade or so before Gregory bought into it. It is doubtful whether many of the guests were interested in either its architecture or its history. Despite the tea dances and parties it hosted, it became better known as *the* place to go for dirty weekends. Discreet and close to London, it became, in the words of one disgruntled local, the biggest brothel in southeast England, though not all the guests may have required paying for their services. It was also a useful location for the proving of adultery as grounds for divorce.

The house was sold in 1939, incongruously enough to the Southern Railway company, which used it throughout the Second World War for administrative and operational control staff, away from the Blitz, safely outside London.[16]

Gregory was careful not to have his name too publicly associated with either the Ambassador Club or the Deepdene Hotel. The name on the title deeds was Mazzina's, shared with a non-executive stockbroker appointed by Barclays Bank called Arthur Bissett. That did not stop Gregory boasting about 'his' club and 'his' hotel. Neither made money and both would go bankrupt in 1936, but Mazzina would continue loyally to send money and to visit Gregory. The young man's other business ventures, the Bristol Grill and the separate Millionaires' Club, both in Cork Street, would also ultimately fail, and in 1943, after a police raid on the club, he was fined £215 for offences including selling alcohol after hours. He was also summoned by Westminster City Council for rate arrears totalling £292"12s"5d, which he could not afford to pay. While police waited to arrest him at his flat in Welbeck Street, he locked himself in the bathroom and hanged himself with his dressing gown cord.

Despite the loss of the political honours touting, Gregory still had *The Whitehall Gazette*, which would be joined on a separate floor in the Parliament Street office in 1929 by *Burke's Landed Gentry*, the companion publication to *Burke's Peerage*. Gregory picked up the landed publication, having been unable to secure both volumes, for a song when the Burke family, who had owned both reference books for a century, went bust. It is doubtful whether it made him any money but then it had only cost him about £2,000 to purchase, a later editor told Cullen. He did not buy it to make money, but maybe for its subscribers' list and certainly for the kudos: one more step on the road to respectability and status.

Gregory also publicly involved himself with a Ukrainian nationalist movement in exile from 1928. This became the Anglo-Ukraine Committee in 1931. Gregory probably saw an opportunity for profiting from the exiles' need to raise cash for their fight to restore the country and because of his hostility to Bolshevism. This also led him into involvement with other exiled Eastern European and Russian groups, some more respectable than others. Ukraine had achieved a short-lived independence from Russia in 1918 following the Russian Revolution. It was led for a few months by a wealthy aristocratic Cossack called Pavlo Skoropadsky, who had taken the title of Hetman (leader) briefly in Kyiv before following the retreating German Army into exile in Berlin. The movement he headed included pro-Russian monarchists, Slavists and landowners, and was never going to be strong enough to counteract the Soviet forces that swept over most of Ukraine.

Gregory's chief contact was a journalist called Volodymyr Korostovetz, who could speak English having been educated by an English tutor employed by his wealthy aristocratic family at their large estates in northern Ukraine. His father had been a colonel in the Imperial Russian army and Korostovetz himself had served as a Russian diplomat before the Revolution forced him into exile. Gregory employed him to write propaganda articles about the Hetmanite movement, and he became a leading spokesman and lecturer at places such as the Royal Institute of International Affairs at Chatham House.

The Ukrainian committee, which Gregory chaired for a while, included cronies such as Lord Southborough and Sir William Horwood. It was not only anti-Bolshevik, but also, conveniently, a useful money-making enterprise for Gregory, for he persuaded Korostovetz that he could be a fundraiser for the cause, raising large sums not only from weekly subscriptions but from large loans and grants given by wealthy and influential individuals. It would be a revival six years on of honours touting. One of those Gregory mentioned was Sir Henri Deterding,[17] the Dutch general manager of the Royal Dutch Shell petroleum company and a strong anti-Bolshevik, who he knew would surely cough up £40,000 for the cause as a pre-payment for the peerage that Gregory would acquire for him. Growing suspicious when the money did not materialise, Korostovetz contacted Deterding's office to discover there was no question of any money being contributed as Sir Henri did not wish to embroil the company in international tensions or abuse British hospitality. Further researches led Korostovetz to calculate that Gregory had pocketed £380,000 for honours since 1925 and had delivered only one knighthood.

Eventually, in February 1932, Korostovetz went to MI5 with his suspicions that he was being deceived and the cause fleeced. He was seen by Harker, the man who had tried to initiate proceedings against Gregory for embezzlement five years earlier. Korostovetz's statement to the police is in the National Archives file on Gregory: 'There was a general sense that the word of the Chief as he was invariably called in the office was listened to in high quarters and that ... money was available or obtainable for those causes that tended to support or revert to the ancient order of things. It emerged ... that the Chief was the Director of Secret Patronage and some years before Korostovetz got a definitive statement that Maundy Gregory was the Chief of the Secret Service.'[18]

Korostovetz was not the first person, nor the last to take Gregory at his word – or by inference – that he was a kingpin of the state and the chief of spies. Gregory could surely not believe it himself, and by now his Ukrainian contact could not have seriously believed it either, otherwise he would scarcely have gone to see Harker.

It must have been a cynical lie, if Gregory ever did believe it even partially, because by now he was juggling sources of income increasingly desperately as it dawned on the Ukrainians that he was untrustworthy. Gregory was at this time receiving subsidies for *The Whitehall Gazette* from Skoropadsky, who in turn seems to have received them from Alfred Rosenberg, the Estonian-German who was the Nazi movement's leading ideologue and antisemite, joining the nascent party in 1919 even before Hitler did. How far Gregory was aware of the Nazi connection is unknown. He did not voice support as he might have done through the columns of *The Whitehall Gazette* for the British Union of Fascists, which was set up by Oswald Moseley only in October 1932, as he had done for Mussolini and his Fascisti and for the antisemitic rantings of the likes of Basil Thomson.

Certainly, however, the money would have been welcome. The Ambassador Club was mostly empty and costing large amounts to keep going, and the Deepdene Hotel was heading for the rocks, too. His lifestyle was still extravagant and so was keeping up with the flamboyance of his appearance and liberality as a host.

Gregory's chief German contact, however, was not an active Nazi or sympathiser, but a conservative businessman named Werner von Alvensleben, who had served during the First World War as an aide-de-camp to Skoropadsky. Gregory had even attended a rally at the Sports Palace in Berlin in November 1930 organised by the League for the Protection of Western European Culture, a fiercely anti-Communist organisation, which was to be addressed by his friend Sir William Horwood. Von Alvensleben was made an honorary member of the Ambassador Club in return, which probably means he paid for Gregory's trip.[19]

Gregory also met the Hetman, who was living in Berlin, during his visit. They got on rather well and Gregory wrote a characteristically gushing account for the *Gazette* on his return: 'As I entered the Sports Palace, Berlin, I was at once astonished and overjoyed. His Highness the Hetman of all the Ukraine told me that he wished the enthusiasm of this meeting could be in some way electronically heard by the people of the Ukraine who are chafing in the toils of Bolshevism.' It seems doubtful that the Sportpalast, which held 14,000 people, was anywhere near full that evening, as it would be for Nazi rallies a few years later, and chafing was a mild term indeed for the Stalin-engineered great famine, or Holodomor, which killed up to five million Ukrainians shortly afterwards.

Gregory returned to Berlin the following year, again as the guest of von Alvensleben, to attend a meeting of the Herrenklub, an aristocratic conservative club, after which he seems to have fallen out with the Germans and Ukrainians, who decided to sever relations. Cullen suggests that this followed an investigation by one of their supporters, a London-based journalist named Kurt Abshagen, into Gregory and the Ambassador Club, which concluded that Gregory was a fraud and a homosexual, lacking political influence. Skopropadsky ordered the dissolution of the Anglo-Ukraine club and ended the subsidy the Hetmanites were sending to *The Whitehall Gazette* every month. Gregory retaliated by publishing a series of articles by one of the organisation's opponents 'in the public interest', and in November that year followed that up with an anonymous letter suggesting the separatist movement was being supported by a foreign (i.e. German) government.

Gregory's version of the high life included a number of expensive private passions. He became a collector of literary first editions, bought quietly from London and Parisian dealers. Some had homosexual or homoerotic themes, including Beardsley or Wilde first editions and a jewel-embossed volume of the poetry of Arthur Rimbaud. He dealt strictly with the same director in each firm where he had an account, supposedly so that only one member of staff would know how much he owed. He was also extravagant. Gerald Macmillan, his first biographer, was scathing: 'To maintain his pose as a bibliophile, he assembled a large collection of valuable books and manuscripts. But he was not a genuine collector. He knew nothing about books or their value and bought solely for appearance or effect ... he made these purchases in a manner calculated to draw attention to himself.' This included, according to Macmillan, a large collection of theological tracts bound in half-calf covers which he bought solely for the bindings.[20]

Then there was the collection of statues of Narcissus, the beautiful, young, mythological Greek hero, who fell in love with his own reflection in a pond: an archetypal gay trope. Gregory amassed several hundred copies, again according to Macmillan: 'He prided himself on his knowledge as a connoisseur and on his ability to judge the true value and proper price of such objects ... but he did not possess the knowledge to make any such judgement. This was often shown by the absurdly high prices he would pay.'

Perhaps most idiosyncratic of all was Gregory's obsession with the writings of the eccentric English writer Frederick Rolfe, who called himself Baron Corvo – Italian for Crow – a title which was apparently bestowed upon him by the Duchess of Sforza-Cesarini, with whom he had stayed for a while in 1890. By the 1930s, Corvo, who had died in poverty in Venice in 1913, was a largely forgotten and obscure literary figure. His novels, of which the most famous remains *Hadrian VII*, the story of an English seminary dropout who rises to the Papacy (a wish-fulfilment exercise in narcissism by the writer who himself had dropped out of training for the priesthood), are overwrought and camp, and Corvo himself was unashamedly gay at a time when homosexuality was frowned upon and, in Britain of course, illegal. A querulous and argumentative man, living in almost permanent poverty when he was not sponging off benefactors with whom he frequently fell out, Corvo's literary talent has always been an acquired and exotic taste.

Nevertheless, Gregory was an enthusiast and not only set about acquiring original manuscripts of Corvo's work but also founded the Corvine Society of fellow enthusiasts which met at the Ambassador Club and held banquets there from 1929. By the look of the menu at that first feast, happily reproduced by Macmillan, they – or more probably Gregory – did themselves proud. The wine list starts with vodka, followed by sherry then Montrachet 1916, Chambertin 1915, Krug Private Cuvee 1919 and Chateau Yquem 1906 with 25-year-old Croft's port and Courvoisier 1811 to accompany their eight-course dinner.

Fortunately, where many of Gregory's activities remain obscure and ill-documented because of his secrecy, his Corvine interest was fully described by a young writer and fellow enthusiast named A. J. A. Symons, who met him in the course of writing his biography *The Quest for Corvo*, which was published in 1934. Gregory called on Symons out of the blue. According to the young author, Gregory was 'a plump, rubicund, middle-sized man in the fifties with an expensive button-hole, an air of constant good-living, an affable smile, a glittering watchchain, good clothes and ... very beautiful boots'. And a fanatical admiration for the works of Corvo. He invited Symons to the Ambassador for lunch and asked whether he might buy any of the original manuscripts the young man possessed: 'He could not hope, he conceded, that I would part with any of the major manuscripts; but perhaps I could spare a fragment or a duplicate? Money was no object, he added, almost regretfully.'[21]

Symons let him have a short poem of Corvo's for £20 ('without hesitation Mr Maundy Gregory's hand went to his pocket; a thick gold-edged wallet appeared ... four five pound notes were taken from an impressive wad'). Over the course of several lunches, Symons came to see Gregory as a very rich and influential man and was much impressed that he kept a taxicab permanently waiting outside ('You see, I own it.')

Symons swallowed Gregory's story whole: two yachts, a house in London, another on the river and a flat in Brighton, a library of many rare books, much fine wine in his cellar: 'Of all these things he spoke quite calmly and with a friendly, flattering assumption that thenceforth I should share in them.' Perhaps just as impressive for an impoverished young would-be author, Gregory told him that he could have unlimited resources to search for more Corvo manuscripts: 'I could draw on him for any reasonable sum to advance these purposes. It was a memorable and delightful lunch.'

All the Gregory tropes were there, showing off to the impressionable Symons as a very rich and powerful man: cufflinks of platinum balls covered with diamonds, a black pearl tie-pin, the breathless late arrival claiming to have been detained at Buckingham Palace on urgent affairs, his important career in the secret service, his intimate links with many royal houses. And the glance around the dining room with the conspiratorial whisper: 'Of course, this place belongs to me.'

Gregory purchased a number of Corvo's letters from Symons for £150: 'exactly six times what I had paid for them'; evidently Symons was a man after his own heart. 'So far from demurring, my host questioned without the slightest irony if I was asking enough.'

This was Symons' summing up of Gregory: 'As I came to know him better … I grew to like this man of mystery … He loved visible things and the physical results of wealth with something between the zest of the parvenu and the joy of the artist. He had at least a dozen gold cigarette cases and never used the same one on two consecutive days, indeed, his personal jewellery (all very valuable and good) would have sufficed to stock a shop. Yet for all the discursiveness of his self-revelation, I could never find out his occupation nor the source of his income … all his payments were made in the crispest of brand-new bank notes or else in the shiniest of brand new money. He really seemed by his behaviour and extravagance to possess a private mint.'

But what Symons did not know was that Gregory was living way beyond his extravagant means and his cupidity and insouciance were about to bring him down.

13. A DEATH IN THE FAMILY

*One of the oddest wills of the millions that
have been stored in the
vaults of Somerset House.*
DAILY EXPRESS, 24 FEBRUARY 1933

Maundy Gregory's cash problems and indirectly his future difficulties with the law originated way back when he accepted
£30,000 from Sir George Watson, the owner of the Maypole
Dairy chain of grocery shops in 1923.[1] Sir George wanted a
peerage to add to the baronetcy he had been awarded in 1912
and he may indeed have felt he was entitled to it from his public philanthropy in Berkshire where he lived and where he had
founded a university chair for the study of American History.
He had been high sheriff of the county, too. The money was
passed over in the form of bonds.

Unfortunately, the peerage did not then eventuate. Gregory
always had an excuse for the delay: as he wrote to Sir George
in June 1926, the General Strike three months earlier had
caused a problem. 'The strike has butted in and caused the
entire side-tracking of our collection of names which was otherwise fully approved,' he wrote.[2] The bonds fell due in early
1930 and, still trusting in Gregory's bona fides, Sir George

replaced them. Then he died during a routine operation in July, presumably causing Gregory a wave of relief. It did not last long. Unfortunately, Watson's heirs and executors proved less patient and demanded the money back, claiming they were following his wishes, now that the purpose of the transaction was void.

Gregory, of course, no longer had the money. As he had with other dissatisfied customers, he tried claiming that there had been no guarantees and that anyway the £30,000 had been a personal gift from Sir George from the goodness of his heart. He denied and wriggled for another couple of years, but the executors could show evidence in the form of letters that Sir George had paid the money in the expectation of a peerage and wanted it to be repaid. They threatened to publish them. As the executors' determination hardened, Gregory found himself obliged to take out a short-term loan from Drummonds branch of the Royal Bank of Scotland in Trafalgar Square, to be repaid at the rate of £10,000 at quarterly intervals. He simply could not afford the public humiliation of having his dodgy dealings as a tout exposed, still less his shortage of money. He settled with Watson's relatives at the courtroom door on 13 January 1932: agreeing to pay £10,000 immediately, then a second tranche on 13 July, and a final payment a year hence, 13 January 1933. Plus, there were court fees of £380 to find.

This was just as he was falling out with the Ukrainians and the Germans, and there were other bills, too, to keep the club running and belatedly paying in the insurance contributions of staff at the Deepdene which had somehow been overlooked. He managed to meet the first payment to the executors, but things were getting desperate by July. Gregory asked whether Edith Rosse could lend him the money. He knew from his accountant, Ben Pengelly, who also did Edith's tax returns, that she had enough: £18,000 in savings. Gregory himself claimed that he had contributed substantially to this, the least of which was a subsidy of £5 a week for life, but there was also an annuity, a generous separation settlement from Fred Rosse[3] who paid her up to £600 a year and about fourteen properties accumulated over the years which Gregory had advised her about buying. They included, of course, *Vanity Fair* on Thames Ditton Island which he had made over in her name in 1910 when he wanted to lie low following the *Dorothy* fiasco. He had been generous, too, with ongoing gifts, for instance he had paid all the expenses for her lengthy holidays to Monte Carlo and most recently a month in Florence, spent with her friend Mrs Dagny MacKinlay. No wonder he felt he was entitled to claim some of her money. Her savings could cover the best part of the outstanding payments.

Unfortunately, Edith did not see it that way. She had not realised (why would she?) that the ever-generous Uncle Jim was desperately short of money, and, anyway, most of her capital was tied up in property and could not be readily accessed. It had been a lifetime's work, successfully lifting the former chorus girl out of penury and into a comfortable lifestyle which she did not want to give up. She also had outgoings of her own, not least her niece Ethel, who was a perpetual trouble to her.

Edith had formally adopted her twelve-year-old niece in 1916 when her father, Fred, Edith's brother, was called up for the forces. Fred, who was an impoverished carpenter living in Islington (not then as prosperous as it is now), looked after five children since their mother died. From the start, though, Aunty Edith's relationship with Ethel seems to have been a fraught one. For a period after she had left school and trained as a secretary, Ethel was persuaded to emigrate at short notice to Canada, but within a few years she was back again, and the atmosphere was soon strained. Edith thought her niece should act as her companion (her letter to a potential companion referred to earlier had evidently not worked out), Ethel thought she should be allowed out on the town and wanted boyfriends (maybe she had a few, too) and Maundy thought she should just leave, preferably forever.

There were regular rows – judging by her lengthy depositions in the National Archives, Ethel was feisty, demanding and rancorous, just like her aunt[4] – and Ethel was regularly moving into the apartment at Hyde Park Terrace and out again after there had been a falling out. The last and most serious of these happened at the end of February 1932 with Gregory insisting that she should never come back, and thereafter Edith met her surreptitiously in Hyde Park, or at the apartment when Gregory was out. She gave Ethel an allowance of £1.10s a week. But even though Ethel was no longer living in the apartment, the rows continued.

A flavour of the relationship is conveyed by a letter from Edith to Ethel on 29 June 1932, which is in the National Archives file. 'Mr G' was disgusted with Ethel's idleness: 'A girl of your age should have enough character to stand on her own but you seem strangely deficient, although in other ways capable and clever. MG like most men is fed up and doesn't see why he should go on. He has put up with you for my sake knowing what troubles and distress I have suffered.'

There was a complication in releasing her savings, even if Edith had wanted to do so, in that she had made a will bequeathing everything to Ethel (and not mentioning Gregory at all) in 1928. At some stage, following a row, that will may have been discarded, but apparently there had been a second will when Ethel was back in favour, though somehow it subsequently disappeared. It was definitely not there in the summer of 1932 when Edith wrote to her brother, Fred, Ethel's father, that July: 'Ever since I had that girl back I have had daily hell. Another terrible scene this morning and I feel half dead as if I have had a bad seizure … I have given her £2 this morning and £1 on Friday. I have absolutely finished with her and she can do as she pleases.' Fred Davies later alleged that Edith must have destroyed the second will at Gregory's behest. At the very least, relations between Edith and Ethel at that stage seemed to be in terminal decline.

On 19 August, a hot and heavy Friday with the temperature up in the mid-eighties and thunder threatening, Gregory and King George of Greece were dining at the Carlton Hotel when they were disturbed by an urgent message from Edith's housekeeper, Lottie Eyres, to call home at once. She said that Edith had been complaining of the heat all morning and that she had said she could not breathe. After a light lunch of a cheese and tomato sandwich and a half bottle of champagne, she had gone towards a window to get more air, but had fallen back and collapsed on her bed. 'Come quickly, Eyres,' she had said. 'Call a doctor. I have never felt so ill.' Eyres and Gregory's housekeeper, Mrs Kate Wells, had got her undressed and into the bed with Edith moaning that Gregory must be sent for, but he might not arrive in time. Lottie thought she had heatstroke.

The doctor who was sent for, Dr Edgar Curnow Plummer, was not Edith's usual physician; Dr Blair, who was not available, may have been on holiday. Plummer and Gregory arrived together. The doctor knew nothing of the patient, her apparent alcoholism or her high blood pressure, and does not seem to have checked as he diagnosed heat collapse and prescribed an aspirin and an ice pack. He was to change his diagnosis of Edith's condition at least four times over the coming three weeks.

It was at this point that Edith seems to have become agitated about her will and asked Gregory to get paper and write a new one out for her. Gregory told the *Daily Express* in an interview published on 20 July 1933 after the paper's crime correspondent tracked him down in Paris: 'Mrs Rosse said to me, "Jim get pen and paper – there is something I want you to write." I put my hand in my pocket and pulled out the Carlton Hotel luncheon menu card … I found there was no writing on the back and so I wrote on that … I had no pen and so I had to write in pencil. She dictated the will without the slightest hesitation. I tried to persuade her that there was no necessity to take the precaution of making her will, but she insisted in going on with it.'[5]

That was Gregory's later version, one wonders quite how hard he tried. If, as is probable, he had not had any idea of getting rid of her before, the will made out entirely to his benefit might well have seemed to present an unexpected opportunity.

The will was a brief hand-written affair on a piece of folded card, dictated by Edith moaning and whispering as if at death's door. Judging by the shaping of some of the letters it seems that Gregory probably wrote it, though in pencil, not in his usual thick-nibbed, black ink gothic-style fountain pen. The will was very brief: 'Everything I have if anything happens to me to be left to Mr J. Maundy Gregory to be disposed of as he thinks best and in accordance with what I should desire.'

Edith's initial attempt at a signature, Edith Marion Rosse, written while she was lying on the bed, ran at a slant across the last two words, so she tried again underneath at the doctor's suggestion, just missing the last line, the letters nearly falling off the side of the card. As witnesses, Plummer signed below, listing the initials of his medical qualifications, and Eyres wrote her name neatly below his. In the top left-hand corner, Gregory, using his usual pen, at some stage squeezed his signature in, too. No one who was present questioned Edith's competence to sign her scrappy new will.

It was frankly unclear how ill Edith was at this stage, beyond being diarrhetic and dizzy. She was able to read and sign the card, after all. Lottie Eyres thought the whole theatrical process was a bit of a sham, and Dr Plummer said later that in signing it he was just humouring her. His prescription of aspirin showed he scarcely thought her condition was serious, or lasting. But he was called out three times that evening and eventually gave her some morphia. Over the following days, Dr Plummer visited regularly, perhaps ten times over the course of the weekend in those pre-NHS days, but after that her condition improved sufficiently that he did not need to come again and her care reverted back to Dr Blair. In the meantime, Gregory was telling Edith's former housekeeper, Mrs Hilda Howard, who rang up to see whether she could come and visit, that she was much too ill to see anyone.

But according to her brother, Fred, she was sufficiently well that she met him at Baker Street Tube station, gave him a pound note for his birthday, which had been the previous day, and had a drink with him at the Globe pub across the road. It seemed to him that she was then back to her usual robust health. A few days after that she was taking an outing in Gregory's taxi up to Hampstead, and Blair, having visited every day since his return, was told he did not need to make any further visits. When they arrived back from the jaunt, though, Edith complained that her eyesight was suddenly bad, and she could not see properly.

Then, in the first days of September, her condition suddenly deteriorated again. Edith and Gregory had supper together in his flat on Saturday the third – liver and bacon and stewed prunes and cream prepared by Gregory's housekeeper, Mrs Wells, washed down with a bottle of champagne which he opened himself, so quite a substantial meal for an invalid. Afterwards, she went back down to her bedroom, which was the house's former billiard room and jutted out into the back garden. In the night she was violently sick, falling out of bed while trying to reach the telephone. Her bedside bell rang in Gregory's bedroom upstairs, and he came down to see what was up. Dr Plummer was called out in the middle of the night – Edith had not been satisfied with Dr Blair, Gregory claimed later – and Plummer diagnosed nothing worse than indigestion. Although Plummer visited Edith at least 27 times during her illness, sometimes three or four times a day, including night visits, his complacency and misdiagnoses make one wonder why he was chosen instead of Blair (who himself came to see her at least eight times). Could it be that it was his incompetence that ultimately appealed to Gregory, or his bedside manner? If so, he concealed it well, for all those who visited the patient said how attentive and considerate he was to Edith throughout her illness and how grief-stricken he appeared when she died.

Edith did not get any better and became bedridden and comatose over the following week, eating only liquified food such as milk and jelly. By this time, Plummer thought she was now suffering from uraemic poisoning caused by Bright's Disease[6] and decided that he had better call in a specialist. Medical men were now hovering regularly, several times a day and sometimes at night, around her bedside, so the bills were spiralling. In moments of lucidity, Edith blamed her wayward niece Ethel for making her ill through stress.

Dr Basil Parsons-Smith, a Harley Street heart specialist, noted her high blood pressure, her enlarged heart and detected uraemia, and for the first time the medical opinion was grave: he gave her little chance of recovery. Two nurses were called in and Mrs Howard was by now staying with Edith, permanently by her bedside and sleeping in the same room. Yet another specialist, a Harley Street surgeon this time, Mr David Levi, was called in (by Peter Mazzina this time) and did not take long to conclude that Edith was dying.

By now, however, it was too late to change her condition and Edith died during the night of 13–14 September with both Gregory and the first doctor in attendance. Plummer gave the cause of death as cerebral haemorrhage and chronic Bright's Disease. Once that was sorted out, Gregory went off to his scheduled lunch appointment with the King of Greece, saying he thought no good purpose would be served by postponing it.

Later that day, Gregory wrote to Edith's former husband, Fred Rosse: 'Poor Edith passed away peacefully early this morning at ten to one … We did everything we could for her – three specialists and two nurses. She did not suffer at all towards the end.' But strangely, perhaps, he did not contact either of Edith's closest relatives, Ethel or her father, Fred. Both were living in expectation that they would ultimately benefit from Edith's will, and both only found out belatedly about her death: in Ethel's case on the day of the funeral when she rang up innocently to find out how her aunt was doing. When she got through to Gregory, he told her about her aunt's death but refused to tell her the cause, claiming bizarrely that it was a professional secret.

This was extremely rash of him since his behaviour was bound to arouse their suspicions, which were only enhanced when Edith's brother, Fred, who had not even known that she was ill, called on Dr Plummer to find out what had happened and was promptly shown the door. Instead of quietening their worries, it only exacerbated them and led them to pursue the case, first with Fred Rosse, who was equally concerned about what had happened to his long-estranged wife and her money, and joined forces with them. All three consulted solicitors, then the registrar of wills at Somerset House and then the police at Scotland Yard. They were, however, too late to stop the money going into Gregory's coffers.

Perhaps Gregory was just too busy to worry about them in his haste to claim Edith's estate. What he certainly did not delay doing was getting the menu card will authorised and laying claim to all Edith's assets as she had allowed him to do with what he willed. The will was proved, perhaps surprisingly quickly, on 8 October, just over three weeks after her death, presumably because at that stage there were no objections to it, as the previous beneficiaries did not know that they had been dropped. Edith left £18,865. 18s. 11d – net £18,699. 5s 7d (nearly £900,000 in today's money) – and not only did Gregory seize it that autumn, but he had spent it all by the New Year, mostly in clearing his current debts to Drummonds Bank and the Watson executors.

Later, in an interview with the *Daily Express*, Gregory claimed to have been shocked by the amount Edith had in her various bank accounts. 'I had a shock when I went through her papers. "Why! Goodness gracious," I said. "The little lady must have been holding out on me. There must be quite

£6,000 here!" I looked through more of her papers and found another £1,000 here and another £1,000 there, until the sum total mounted up to £18,000 odd. I was never more astonished in my life.'[7]

This, to say the least of it, was a highly unlikely story, since he and Edith had shared an accountant, Benjamin Pengelly, since 1921, the man who would subsequently go to prison for attempting to blackmail Father Barlassina, who certainly knew all about Gregory's money. He would testify later that he had discovered that a lot of pages had been torn out of Edith's bank passbook after her death.

Gregory also acted suspiciously to get Edith buried quickly and chose an equally strange way to do it. Apparently, St. Nicholas Church, Thames Ditton, which would have been the nearest parish to the island where their cottages were, was somehow not suitable: perhaps the graveyard was not close enough to the river. The day after Edith's death, Bramley drove Gregory in the taxi up along the Thames Valley after lunch looking for suitable churchyards, without worrying that she had not had a connection with any of them. What he seems to have been looking for were churchyards right next to the river. Initially, he thought of Whitchurch near Pangbourne, but that did not work. Edith had always said she would like to be buried besides the Thames, closeness unspecified, but probably the churchyard of St. Mary the Virgin was not quite near enough to the river for his purposes. Gregory had called in Harrods' Funeral Service as soon as he had registered the death on the morning after Edith died and he ordered a lead-lined coffin for her. When the undertaker inquired whether the lead lining of the coffin was to be sealed so as to be watertight, Gregory apparently replied that that would be too drastic.[8]

Heading back towards London, none of the village churchyards seemed quite right, or, if they were, they were already full or reserved for parishioners. No good at Mapledurham, or Reading, or Caversham, or Sonning or Shiplake or Wargrave or Henley or Remenham: in each case the churchyards and cemeteries were for locals only. At last, they came to Bisham, a village just south of Marlow. The ancient church of All Saints is so close to the Thames that from the other side of the river it appears almost to float on it and the churchyard next to it, protected by only a low wall, also seemed likely to flood. Securing a place right next to the river required some fast talking to the vicar and a fee – essentially a bribe – of 100 guineas for church funds and the permission was obtained. A churchwarden, a local butler, was dragged out of a whist drive in the nearby parish institute hall to receive the money. The funeral would be in two days on 17 September, only three days since Edith had died. Speed was of the essence, even if it was a little undignified. With luck, by the time her relatives, especially Ethel, found out she would be safely buried and beyond all fuss. The death notice appeared in *The Times* the day after the funeral.

Surmounting the grave was a concrete plinth and a plain cross with a metal figure of Christ crucified attached, floridly inscribed, obviously by Gregory: *'IN LOVE EVER REMEMBERED EDITH MARION ROSSE (Milady) who peacefully fell asleep in London upon 14ᵗʰ day of September 1932. Requiescat in pace.'*

Below was added: *'They shall hunger no more, neither thirst any more; neither shall the sun light on them nor any heat.*

'For the Lamb which is in the midst of the throne shall feed them and shall lead them into living fountains or the waters of life, Apocalypse of St. John the Apostle. Chapter 7, verses 16–17.'

Interestingly, the translation of the text used is a Catholic one. Edith was not a Catholic and was buried in an Anglican parish graveyard, but Gregory now was, having converted nine months earlier.[9] The grave is still intact and was in good order when I visited in the autumn of 2024. It sits maybe twelve feet from the edge of the River Thames which is wide and free flowing at that point with the graveyard shielded by the low wall. It is not noticeably closer to the river than other later graves. Edith's grave is surrounded by a low concrete edge only a couple of inches deep and the grass covered grave has sunk slightly. The cross and plinth are still solidly upright but the inscription is barely decipherable with only the words 'IN LOVE … EVER REMEMBER' still clearly visible.

The speculation ever since has been that Gregory deliberately chose a site that would flood easily and an unsealed lead lined coffin that would fill with water. It was to be buried to a depth of only eighteen inches – 'I did not like to think there should be a great weight of earth over poor Mrs Rosse,' he told the *Daily Express* – and the lead would mean the inside of the coffin stayed saturated. The corpse inside would be soaked and, perhaps with luck, any cause of death would be impossible to discover. It was a trick previous poisoners seem not to have thought about. Had Maundy Gregory poisoned his old and closest friend Edith Marion Rosse? No one had seen him do it, but then that was not so uncommon: most such murderers did not let anyone observe what they were up to. That winter the graveyard did not flood, but water still leached into the grave from the nearby riverbank.

14. NEMESIS

The offence is of a highly mischievous character.
SIR ROLLO GRAHAM-CAMPBELL,
CHIEF MAGISTRATE OF THE
METROPOLIS, MARCH 1933

Edith's money had only temporarily eased Gregory's problems, and by the start of January 1933 he was desperately short once more, so much so that he was not even able (or perhaps willing) to pay the undertaker's £82 bill for her funeral. The urgency for money made him revert to old habits, and they would bring about his downfall.

The scheme was to entice a new victim willing to pay for a knighthood. In other words, it was the modus operandi which he must have thought he could get away with by a discreet approach, all being conducted privately. Perhaps he thought he might not even have to obtain the honour and could keep the money, even though that ploy had failed with the Watson executors, which was why he was in the peril he was.

Unfortunately, the man he, or his crony James Douglas Moffatt, chose did not need a knighthood and was not willing to pay for one, though he could have easily afforded to as he had recently inherited his father's 52,000 acre South Australian cattle and sheep farm. He could have lobbied through royal contacts had he wished for an honour and, worst of all, he was prepared to go to the police if he was suborned. He was, therefore, entirely unlike the provincial businessmen and hard-faced men who had done rather too well out of the war who had been tapped up by Gregory a decade earlier.

The man was a retired 37-year-old Anglo-Australian Naval officer and war hero, Lieutenant-Commander Edward Whaley Billyard-Leake DSO. He had gained a certain amount of fame during the Zeebrugge Raid of April 1918 when the British fleet had attempted to block the harbour of the Belgian port which was used by German U-boats and cruisers as a safe haven from which to attack shipping in the English Channel and further afield. Billyard-Leake had been in charge of the *Iphigenia* that day, one of three aged British naval ships which were filled with concrete and sunk at the entrance to the canal leading to the docks. He was the last to evacuate the ship right in the entrance to the canal. It was a daring and dangerous manoeuvre which won the officer not only the Distinguished Service Order but the Croix de Guerre and the Legion d'Honneur. Unfortunately, other parts of the raid did not go so well, the ships did not completely block the port entrance and within days the U-boats were out in the Channel again. But Billyard-Leake was an authentic hero, 'a cool-headed young officer … one in a thousand' according to the admiral of the fleet, and he was commemorated in a painting of the raid.

Clean-cut, blue-eyed, tall and handsome, his wartime exploits had given him friends in high places including Lord Louis Mountbatten, cousin of the Prince of Wales, who had chosen him to be a godfather of his daughter. Billyard-Leake, already on his second marriage, would shortly move on to his third, marrying the West End actress Betty Chester.

It is not clear whether the approach was initiated by Moffatt or sanctioned by Gregory. Whoever it was had not done any thorough research: they could have looked him up in *Who's Who*. Billyard-Leake was at home in 15 Lowndes Square, Belgravia, in December 1932 when he received a letter from Moffatt – the man's usual mode of approach – on Sports Club headed notepaper asking cryptically for a meeting. It stated: 'Dear Sir, I am requested to place before you a social matter of a very confidential nature which it is thought may be of interest to you. Will you kindly let me know whether you can suggest a meeting within the next few days in London or elsewhere. I cannot put more in a letter.'

Billyard-Leake dimly recognised the name as someone from the horse racing world but could not imagine what Moffatt could want from him and so ignored the initial approach. Then, when Moffatt wrote again, he instructed his secretary to find out what he wanted. A telephone call followed in mid-January, which caught the naval man off guard as he happened to pick up the telephone. Warily, he agreed to have lunch which was then postponed to 23 January 1933 because Billyard-Leake had flu.[1]

The two men eventually met on that day at the Sports Club in St. James's Square at noon. They chatted about general subjects for twenty minutes then Moffatt said: 'My business is very confidential and comes from the highest authority in the country. Would you like to have a knighthood?' Billyard-Leake simply asked 'Why?'

Moffatt replied: 'People thought [you] ought to have it.' In his statement, Billyard-Leake said that 'No such idea had ever entered my head. Then [Moffatt] said there was someone who wanted very much to meet me and discuss the matter. He said that it would cost about £12,000.' Then Moffatt produced a copy of *The Whitehall Gazette* listing the guests who had attended the last Derby Night dinner and said: 'I want you to meet Maundy Gregory. You see from this list the sort of people with whom he associates. He can get the knighthood for you.'

Intrigued but suspicious, Billyard-Leake agreed to play along. Clearly there was not a moment to lose as Moffatt wheeled him straight round to Hyde Park Terrace by taxi to meet Gregory at 3pm the same day. There, Gregory, 'whose name was unknown to me', told him: 'The highest authority in the country has been considering for a long time whether you ought not to have a baronetcy [or a knighthood, I forget which] promised to your father.'[2]

During the course of their conversation, Billyard-Leake said he gave out a great deal of general information about himself because he wanted to instil confidence in Gregory, of whom he was wary.

Gregory said to him: 'Of course you will understand that certain doors require unlocking and the sinews of war are necessary for unlocking them. We are gentlemen and understand one another.' Billyard-Leake asked for further details about these sinews and Gregory said 'they would amount to something in the vicinity of £10,000 in my case, that a baronetcy cost over £10,000 and that in Mr Lloyd George's time in the case of war profiteers from £15–20,000 had been demanded and paid. I said the sum was a substantial one and I must talk about it to my wife.' Ten thousand pounds, of course, was precisely the sum Gregory owed to be paid to the Watson executors by the end of the month.

Gregory must have been desperate to close the deal by offering a cut price special offer on the honour. He told Billyard-Leake: 'After all you have told me, of course you ought to have a baronetcy.' A new list was already being prepared and was very full but he thought his name could be squeezed on to a supplementary list in February: 'in which I think I can secure the inclusion of your name'. Otherwise it would be on the King's birthday list in June.

Gregory went on to boast about his highly placed friends including the King of Greece and Mussolini and how he was entitled at all times to direct access to the Pope. He suggested having lunch two days later at the Carlton Hotel.

After he left Gregory, Billyard-Leake went straight round to see a contact of his, Sir Godfrey Thomas, who was private secretary to the Prince of Wales (with friends like that he really did not need to buy an honour). Thomas told him to go ahead with the meeting but to keep a careful note afterwards. So the two men met again at the Carlton Hotel as arranged. Over a cocktail, Billyard-Leake told Gregory that his wife wanted proof of his bona-fides, at which Gregory pulled out a sheaf of typewritten sheets about himself. He was, of course, himself directly descended from royalty in the shape of Edward III. And he was the recipient of numerous Papal and Catholic honours: Commander of the Most Venerable Order of the Hospital of St. John of Jerusalen in the British Realm, Grand Cross of the Equestrian Order of the Holy Sepulchre, Knight Commander of the Most Noble Order of Pius IX, Commander of the Most Noble Order of the White Rose of Finland, Grand Cordon of the Royal Montenegrin Order of Danilo and Grand Cordon of the Tunisian Order of Nichan Ifitkhar.[3]

If that was not enough, he had received an apostolic blessing from Pope Pius XI only four months earlier. Then there was his work in counter espionage during the First World War, employing a thousand agents, his assistance to the Grand Duke Nicholas of Russia ('with regular quarterly emoluments paid entirely confidentially'), his active assistance with the affairs of the Montenegrin Royal Family; his role as a principal co-organiser of the great secret anti-Bolshevist movement. And his public benefactions: financing the gilding of the choir stalls at Westminster Abbey, obtaining a gold and jewelled processional cross for the abbey and 'confidentially handing over an anonymous gift of £20,000 towards saving the roof of St. George's Chapel, Windsor'.[4] It certainly sounded impressive.

Gesturing round, Gregory pointed out two or three people in the restaurant for whom he said he had obtained honours,[5] and then mentioned Admiral 'Blinker' Hall and Vernon Kell of the intelligence services with whom he claimed to be on intimate terms. He also named another admiral, Sir Lionel Halsey, who was now the treasurer in the Prince of Wales' household and yet another admiral, Sir Sydney Fremantle. The number of admirals was piling up, presumably to impress Billyard-Leake with his naval connections. Perhaps Gregory did not realise that his guest might actually know them. Rounding off the list was General Seely, the former cabinet minister who presided over the annual Derby dinners. Billyard-Leake could contact any of them, Gregory said, to check him out, except for Halsey, who had been involved in a financial transaction of which Gregory disapproved. Perhaps Billyard-Leake would like another lunch, this time with another contact, Lord Southborough?

Playing for time, Billyard-Leake said he had not yet had a chance to discuss things with his wife, which must have come as a bit of a disappointment to Gregory in the circumstances. To hurry him along, Gregory then said he had discussed the matter again with people in authority and they were willing to have the matter arranged for no more than £10,000 in his case. It would be made a certainty if Billyard-Leake could deposit part of the sum on account immediately, say £2,000. None of the money would be going to party funds, said Gregory, without mentioning where it would really be going. Billyard-Leake promised once again to discuss it with his wife and Gregory suggested they should have a further lunch in another two days, on 27 January. It was to be at the Carlton again with Lord Southborough this time and would apparently help him 'just to complete data'. Including the lunch with Moffatt, that would make three lunches in four days. Gregory was so desperate that he does not seem to have smelled a rat. Had he done so, he might have realised that the naval man did not need any special access to the sort of names he was dropping and indeed probably knew them better than he did himself.

Instead of going to the lunch, though, Billyard-Leake spoke to Thomas again and was put in touch with 10 Downing Street. Sir Patrick Duff, the principal private secretary to the Prime Minister Ramsay MacDonald, called him back and put him on to Sir Maurice Linford Gwyer, the treasury solicitor in charge of legal advice to the government. It was a sign of how seriously senior sources were now taking the case, probably realising that they had the chief honours tout in their sights at last. There had been previous complaints about Gregory but none by people who would agree to be publicly identified or give evidence in court. Anyway, as advised, Billyard-Leake cancelled his next lunch with Gregory, telephoning him from the treasury solicitor's office at Storey's Gate (just across Whitehall from Gregory's office, almost literally a stone's throw but for the treasury in between) and telling him that he would give a definitive answer the following week. What about another lunch, said Gregory, this time with the King of Greece? Alas no, said Billyard-Leake. He said he hoped it was understood that whether the deal came off or not, there would be no bones broken. Then he decamped for a long weekend in Ayrshire where the family also had property.

Before he left, however, Billyard-Leake gave a statement to a solicitor from the treasury department that he was willing to give evidence against Gregory, but only if there was a reasonable certainty of a successful prosecution. He was clearly taking no chances himself. In his statement, he explained his motivation: 'I was exceedingly indignant at the suggestions made to me by Maundy Gregory and I wish this sort of thing to be shown up and stopped so far as possible.'

It had not been the first time he had been approached, he said. He had received an invitation from Lord Southborough – a person he had never met – to join the Ambassador Club, and that Southborough told him that he had already proposed him for membership.[6]

Billyard-Leake was particularly outraged by such surreptitious approaches: 'I now believe that Maundy Gregory is mixed up with the Ambassador Club and a gang of people there who are concerned with extracting money from various people though I have no definite proof of this.' And he added an even more scandalous allegation: 'A girl I once met there told me she had been asked to make up to me and that it was believed that I would be willing to pay a substantial sum for a baronetcy in which case she would get her share for what she had done.' This implies that Billyard-Leake knew more about the club than he had previously let on. And that maybe Gregory was prepared to pimp a young woman in pursuit of cash for honours.

His statement was immediately forwarded to the Director of Public Prosecutions Sir Edward Tindal Atkinson with a covering note from Gwyer: 'You will find all about Billyard-Leake in *Who's Who*: he has a DSO, Legion of Honour and Croix de Guerre and impressed me as a witness of truth ... He says he has been keeping Maundy Gregory in play as long as he can and doubts whether he could successfully continue to do so. The matter falls in your sphere not in mine and I therefore hand it over to you.'[7]

Atkinson called Billyard-Leake in as soon as he returned from Scotland and the two met on Thursday, 2 February. Getting home to Lowndes Square later that evening with a friend named Michael Isaacs, there was a note waiting from Gregory asking him to ring. Billyard-Leake did so, but not before asking Isaacs to sit close to the telephone so that he could overhear what was being said. He wanted a witness to the conversation.

Billyard-Leake told Gregory that he had talked the matter over with his wife and definitely did not wish to continue. Gregory replied with the dodgy salesman's age-old patter about an unrepeatable offer: 'It is very regrettable as the matter is now practically complete. If you adhere to your decision the matter must drop and I cannot revive it. Couldn't you give, say, £2,000 or £3,000 on account to keep the pot boiling?' The commander replied: 'I told you that my decision would be final.' 'Will you not consider the matter and talk it over again with your wife tonight?' Gregory wheedled. Billyard-Leake said he would give him a call if he changed his mind.

The following morning, Friday, 3 February, Chief Inspector Arthur Askew, one of Scotland Yard's senior detectives with nearly 27 years in the force, was called to the Assistant Commissioner's office and told to obtain a summons for Maundy Gregory's arrest under the Honours Act. That evening, he and a detective sergeant arrived on the doorstep of 10 Hyde Park Terrace to be told by the housekeeper, Mrs Wells, that Gregory was out and she did not know when he would return. 'Mr Maundy Gregory is a very busy man indeed,' she told them. 'His hours are most irregular.'

Perhaps surprisingly, the two policemen left then but they were back on the doorstep at 8am on the Saturday. This time when Wells told them that Gregory had been called away unexpectedly, Askew told her they would wait. The housekeeper disappeared and then returned to say that Gregory would not see anyone until after breakfast. Another servant – presumably Edith's former housekeeper Mrs Eyres – later appeared to say that Mr Gregory had already had breakfast and gone out. Askew told her he believed he was in and would wait until he had seen him. He handed her his card which was duly taken upstairs.

The policemen waited for Gregory to appear in what had been Edith Rosse's drawing room on the ground floor, admiring as they did so a large poster advertising *The Desert Song*, the then popular Sigmund Romberg operetta. Meanwhile, Wells chattered away telling them that Edith had died the previous September.

It took Gregory an hour to get ready, and when he finally appeared he apologised for the delay, saying he was worried about imposters. This did not impress Askew, who told Tom Cullen forty years later that Gregory had been like an actor expecting a round of applause. 'He came trailing clouds of after-shave lotion, or of some other scent and this combined with the hair oil and all those rings, not to mention the unctuous manner, made a bad impression on me from the start.'[8]

Gregory asked what he could do for them and Askew handed him the summons with the customary caution that anything he said might be taken down and used in evidence against him. He was to be charged that he had tried to obtain £10,000 from Commander Billyard-Leake DSO as an inducement for endeavouring to procure the grant of a dignity or title of honour for him. He was to appear before the court of summary jurisdiction at Bow Street Police Court on 16 February. Special Branch was given his passport number for circulation to ports so that he was to be arrested if he tried to leave the country.

It might be thought that a summary hearing for a crime which carried the potential of two years' imprisonment and a fine was rather underplaying the case, but clearly the authorities wanted as little publicity as possible – though they could not have hoped for none at all as Bow Street magistrates was covered by the press every day because it was the central London court, hearing about the misdeeds of celebrities and extraordinary crimes in the capital every day. News of the summons started leaking out to the press in the London evening papers on the 7th, then *The Times* carried a report on 8 February. Reporters would hardly ignore a case which would be prosecuted by the Attorney General Sir Thomas Inskip, and with a defendant represented by Norman Birkett KC, one of the best-known and most successful barristers in the country, a man often to be seen defending or prosecuting murderers and fraudsters at major trials. Birkett knew Gregory since they had a shared interest in the work of Baron Corvo, and the lawyer had attended at least one meeting of the Corvine Society.[9]

In the fortnight before the hearing, Gregory had to rustle up some money and he seems to have done it by soliciting former honours clients with warnings that they might care to help him out if they did not want to see their names disclosed in open court, which would have laid them open to prosecution, too, as well as being unwelcome and embarrassing publicity. He was able to pay Birkett's 300 guineas' fee in advance, but also allegedly raised more than £30,000 by his blackmailing tactics, suggesting confidentially that 'a couple' of grand would be helpful in forgetting their names. Even so, with his career now in freefall, he took the precaution of moving silverware and other valuables, including the wine cellar out of the Ambassador Club to the Deepdene Hotel and furnishings from Hyde Park Terrace down to the flat in Brighton. Contemporary gossip also had it that many of his marks also found it prudent to disappear: Cullen quotes one saying: 'London in mid-February was as deserted as when the grouse season opens in August.'[10]

His former clients were not the only ones who were worried. So was the Conservative Party, even though Gregory had mainly sold honours for Lloyd George's party funds. At his initial hearing on 16 February, Gregory pleaded not guilty to the charge, opening the possibility that all sorts of things might come out if there was a full trial. As J. C. C. Davidson, the former Tory Party chairman who had instigated the squeeze on Gregory's honours list nominees and was now in the cabinet as chancellor of the Duchy of Lancaster, noted it was a matter to be taken very seriously. Careers might be ruined and worse. As he wrote later: 'Nobody knew to what extent Maundy Gregory would betray his past in his desperation and financial stringency. We accordingly organised someone to go and see him, who told him that he could not avoid a term of imprisonment, but that if he kept silent we could bring pressure to bear on the authorities to let him live in France after his sentence had been served.'[11] It was a price worth paying.

A memorandum in the National Archives file shows that the government was taking the case extremely warily, too. Written anonymously on 7 February, presumably by someone at Scotland Yard, it states: 'Before any proceedings were set on foot Downing Street was consulted and it was only after considerable hesitation that the decision to proceed was taken.

The Attorney General is fully aware of all the implications of this case. What would be of most use to the DPP is a list if we can provide one giving any indication of those who have been approached by Maundy Gregory in the past with a view to obtaining honours through his good offices. The DPP is of course fully aware that the sources of information that he obtains from us must on no account be divulged except to the Attorney General and his junior Mr Fulton.'

The case against Gregory was outlined at the initial hearing in front of the Chief Magistrate of London, Sir Rollo Graham-Campbell, who himself was newly knighted to accompany his promotion to the job the previous month. The attorney general guided Commander Billyard-Leake through the evidence for the prosecution. He pointed out the letter-writing Moffatt sitting uncomfortably, but uncharged, in the public gallery and explained his meetings with Gregory clearly and concisely. Isaacs was also called and led through what he had overheard from the telephone call, and the commander's chauffeur was able to confirm the dates of the lunches at the Carlton Hotel.

Birkett reserved the defence through all this and asked the magistrate's leave to postpone his cross-examination until he had had a chance to consider the position, as he had only recently been appointed. If he had not thought so before, Birkett would certainly have realised that the case against his client was formidable, the evidence strong and the witnesses unimpeachable. It is likely that he, too, had been under pressure to persuade Gregory that it was in everyone's interest that he should change his plea to guilty. If he persisted to deny the charge the case would be heard in front of a judge and jury at the Old Bailey, there would be detailed cross-examination on the Billyard-Leake case only, with no opportunity to name other names, and the full force of the law would come down on him: two years' imprisonment and a £500 fine.

The hearing was adjourned for five days. On the following Tuesday, Gregory changed his plea to guilty, and Birkett got to his feet to make the best case he could for leniency. The object of the prosecution, he said, had been fully achieved and Gregory's activities were now completely at an end. No useful purpose would be served by suggesting explanations or anything of that kind. It was difficult to do justice to Gregory and not to do injustice elsewhere. He hoped that the magistrate would feel justice would be met by a monetary penalty and payment of costs: 'I submit that would be a proper ending to this disturbing case.' In other words, closing of ranks, nothing to see here. Birkett had done his best to minimise and mitigate.[12]

Not quite all: Chief Inspector Askew was called and asked by Eustace Fulton, Inskip's deputy, whether the police had other complaints of a similar character against Gregory. Yes they had, but Fulton did not press the question, and when the magistrate questioned what those similar transactions might be, he was satisfied with the answer that others had paid or been asked to pay money to receive honours. That was as far as it went; no names, no further information required. Askew complained to Tom Cullen decades later that he had been gagged: 'I had uncovered a lot more concerning Maundy Gregory but I was not allowed to make any allusion to this other evidence.'[13]

Sir Rollo was nevertheless not falling for the argument that a monetary penalty would cover the case. The offence was of a most mischievous character – highly mischievous in itself and doubly so because anyone who committed an offence under the act endeavoured to induce some other person also to commit a criminal offence. Fortunately, on the present occasion, the attempt was unsuccessful owing to the very proper attitude taken by Commander Billyard-Leake. 'In my opinion, the maximum fine of £50 would be wholly inadequate to meet the facts of the case. On the other hand, as this is the first case under the act, I do not propose to impose the maximum penalty of three months' hard labour. You will go to prison for two months and pay £50 with 50 guineas costs.'

His words were taken down assiduously by the reporters – and perhaps coordinated afterwards to check the quotes – as they were all identically verbatim in the next day's newspapers. The story was widely, if not extensively, covered and several had photographs of Gregory looking dapper in wing collar and homburg hat outside the court, a faint smile playing across his lips. The *Express'* eulogistic profile has already been quoted in chapter one, but the *Daily Sketch* also carried a lengthy article about 'the man of mystery who made prominent personages his friend, revelations cause concern in high quarters'. He had had an amazing career, it said, with the hyperbolic sub-heading: 'Actor becomes counsellor of kings'.

The piece was so eulogistic that it could almost have been written by Gregory himself for one of his profiles in *The Whitehall Gazette*: 'Who is Maundy Gregory? That is the question the man in the street has been asking ever since the *Daily Sketch* announced exclusively a fortnight ago that a summons had been issued at the instance of the public prosecutor ... Maundy Gregory though his name was unfamiliar to the general public was well known in the highest places in London. His circle of acquaintance was select and it embraced a host of the most notable people of the day. Princes and Prelates, peers and distinguished commoners, statesmen of high rank, leaders of the arts and of the sciences – all alike came within his ambit. He was on closest terms with men and women whose names have been household words for two decades or more. But while many sought his counsel and help and many more accepted his hospitality few understood Maundy Gregory. To all he was a man of mystery. Exactly his position in the scheme of things no one really knew.

'By some he was assumed to hold a high position in the British Foreign Office, by others he was regarded as the head of the secret service and again by others to have indefinable influence in affairs – an influence that was as powerful as it was quietly exercised.' It listed his honours and his charity work and 'much activity in the role of anti-Bolshevik agitator' and noted that his home was 'tastefully furnished'.[14]

The *Sketch* and other papers were, however, suspicious that not all had been revealed about his influence: 'had these cases been gone into the names of many prominent persons, titled or otherwise, would have been introduced ... the money involved in the allegations would have amounted to hundreds of thousands of pounds.' Its columnist Candidus (those were the days when tabloid columnists could at least affect Latin names) wrote that: 'it would have been more completely reassuring if it had been proved that Gregory never had any sort of authority, direct or implied, to negotiate or if he ever had, when so scandalous a connection existed and when it ceased.'

Fortunately, the *Daily Telegraph* was on hand in an editorial to offer its readers reassurance. While the court case had been 'a salutary warning' it added: 'There is nothing to show that Gregory really was in touch with any person, official or otherwise, who could exercise the slightest influence in procuring the bestowal of an honour.'[15]

In the circumstances and considering the amount of money he had made over the years, Gregory had got off very lightly indeed. He was taken away to Wormwood Scrubs to serve the full eight weeks. Gregory was to be a 'second division' category prisoner under the terms of the 1898 Prison Act, which meant he would not be subjected to hard labour and could be given rehabilitation training. He served his sentence in the prison library. Gregory would claim to the *Daily Express* a few weeks later that his imprisonment was 'not a blot on your escutcheon, it does not deprive one of any civil rights or title or orders'.

15. THE WHOLE STORY

Maundy Gregory was let out from Wormwood Scrubs early on the morning of 12 April 1933. Having served seven weeks of his sentence, he was released early for good conduct. Waiting for him outside was Tom Bramley in the taxi and Captain Richard Kelly, a shadowy figure who knew Gregory from the Ambassador Club and who had attended at least one of the Derby Eve dinners. J. C. C. Davidson in his notes about Gregory did not name Kelly, referring to him only as 'a friend of mine', but he appears to have been much more than that. Kelly's official job was as a lobbyist for the brewing industry, but he seems also to have been an assistant to Admiral 'Blinker' Hall, the former wartime director of Naval military intelligence, who by the 1930s was a Tory MP. More than that, Hall was the founder of an organisation called National Propaganda, which became the Economic League, dedicated to countering Bolshevik infiltration and industrial subversion – its director by 1933 being John Baker White, last seen in this story keeping an eye on Gregory at the club with Colonel Harker of MI5. Kelly was secretary of the National Publicity Agency, which despite its title was also concerned with tracking left-wingers and weeding them out of trade unions and companies. It was just the sort of undercover work that would have appealed to Gregory and which he would probably have claimed at one stage to have initiated.[1]

The taxi took Gregory and Kelly to the latter's home where they had breakfast, and later in the day they motored down to Newhaven in Kelly's car to catch the ferry to Dieppe – a quieter route and one where it was thought that Gregory was less likely to be spotted than on the Dover to Calais sailing. From there to Paris, where Gregory was booked in to the Hotel Lotti, centrally placed in Rue de Castiglione, between the Place Vendome and the Tuileries Garden, under the name Peter Michael, which at least made use of two of his Christian names. Like a remittance man of old, Gregory would never set foot in England again and would be sustained by regular payments from the Conservative Party, channelled through Captain Kelly and the National Publicity Agency. Davidson and the party leader Baldwin, who had professed themselves so outraged by honours touts a few years earlier and so determined to root them out, had ended up closing down Gregory's trial in return for his guilty plea before subsidising his exile, paying for his silence about the honours he had procured and the names of those who had paid him.

As Davidson noted, they had taken him to France, 'ensconced him in previously arranged accommodation, (given) him a sum of money and promised him a quarterly pension, on condition that he never disclosed his identity or made any reference to the past ... Maundy Gregory did keep his word and as far as we know he never betrayed his identity to the French police or to the public or the people he consorted with in Paris and we kept him until the end.'[2]

Sanctimoniously, Davidson added: 'I would far rather raise £1,000 by half-crown[3] subscriptions in the constituencies than by one cheque from a rich industrialist.'

Perhaps Davidson had a memory lapse because Gregory was very much out and about in the British media and far from keeping his head down. Even on the day after his sentencing in February, the *Daily Sketch* was raising questions about Edith's death under the headline: 'Police and Woman's Death Secret … Composer's Wife Who died in the House of J. Maundy Gregory, Defendant in the Sensational Honours Case.'[4] The insinuation in the article was clear and Gregory immediately issued a writ for libel. The *Daily Express* was also incredulous about the will, though it steered clear of potential defamation by not casting aspersions: it was 'one of the oddest wills of the millions that have been stored in the vaults of Somerset House. It disposed of a fortune of more than £18,000 in thirty words written on the back of a Carlton Hotel menu … Mrs Rosse is believed to be the first testator to use a menu card.' It also tracked down Gregory's mother, aged 84, living in the home for the widows of indigent clergy in Winchester and noted that his brother Stephen was living in Canada.[5]

It did not take long for Percy Hoskins, the *Daily Express*'s crime correspondent, to track Gregory down to his Paris hotel suite for an article headlined: 'Maundy Gregory Tells the Whole Story.'[6] It began in true breathless first-person tabloid style: 'Gregory was astonished when he found I had tracked him down. It was a long time before he could bring himself to talk freely,' and continued in ghost-written, first person prose: 'It is not I who have anything to fear from the truth being told and I shall take strong action if necessary to defend myself against accusations or insinuations that there was anything disgraceful about my association with Mrs. Rosse.' That was as far as his legal action would go, though the *Sketch's* story had clearly irked him and he wanted to shut down any more inconvenient aspersions

For by then, on that very day, an inquest was being held in London into the suspicious death of Edith Rosse. Complaints about what had happened surrounding her death and particularly her will had come initially from Ethel Davies and her father Fred. As far as they knew, her 1928 will had never been revoked. Their suspicions were compounded by Gregory's extraordinary insouciance towards them. He had not bothered to contact them during Edith's month-long illness, nor to tell them how and why she had died. Instead, he had brushed them off and so had Dr Plummer. Fred at least got a brief letter saying Edith had died of a 'heart stroke'; Ethel was told when she finally reached Gregory over the telephone that her aunt was already buried near Marlow and he did not wish to discuss it further as he was suffering from influenza. When Fred asked for an appointment to see Plummer, he received this letter:

> Dear Sir,
> Respecting your telephone inquiry about the late Mrs Rosse, I think no useful purpose will be gained by seeing you: you will of course understand that any information of a medical nature is a matter of professional secrecy and I am not in any way concerned with her private affairs.
> I have no wish to be discourteous, but there is no use in wasting your time and mine in a discussion which will lead nowhere.
>
> Faithfully yours,
> E.C. Plummer[7]

The letter prompted Fred Davies to approach the Paddington Green coroner's office about 'something not being right' about Edith's death – he was told to get a solicitor – and also to write again to Maundy Gregory to query her burial at Bisham when there was a family plot at Edmonton, which his sister had known about, and to ask for more details about the will. The letter he received back from Gregory's private secretary, George Pratley, on 10 October was warmer in tone but no more satisfactory. Gregory, it said, was searching for information about the grave in north London: 'He has been intending to write to you for some days to tell you that he would like a little later to consider personally making you some little gift from himself as a memento.' The letter was written a week after he had been granted probate on Edith's estate.

This idea was scarcely satisfactory. Over the next few months, Fred and Ethel, neither of whom had much money – Ethel was currently living in a convent hostel and working part time at Selfridge's – managed to track down Edith's death certificate at the Paddington registrar's office and her will, such as it was, at Somerset House. The author Andrew Cook points out that Edith's replacement will was placed with Somerset House on the day it was made, 19 August 1932, which was a Friday, and since Edith fell ill in the early afternoon after lunch, Gregory must have rushed immediately down to the registry of the probate office on the Strand to lodge the will before it closed for the weekend. At that stage, of course, it was still thought by the doctor that Edith was suffering from heatstroke and nausea.[8]

Fred wrote again to Gregory in late October: 'Everywhere I make enquiries people seem to be under the impression that *you* were Mrs Rosse's brother … I must inform you that she desired me to participate. I must ask you to give me full details … we must be able to settle this dispute amicably … I am entitled to the information I seek.' That received no reply.

The couple contacted Edith's former husband, Fred Rosse, who became equally agitated because he disclosed that he was still officially her next-of-kin. He had been paying her a monthly sum for the last eight years and could not understand how she had accumulated so much money: probate had been granted on 3 October, less than three weeks after her death, so they now knew she had left nearly £19,000. Fred Rosse engaged solicitors to stop the disbursement of the estate but they were already too late: the money had gone and, as far as they were concerned, the will was legitimate.

On 8 February 1933, probably spurred on by press reports of Gregory's forthcoming court case, Ethel went to the police at

Scotland Yard. She also must have tipped off the *Daily Sketch* that she had done so or the newspaper could not have written its story about the 'death secret'. At the Yard, she dictated to detectives over the course of several days a lengthy and meandering account of the ups and downs of her relationship with Edith, her knowledge and suspicions of Gregory, and the saga of the wills, the most recent of which on the back of the menu card might have been forged because it was largely in his handwriting. Her statement was laboriously written down on 60 sheets of foolscap paper, but if Ethel thought that it might affect the hearings at Bow Street Magistrates' Court she was mistaken. She was also seen by Chief Inspector Askew because he had been involved in the Billyard-Leake case. He was not particularly impressed with Ethel: 'She is a most garrulous person and I found her very difficult in keeping to the point,' he wrote in a report to his superiors. Fred Davies was also interviewed and was equally unimpressive: 'He is apparently a man of rather low mentality and not a person on whom a great reliance can be placed.'[9]

Little account was taken of the father and daughter's desperation – both were now out of work and needed the money that they thought was rightfully theirs – or of the dismissive way they had been treated by Gregory and Dr Plummer, who had clearly believed they would just go away if they were stonewalled. Anyway, the Gregory court case was about to start and Askew was busy.

Nevertheless, Fred Rosse was interviewed the following week, two days after Gregory had been sent to prison, and he insisted that his wife would never have made a will on the back of a menu card: 'knowing her thorough business mind I cannot conceive her making such a will … I am convinced that in her normal state of mind my wife would not have used a pencil to make her will and I am not satisfied with the execution of her will which I am given to understand is in the handwriting of Maundy Gregory. I certainly think the matter calls for a police inquiry. I certainly think the doctor and the housekeeper should be called.'

Askew filed his report on 25 February, outlining all he knew about Gregory and his associates. *The Whitehall Gazette* was 'undoubtedly used to influence his dupes in the belief that the journal was an official or semi-official organ whereas it was run at a loss and had no official status. Gregory was also the controlling spirit of the Ambassador Club in Conduit Street and rendezvous of people in his pay or closely associated with him in his inducements to get people to part with large sums of money … to procure titles. The club was managed by one Peter Mazzina, a naturalised British subject who is said to be an associate of known receivers of stolen property the most notorious of whom is "Hubby" Distleman and a man named "Biff" Byfield who are said to have displayed very valuable jewellery at the club. I am given to understand the Ambassador Club was conducted at a great loss and the bailiffs are in there. Also that Drummonds Bank is involved in the loss to the extent of many thousands of pounds. Distleman is well known to myself and most West End officers as a thief. He will receive close attention.'[10]

Although permission for a suspicious death inquiry was given almost immediately, it was another two months before the investigation got properly underway, a few days after Gregory had been whisked away to France. The delay was surely deliberate. Similarly, a petition for bankruptcy was only filed at the High Court on the day of his departure on the ferry. Having kept Gregory quiet so far in return for a light sentence, the authorities certainly did not want him to come back and start spilling beans. The debts were quite staggering; there were bank overdrafts of £3,150 and a loan of £1,500 from the National Provincial Bank on the lease of Hyde Park Terrace; £300 to the tax authorities; debts to Sun Life Assurance and rent to the Paddington Estate; the rent on the Parliament Street office had not been paid, nor the electricity and gas bills. He owed £892 to the Goldsmiths and Silversmiths' company, presumably for presents, £800 to a jeweller named Plante and £389 to Cartier, £41 for his broad-nibbed pens, £160 worth of cigars, £107 to his wine merchant, £46 to his optician, £98 on clothes and £95 to the Carlton Hotel for unpaid lunch bills. He owed the printers and stationers £832; he needed to pay £550 for car hire, boatbuilders were owed £155, booksellers £85; three solicitors' firms were waiting for £500 each, one of which had also loaned him £250. Dr Plummer had not been paid, nor had Harrods the £82 for Edith's funeral, and there was also legacy duty on Edith's estate of £1,750. None of these had been paid, nor had individuals who were also owed money, such as Ben Pengelly. Gregory was made bankrupt at a creditors' meeting on 9 June. The Home Office eventually paid for the cost of Edith's funeral.[11]

The exhumation of Edith's grave at Bisham took place on the evening of 28 April, exactly a fortnight after Gregory left the country and seven and a half months since the burial. It was not exactly a private affair: there were grave diggers, constables from the Berkshire police, detectives including Askew sucking on his pipe, the Home Office pathologist Dr Gerald Roche Lynch and several journalists, including a man from the *Daily Mail* and Hoskins from the *Express*. Lynch took soil and separate water samples from inside the grave and the surrounding area. The grave diggers required a tripod, pulley and chain to winch the heavy coffin back into the daylight, for even though it was only buried eighteen inches deep, it was full of water. As they lifted it, the water poured out. Hoskins told Cullen 40 years later that he heard Lynch murmur to his assistant: 'Not a chance – not a bleeding chance.'[12]

The coffin and its contents were driven by lorry overnight up to Paddington mortuary to await the postmortem by Dr Lynch and Sir Bernard Spilsbury, the leading criminal pathologist of the day, a man whose punctilious delivery of evidence in court had hanged many criminals convicted of murder over the previous 25 years. First, Fred Rosse had the distressing duty of formally identifying his former wife and then the pathologists got to work. It was as Roche had feared: the body had been immersed in water for several months over the winter because the Thames had leached into the lead coffin.

It took two and a half months for the inquest into Edith's death to be held, probably because it took several meetings for Spilsbury and Lynch to agree their conclusions, but maybe also because of nervousness on the part of the authorities about what the findings might show. If they thought that delay would cause the story to fade away, however, they were mistaken. By late June, the *Daily Telegraph* was querying what was taking so long: it was, the paper said, 'one of the most mysterious cases that has ever been brought before a coroner's court'.[13] Why had the inquest taken so long to come to court, Fred Seymour Cocks, the Socialist MP for the Nottinghamshire constituency of Broxtowe, demanded to know in the Commons. There was no desire other than to conduct the fullest possible inquiry, replied Sir John Gilmour, the home secretary, smoothly.[14]

Meanwhile, according to Cullen, who spoke to Gregory's friends who had seen him in Paris, the man himself was holding mock trials in his hotel room and recruiting them to rehearse what might happen if he was extradited and taken to court. He was not going to return to England if he could help it, and he recruited a solicitor called Walter Frampton to safeguard his interests.

He need not have worried. When the inquest was eventually held on 19 July, the Central London Coroner, Samuel Ingleby Oddie, refused Fred and Ethel's solicitor's request to delay the proceedings until Gregory was present. Dr Plummer, as might be expected, dead-batted questions: did he think that Edith's vomiting and diarrhoea might have been caused by other than natural causes, or something she had eaten? No. The terms of the will had not aroused his suspicions? No, not in the least. He had been perfectly satisfied by his diagnosis of the cause of death. Why had he treated her relatives with scant courtesy? Because he had not known what their standing in the matter was.

The coroner asked: 'Were you not rather rude to Mr Davies when he called to see you?' Plummer answered: 'I was a busy man. It was after Mrs Rosse's death and Mr Gregory told me he had had a great deal of trouble with them ... under these conditions I think it is a matter of general principle among the medical profession not to impart information without the authority of the relatives of the deceased ... I regarded Mr Gregory as the natural representative.' He had, he said, listened to what Fred Davies had said: 'I did not immediately show him the door.' The coroner said: 'Perhaps you got a bit irritable?' 'Possibly.'

Much more seriously for Plummer's reputation came the evidence of the pathologists. Spilsbury was asked by Ingleby Oddie whether there had been a brain haemorrhage. There had not. Any sign of Bright's Disease? No. 'Is it a fact that the death certificate is quite wrong?' Yes.

Lynch, who said he had never seen such a shallow grave, was asked whether there had been any trace of poison in the body. He answered: 'In view of the time that elapsed since death and the condition to which the body had been subjected ... It is quite possible that certain poisons could have become decomposed, thus rendering their detection impossible.' He was asked: 'Are there poisons which might have produced symptoms or signs similar to those Mrs Rosse suffered from?' Yes. 'Is it a well-known fact that after prolonged exposure certain poisons do decompose?' Yes ... owing to conditions there may have been poisons which had decomposed.

Gregory's solicitor, Walter Frampton, asked: 'You examined for poison?' Yes. 'You found none?' None.

Dismissing the Davies' solicitor's further request for the inquest to be adjourned until Gregory was present as a material witness, Ingleby Oddie drew the hearing decisively to a close. It was an open verdict: 'I am certain that a more careful analysis has never been made than that in this case,' he said. 'The result is a negative one ... All I will say is that no poison has been found and no poison will ever be found in this body. Therefore, no possible charge could arise out of this inquiry.'[15]

And that was that. Any further questions about Edith and her final illness were left unexamined and there was no attempt to extradite Gregory to answer them. Nor was there any attempt to examine Ethel or the two Freds, Davies and Rosse. Why had Plummer misdiagnosed Edith's condition no fewer than four times and ultimately entered an erroneous cause of death? Why had specialists not been called in earlier? What was the significance of her symptoms, including the eyesight problems, that afflicted her during her illness? Why had Gregory sought to have her buried in a shallow grave next to the Thames in a parish with which she had no connection when she could have been buried at Thames Ditton where she had lived, in a graveyard which was only a few yards further from the river? What, if anything, was the significance of the bottles of chemicals that the police had removed from the attic at Hyde Park Terrace?[16] What had happened to Edith's previous wills and why had the requests for information from her brother and niece been ignored? Unsurprisingly, such unanswered questions led to speculation then and subsequently that Gregory had murdered her and covered up the crime. Certainly, the inquest was curtailed. An inquest's purpose is to determine the cause of death, not prejudge a criminal investigation, and an open verdict was probably the only realistic finding, but there is certainly a sense that the coroner did not want to probe too deeply. Almost certainly the authorities were as anxious as Gregory himself that he should not appear

Does the circumstantial evidence, the scrappy will, the convenience of the bequest of all Edith's savings to Gregory immediately after she had refused to help him and at a time when he was desperately in need of funds, the hurried search for a particular grave site, the dismissal of relatives' concerns, all amount to more than a suspicion of murder by Gregory? For his book, *Cash for Honours*, Andrew Cook consulted a forensic medical specialist, Professor Derrick Pounder of Dundee

University, who examined the medical notes of Dr Parsons-Smith, the heart specialist who was briefly called in at the very end of Edith's illness. He suggested that these showed that Edith was suffering from very high blood pressure by then (184/124) and that her reported symptoms of headaches, blurred vision and vomiting were characteristic of hypertension.

Edith was known to have been a heavy drinker and a hysteric, but Plummer did not take any account of this. Further, the albumen that Parsons-Smith noted in her urine indicated kidney disease had probably developed from cystitis, so Plummer's diagnosis of Bright's Disease may not have been so far from the mark.

Pounder suggested that Spilsbury's assessment was far too dogmatic – a common criticism of the great pathologist's assertions made by forensic scientists who have reviewed his cases in recent years – and that he should not have ruled out the possibility of a stroke, or strokes, or have been able so quickly to dismiss the likelihood of kidney disease, given the state of Edith's body when he saw it. Pounder concluded that Edith had died from natural causes.[17]

People who knew Gregory at the time thought he was unlikely to have had a killer instinct, though, as we know, that does not necessarily prove anything: there have been plenty of upright and mild-mannered poisoners. Colin Coote told Cullen that he believed Gregory was essentially kindly, not a killer: 'Flamboyant but not ferocious, more of a leech than a lecher, more vulgar than vicious.' But Chief Inspector Askew, who dealt with more murderers than most, was resolute: he told the author forty years on: 'I am convinced that Gregory murdered Mrs Rosse. Furthermore, if he had not skipped out of the country on his release from Wormwood Scrubs, I would have rearrested him on the murder charge.'[18]

16. MONSIEUR DE GREGOIRE

Maundy Gregory soon moved out from the Hotel Lotti into a
small second floor apartment fairly close by at 8 Rue d'Anjou.
Its facilities were basic: an entrance hall, sitting room, kitchen
and bathroom. It was a far cry from 10 Hyde Park Terrace. His
chief companion was a small brown, yappy Pomeranian dog,
which he named Monsieur Le Beau and which accompanied
him everywhere, including to the American bar of the Hotel
Meurice, a short walk from his flat, past the Madeleine church
where he worshipped, down Rue Royale, skirting the Place de
la Concorde and then along the Rue de Rivoli to the hotel. He
was in the bar most days, drinking whisky and clearly in deep
depression. He complained that he was lonely and sometimes
started weeping. Captain Bertie Phipps, a long time Paris resi-
dent, was asked by people in London to keep an eye on him and
told Cullen: 'Monsieur le Beau was all that kept Maundy from

going round the bend. Maundy lavished all of his affection on that dog, which was a horrid little beast, always yapping at anyone who came too near it. But Maundy would spend hours grooming it and he never ate himself until Monsieur had been fed, usually off the best Sevres china.'[1]

Gregory regarded the bar at the Meurice as his headquarters. Ronnie Russell, the English barman who worked there for forty years before retiring in the mid-sixties, told Cullen that he found the new arrival in 1933 arrogant: 'He stood in the doorway with his friend Captain Phipps surveying the scene as though he was planning to buy the hotel ... inspecting the bar arrangements including the clientele ... He introduced himself to me as Sir Arthur Gregory.[2] He said that he was planning to be in Paris for some time and that he would like to run up a bar bill, explaining that he received his remittance from home once a month.'

From then on at the start of every month, Gregory would go in with a brown paper parcel fastened with red sealing wax and put it down on the bar, check his bar bill against the tally he had written in a small notebook kept in his waistcoat pocket, invariably pronounced the debt accurate, then opened the package, drew out some bank notes and handed them over. Russell said: 'I thought to myself, this man must be crooked or he would not suspect other people of being crooks.' The barman knew precisely who he was because he recognised him from the photograph in the European edition of the *Daily Mail*. He said he worried about Gregory – by now bald, portly and red faced, looking older than his 56 years – walking home through the middle of Paris late at night with his pockets stuffed with bank notes.

At some point in the 1930s, Gregory discovered Dieppe on the channel coast for weekends by the sea. It was a town well known to British exiles such as Oscar Wilde, who had lived there for a time after his release from prison in the 1890s. Gregory stayed with an Anglophile French family called

D'Roubaix, whose house the Villa La Case was on the west cliff overlooking the sea and the port's harbour. He was apparently ostracised by the town's small English expatriate community. According to Phipps, he was questioned by the English wives over tea in a local café about why he associated with 'that wife poisoner'. Phipps was surprised by the vehemence of the attack: 'What is this, I asked, a tea party or an inquisition? Ironically there was hardly a member of the English colony who wasn't being paid to keep out of England for one reason or another.' They took exception to his knighthood and Gregory disdained them in return.

The chilliness of the welcome did not stop him moving there full time in 1939, though he kept on the Paris apartment. He stayed with the D'Roubaixes. 'We were the only family in Dieppe who would receive Gregory,' the family's son Mickey, who had been a teenager in the late 1930s, said. 'People used to ask us: what do you see in that imposter? But father found him amusing, besides Gregory was extremely thoughtful in the way he repaid hospitality. At Christmas he would leave an expensive gift beside the dinner plate of each member of the family.'

Gregory was also welcomed to the family because he was by now a devout Catholic, attending Mass every day. He was drinking heavily. D'Roubaix said: 'I have known him to bring a whisky bottle to the dinner table when he stayed with us. He would sip whisky during the meal while the rest of us shuddered and drank our wine. He kept a bottle of whisky on the night table as well: "just in case I wake in the night". He was never drunk, but then he was never sober.' Cullen speculates that this was the only family Gregory had lived with since he was growing up in Southampton more than forty years earlier.

When in Paris, Gregory occasionally raised his profile, having lunch at the British Pavilion during the International Exposition in 1937 and once, in 1938, during a state visit by the King and Queen, following the entourage down the Champs Elysees in an open topped car, waving to the crowd.

Perhaps he felt entitled to do so, having been at their wedding fifteen years earlier. But he was more and more seen in Dieppe, limping with his little dog along the promenade while dressed in an absurd shaggy fur coat tied with a pyjama cord around his middle. It reached right down to his ankles, and it covered his increasingly gaunt frame: he had lost weight and his old suits hung loosely about him. By now he was also suffering badly from gout.

Once the war broke out, Gregory's previous chatter about having been a spy master in the First World War came back to haunt him. When German planes bombed the town, aiming at the hotels which had been turned into hospitals for wounded British troops, he was sure that he was the real target. None the less, when the evacuation of British civilians began in the spring of 1940, he did not join the rush to go back to England as the German forces approached. Phipps told him that unless he got a move on it would be impossible to get away and he was even offered sanctuary at Captain Kelly's home in Sussex. But he did not take it up, probably fearing a court case back in England where the bankruptcy proceedings against him were still to be concluded. At one stage he even thought he might return to Paris to collect his property left behind. He did not get there and all his effects, including his piano, were lost. He never did return to the apartment.

But soon it was too late. By the end of May, the trains had stopped running and the British army was reduced to the salient up the coast at Dunkirk. Peter Taylor, the British consul in Dieppe and one of the last to leave, said Gregory commandeered a bicycle and fixed a basket to the handlebars for the dog, and the last he saw of him he was steering down the road out of town: 'I saw them start out on that Sunday morning on the road to Rouen, Maundy with his fur coat flapping around him and wobbling uncertainly as he tried to get his balance, the dog yapping furiously at the unaccustomed indignity of the basket. A more ludicrous pair it would be hard to imagine.

I wondered whether they would get beyond the outskirts of Dieppe – Maundy had a game leg remember – and then I promptly forgot about them as I had too much on my mind.'

Somehow, Gregory managed to get himself 170 miles south from Dieppe to Le Mans along roads which would have been full of refugees fleeing the advancing Germans. He must have ditched the bike or swapped it, but he kept the dog. Perhaps he managed to get on a train, or maybe he hitched a lift: it would have been a circuitous route if he was really still trying to reach Paris. But at Le Mans he seems to have fallen in with a Parisian dentist named Fevrier and his family who were heading westwards, as far away from the capital as they could get. They had booked a room at a country hotel named Belle-Vue in the small Breton town of Chateauneuf-du-Faou, a few miles inland from the far western coast of Finistere at Quimper, and it was there on 5 June, ten days after leaving Dieppe, that Gregory also secured a room where he would stay in hiding for the next four months.

When Cullen visited the Belle-Vue in February 1972, it was still functioning as a hotel and the chatelaine, Madame Anne Yvinec, remembered Gregory when the author showed her his photograph. One would never forget a face like that, she told him, even though when he came here he was a lot thinner. He had signed in as Monsieur de Gregoire and Cullen took the small room that he had had on the second floor.

Gregory, still with Monsieur Le Beau, stayed in his room and had his meals there, only emerging to go to the bathroom at the end of the corridor and occasionally at night to walk the dog. However much he was lying low, however, many in the town were aware of l'Anglais du Belle-Vue.

Things grew much trickier for Gregory when German troops arrived a couple of weeks after him and were actually billeted in the hotel, occupying thirteen of the rooms. He initially moved up to the attic, sleeping on a chaise longue and creeping around in slippers taking care not to step on any floorboards that creaked, but after a while he began to come downstairs and creep back to his room. If he met any Germans in the corridor, Mme Yvinec said, he pretended to be deaf or dumb. Gregory could not speak much French, but his acting ability, which had stood him in such good stead for so long, had never quite left him. Eventually, in early November 1940, growing bored in confinement, he started going out at quiet times of day when the occupiers were guarding the coast or acting as customs officials, and it was on one of these excursions that a local shopkeeper betrayed Gregory to a German officer as he walked past his shop. When the German said that his fellow guest at the hotel must be French, he was apparently told that everyone in town knew he was an Englishman.

Gregory was arrested at the hotel the following morning and insisted on finishing his breakfast before accompanying the troops sent to arrest him. He made no attempt to hide his identity and was loaded onto a lorry to be taken back to detention in Paris. Monsieur Le Beau was left in the care of Mme Yvinec. The bill for his accommodation, food and especially drink, went unpaid, and Madame, whose sheltering of the Englishman might have got her into serious trouble, does not seem to have suffered: perhaps the Germans in the sleepy country town were happy to remain boarders in her hotel, or perhaps she convinced them that she had really thought Gregory was French.

Gregory arrived first at the Drancy internment camp in the northeastern Paris suburbs where he was held with other British citizens who had failed to get out of France in time: it would only later become a holding camp for Jewish people about to be transferred to the death camps. The British themselves were a mixed group, ranging from people who happened to have passports to jockeys working for French trainers and the Duke of Windsor's former butler, James Hale.

Gregory at least had his fur coat, and such an encumbrance when fleeing Dieppe the previous summer kept him warm throughout the Parisian winter. Cullen found a fellow internee who had been at the camp as a teenaged merchant seaman, Leonard White, who told him that the coat had been the envy of the other inmates: 'that and his boots that were fur-lined sabots with wooden soles: most of us would have given a month's pay to own those'. He recalled that Gregory had been kind to him, helping him to learn some basic French as they limped around the camp. Painfully thin and weak and lacking access to the whisky which had previously sustained him, Gregory spent some of the winter in the camp hospital being treated by a Canadian Jewish doctor.

The following summer, he was moved on to another internment camp at the nearby suburb of St Denis where he was found by Ronnie Russell, the barman from the Hotel Meurice. 'I was shocked by his changed appearance. He was much thinner than when I had seen him last; he looked haggard and ill,' Russell told Cullen. 'He seemed embarrassed to see me. He took me to one side and whispered, "Pretend that you don't know me all that well and don't come to see me that often."' Russell thought Gregory was ashamed to be seen with a barman, particularly as he had by then made the acquaintance of some Benedictine monks at the camp and thought they might be judgemental. Russell believed that Gregory had managed to get hold of a supply of miniature whisky bottles from Red Cross food parcels which civilians were entitled to receive. They were probably not enough to sustain him.

In August 1941, Gregory collapsed and was taken to the Val de Grace hospital, which was run by the Germans. They realised that he was dying and offered to release him, but Gregory refused – he was not going to collaborate in any way, apparently telling them: 'You arrested me, now you can jolly well keep me for the duration of the war, and what's more we're going to win.'

If so, it was a last defiant gesture. On 21 September, Gregory made a will leaving everything to his old friend Marcel

D'Roubaix-Bulger, who had first put him in touch with the family with whom he had stayed at Dieppe, 'leaving everything I possess in England, France and any other else place'. There was pitifully little. His Paris flat was at some point emptied by a man or men who had a key and told the concierge that they were acting on behalf of a dentist named Fevrier, who must have been the man giving Gregory a lift in June 1940. Perhaps Gregory gave him the key, or perhaps he stole it. Madame Yvenic from the Hotel Belle-Vue visited the flat after the war in the hope of getting some of what she was owed but found there was nothing left.

Later, Mickey D'Roubaix, the surviving son of Gregory's Dieppe friends,[3] boasted to the *Daily Express* that he had been left a vast fortune, but that must have been Gregory being economical with the truth one last time. He was still seeking to trace Gregory's assets in 1955, but there were none to recover. In any event, searching for whatever might have been left must have been very difficult indeed, and Gregory's Tory Party pension would have stopped with the German invasion of France. The will was witnessed by a doctor and an orderly, and Gregory died a week later on 28 September 1941. He was three months past his sixty-fourth birthday. According to the hospital records, he died from 'progressive cardiac insufficiency' having been admitted to the hospital in 'a very bad condition, absolutely fleshless with notable dwindling of the muscles and a swollen liver'. Russell said: 'Maundy died from a lack of booze. The Germans had cut off his whisky supply.'

Gregory was buried in a cheap grave at the Ivry-Paris new cemetery – it is unknown who paid for the burial but probably the D'Roubaix family – the grave space being rented for five years. After that, in the post-war period, no one was prepared or able to sustain the annual 250 franc renewal cost of the plot so his bones were removed to an ossuary.

The National Archive files show that security services continued to keep an eye on Gregory as far as they could during the war. A War Office note initialled SAH dated 20 March 1940, while he was still in Dieppe, stated: 'While we have no reason here for suspecting Gregory of engaging in espionage activities with the Germans, I am perfectly prepared to believe anything of him.'[4] The French police were asked to track his mail and forward anything of interest, but how far that was possible in the chaotic circumstances of the period may well have been open to question. There was also a later rumour that Gregory had been approached by the Germans to broadcast propaganda to Britain in the manner of Lord Haw-Haw[5] and a number of other British Nazi sympathisers in Germany, but there is no evidence that he was ever asked to do this and his robust answer when offered his freedom in the hospital would seem to show that, whatever his earlier sympathies had been in the early 1930s when he was editing *The Whitehall Gazette*, he had no intention of assisting the enemy.

It did not take too long after the war for the British authorities to learn what had happened to Gregory. Captain Kelly, the man who took him to Paris, had a good idea of his demise by May 1946 when he wrote to a friend: 'It is very sad to think that his end was so horrible and I only hope he was not ill-treated.' This was amplified in a note from an immigration officer named Percy Eade at Gatwick to Major Guy Liddell of MI5 in December 1946 which stated: 'Sir John Maundy Gregory was interned at St Denis concentration camp, a fellow inmate states ... while [there] he was a very sick man, fussy, erratic and secretive. Most of the time he was an inmate of the camp infirmary, later sent to Val de Grace military hospital where he died. Immediately after his decease a Polish Jew named Homeski (interned by error as a British subject) stole Gregory's watch and chain claiming they had been bequeathed to him verbally but the Germans had different views, stealing and looting being a German prerogative.'[6]

Four years later, in December 1950, Detective Sergeant Groombridge of the Metropolitan Police compiled a report for the Official Receiver in Bankruptcy stating Gregory's occupation in Paris was not exactly known: 'he regularly received considerable sums of money from England which enabled him to live very comfortably'. Presumably no one could tell him where that money came from, or what had happened to it.

Percy Hoskins of the *Express* was still on Gregory's trail in August 1950 with an article headlined 'Death Secret of Maundy Gregory Revealed after Nine Years: His end came under Nazi Rule.' The fact that the details had been known by then for some years was not disclosed to the paper's readers. 'Today in a cemetery at Ivry I stood by the grave of a man who in his day was a guardian of state secrets … Princes and Prelates, peers and distinguished commoners, statesmen, leaders of the arts and of the sciences – he was on the closest terms with them all.' It somehow seems appropriate that by then Maundy Gregory was no longer there, his remains forever somewhere else.

17. CASH FOR HONOURS

> *Cash for Honours, it seemed to me, had*
> *been a fact of life for ever.*
> LORD MICHAEL LEVY, *A QUESTION*
> *OF HONOUR*

Leaders and rulers have awarded their loyal followers with honours since time immemorial. Land and lordships for loyalty in the medieval period, with the proviso that royal favour was fickle and both could be cut short: remember the awful warning of Thomas Cromwell, created Earl of Essex in April 1540, only to lose first his title and then his head three months later when Henry VIII changed his mind about him. Elizabeth I, largely free of internal challenges, was most notably parsimonious with honours; only eight were created during her entire 45-year reign, and the number of peers actually shrank from 62 in 1560, shortly after she came to the throne, to 59 in 1603 when she died because a number of noble families had petered out.

It was under the Stuarts who followed Elizabeth that the peerage expanded exponentially, due to their perennial need to raise money, and indeed the title of baronet was introduced by James I in 1611 specifically to sell as successive parliaments grew increasingly reluctant to underwrite royal expenditure, this became especially so after Charles I came to the throne. Previously excise duties had been granted to monarchs for their full reigns when they acceded, but the Commons only allowed them to the new king for a year at a time, so he needed to find other revenues. By 1629, the number of peers had more than doubled since Elizabeth's day, with 72 added: 46 by James in his 22-year-long reign and 26 in his son Charles' first four years, a by-product of James's mountainous debts and parliament's attempts to rein in Charles' spending and increase their control. Thus, peerages were openly sold at a going rate it seems of £10,000, initially traded through the Duke of Buckingham. A sideline was added in, first, Irish peerages from 1619 (limited to 100) then Scottish peerages (150) five years later in 1624, though they proved less popular and were accordingly cheaper. They were available for Englishmen, too.[1]

The Restoration of Charles II saw a further exponential rise after 1660: 29 new dukedoms – 64 peers in all between 1649 and 1685 – and the professional touting of baronetcies with agents scouring the country, armed with blank letters patent to be filled in when they found a purchaser. A further twelve dukes were created by William and Mary after the Glorious Revolution secured the Protestant ascendancy once and for all, and Queen Anne added thirteen more. George I created eighteen dukes, but now the honours were being subcontracted to prime ministers: which meant that the floodgates began to close and the title of duke was henceforth largely limited to members of the Royal Family, with occasional exceptions for war heroes such as Marlborough and Wellington.

The rationale for the award of honours changed as ministers effectively took charge of them. Sovereigns were no longer selling them and prime ministers began using their recommendations as rewards for political loyalty in the Commons, to boost their majorities in the Upper House – and as a threat if they were thwarted in the Lords by other parties. In 1783, William

Pitt the Younger, with the connivance of George III, created 141 new peers and thereby established an inbuilt Tory majority in the Lords. Altogether during George III's 60-year reign, 388 peers were created, though of course not all survived beyond the first generation. Fifty years after Pitt, Lord Grey threatened to redress the balance in the Upper House by recommending to the King the creation of 80 new Whig peers to ensure the passage of the 1832 Great Reform Bill, though in the end he did not have to do so. The threat to create an influx of politically loyal peers recurred in the parliamentary crisis of 1910–11, to force through the Liberal People's Budget, but then again the threat was eventually enough to make the recalcitrant Tory members of the Lords back down from a constitutional confrontation.

During the nineteenth century, however, the character of the peerage and the honours system began to change anyway. Political parties needed to secure funding not only from the traditional source of the landed aristocracy but also from the rising business class clamouring for the recognition and influence that an honour could bring and who were willing to pay for it. Without rotten boroughs and with the gradual expansion of the franchise, aristocratic patronage's influence on seats began slowly to wane, though Lord Palmerston, the prime minister in 1857, happily mentioned to Queen Victoria the electoral advantage that one of his recommended nominees would bring to a particular constituency. But, as he added in a letter to an impertinent correspondent seeking an honour, 'The throne is a fount of honour; it is not a pump, nor am I a pump handle.'

More high-minded still, Sir Robert Peel, the Tory prime minister between 1841 and 1846, spoke to Richard Cobden, the Radical MP and organiser of the Anti-Corn Law League, of 'the odious power that patronage confers', adding in a letter to an aspiring honourand: 'The voracity for these things quite surprises me. I wonder people do not begin to feel the distinction of an unadorned name.' He himself was a 2nd baronet, whose hereditary honour was first awarded in 1800 to his father, the hugely wealthy Lancashire calico manufacturer also named Sir Robert Peel.

Baronetcies by mid-century were seen as a useful way to reward long-standing backbenchers, and suitable also for businessmen, lord mayors, judges, community leaders and other worthies. Retired senior civil servants might hope for a peerage and even a brewer: Sir Arthur Guinness in 1880; a scientist, Kelvin; and the poet laureate, Tennyson, were honoured in that way, the first time men from such backgrounds were ennobled. Also, for the first time, a loyal Tory newspaper proprietor, Algernon Borthwick of the *Morning Post*, was given a peerage to become Lord Glenesk, recommended by the Tory Prime Minister Lord Salisbury in 1895. These awards did not need to be paid for, but indicated that peers did not necessarily require large landed estates or an aristocratic ancestry to qualify either, although they did need a certain amount of money to maintain their status, generally thought to be at least £5,000 a year in stocks if not in land. The Queen, like many Tories, did not much care for the idea of the House of Lords being opened to moneymen, and in 1869 refused to ennoble the Jewish banker Lionel de Rothschild because he had made money from 'a species of gambling far removed from the legitimate trading which she delights to honour'.[2]

The 1884 and 1885 Parliamentary Reform Acts together greatly expanded the (male) electorate and aimed to create uniform-sized constituencies across the country, both of which meant there was an urgent need for more money to be raised by the political parties for their central administrations, to conduct elections and to recruit more candidates. They needed to field men in every seat because the electoral outcomes were suddenly uncertain. The Liberals' election fund was £30,000 in 1880 but up to £80,000 by 1895 and £120,000 by 1906. The chief whips, on whom the task of raising money usually devolved, had to find more revenues urgently and try to choose suitable candidates to fight campaigns. Donors tended to require a quid pro quo for their support and the parties became less choosy who they tapped up for funds. The public also began to realise that politicians could be bought as could the honours bestowed on them.

An importunate trade developed: the Bishop of Peterborough was offered £50,000 for diocesan funds if he could secure a baronetcy for a donor, and Lord Suffield, a friend of the Prince of Wales, was promised a sea wall to guard his estate at Cromer in north Norfolk if he could procure a peerage (he also received a rival offer of £250,000 from someone else for the same thing). Even a rogue such as Ernest Terah Hooley,[3] who bought up peers to promote the companies he invested in during the 1890s and was known to be dodgy, offered £50,000 to the Conservative Party – well above the odds – to buy the respectability of a baronetcy and joined the Carlton Club for an extra £1,000 to party funds even as proceedings for bankruptcy were being launched against him.

Even that paragon of Victorian rectitude William Gladstone was not averse to creating peers and at least acquiesced in using honours to raise money for the party. Much of his time in dealing with the Queen seems to have been devoted to supplicating for honours – about a quarter of all his letters to her dealt in some way with the subject. In 1869, he requested Queen Victoria to create a dozen Liberal peers to assist getting the Irish Church Disestablishment Bill through, but also to boost the party's support in the Upper House more generally. The Queen, who loathed Gladstone, nevertheless acceded though with ill grace.

In 1894, much later in his career, Gladstone even arranged for the sale of two honours. Both candidates were wealthy Liberal MPs but known to be keen to become peers. The first nominee was Sydney Stern, a banker and Liberal donor, who had been an MP for Stowmarket in Suffolk for only four years but whose money was desperately needed to build up a national electoral fighting fund. The second was James

Williamson, the MP for Lancaster, whose family firm had made a large fortune in the town from the manufacture of oil cloth. Both men were evidently needed more by the party for their money than their presence as MPs, but when their names were put forward, Lord Rosebery, Gladstone's successor that year as Liberal leader, refused to support their elevation until he received a letter from the Grand Old Man himself, asking him to put their names forward, which duly came. It caused controversy because Rosebery was supposedly committed to reforming the House of Lords, not buttressing the system by creating more political appointees to the red benches of the Upper House. Nevertheless, Stern was made Lord Wandsworth, and Williamson, who loudly protested that he had not made any donations to secure his peerage, became Lord Ashton. The Liberal *Truth* periodical wrote: 'Both Mr Stern and Mr Williamson are no doubt very estimable persons in private life ... but it is obvious that in these cases the transaction has been a monetary one for politically they are mere zeroes. Such bargains are ... in their nature corrupt.'[4] The furore and ridicule was so great that Ashton retreated into private life, devoting his philanthropy to good works in Lancaster. In a similar way, though it did not require a monetary transfer, Captain Herbert Naylor-Leyland, the Tory MP for Colchester, stood down unexpectedly in 1895 and announced his conversion to Liberalism just in time for a crucial vote, and was duly rewarded with a baronetcy within six months. 'It does not smell ... but the money brought in by this trafficking in hereditary legislatorships reeks of corruption. It stinks!' said *Truth*.

The Conservatives were just as bad. Major donors such as the Newcastle arms and shipbuilding manufacturer William Watson-Armstrong and the American William Waldorf Astor both eventually secured honours.

Neither party was able or prepared to end the link between payment and honours for it was their most lucrative source of income and it became generally and complacently accepted as a way of raising money within the political class, although the issue was periodically raised in Parliament from 1894 onwards. The attitude was summed up neatly by Sir Henry Campbell-Bannerman, the Liberal leader in the Commons in May 1900: 'We in this country have happily been free for two or three generations from any imputation of mercenary or corrupt motives on the part of our public men, a thing that can be said of few other countries.'[5]

There was little incentive to change practices which had come to seem normal. David Lloyd George, the young Liberal MP for Carnarvon Boroughs, was first elected as an MP in 1890, so if he was not in the chamber to hear his party leader's words that day, he must certainly have read or heard about them. Little wonder then that twenty years later, when he was prime minister in desperate need to raise money, he saw little wrong in allowing his associates, successive chief whips, the Master of Elibank and Captain Freddie Guest, to employ an unprincipled tout like Maundy Gregory to do the unsavoury 'brown cap' job of raking in the money by promising honours on a business-like basis to wealthy supplicants. Lloyd George, the first prime minister from a genuinely impoverished background, had seen the Tory controlled House of Lords attempting to frustrate his genuinely radical 1909 People's Budget with its old age pensions and national insurance provisions paid for by taxes on wealth and land.

He had little love for the Upper House. As he said: 'Should 500 men, ordinary men, chosen accidentally from among the unemployed, override the judgement – the deliberate judgement – of millions of people who are engaged in the industry which makes the wealth of the country?' Except, of course, that the men Gregory was tapping up were not unemployed and they would have said that they were the real creators of the wealth of the country. The industrial scale of the honours system that Gregory set up though was so obviously a corruption of it that it was eventually bound to fail as he recruited more and more unacceptable candidates without the common sense or political nous to select men more judiciously. That made it inevitable that the practice was brought into disrepute, though the legislation devised to outlaw the sale of honours was so badly flawed that it has only ever been deployed once, eventually against Gregory himself.

In the century since the passage of the Honours Prevention of Abuses Act, a great deal has changed in parliament, not least the 1958 Life Peerages Act, which resulted in the virtual end of the hereditary principle for appointments to the House of Lords[6] – a process which the current Labour government may take to the ultimate stage by the removal of hereditary peers from the chamber altogether.

The entwining of the awarding of honours with donations to parties has continued to cause controversy, especially when the practice appears egregious. They are even occasionally defended, as when the former Tory minister Francis Pym suggested in 1998, long after his parliamentary career, that a political donation might even be a point in favour of a nominee because it indicated an involvement in public life – a view that would have appealed to Lloyd George. The linkage can be complicated as when the Scottish businesswoman Michelle Mone, who was made a life peer in 2015, was found to have made a £30m profit from a contract for which she had lobbied on behalf of a company, PPE Medpro, with which she was connected. The contract was for the company to sell personal protective equipment which was later found to be unusable to the National Health Service during the Covid pandemic in 2020. The £200 million contract was awarded to PPE Medpro in emergency circumstances as it was allegedly a favoured VIP contractor because of Mone's husband Doug Barrowman's previous political donations to the Tory Party. Mone took a leave of absence from the Lords in 2022, she said in order to clear her name after the allegations were made. She also admitted lying in earlier interviews with the media in which she had denied any link with the company, claiming it was not a crime to lie to journalists. The difference here, of course, was that Mone was not a supplicant for honours, prepared to pay for her peerage at that point, but was a beneficiary of allegedly favourable and profitable treatment because of the political donations that had been made to the Conservative Party.

Both main parties have been implicated in cash for honours questions. The nearest that the 1925 legislation has come to being evoked in the last ninety years since Gregory's conviction was with the 2006 Cash for Peerages scandal in which Labour's chief fundraiser, the businessman Lord Levy, was alleged to have promised honours to potential donors in return for making loans to the party's funds. Several men nominated for honours by the then Prime Minister Tony Blair were rejected by the House of Lords appointments commission on suspicion of making loans in return for the prospect of peerages. Levy was arrested and an inquiry led by the Metropolitan Police's assistant commissioner John Yates took a year to decide that there was no case for him to answer. One of the men, Gulam Noon, the 'curry king' of the Indian food industry, was asked by the *Daily Telegraph* whether the £220,000 he had donated to the Labour Party had helped to get him nominated for a seat in the House of Lords and he answered: 'If a peerage was so cheap, all sorts would buy one.' Levy himself insisted: 'Appointments to the House of Lords are not in my gift. They lie solely with the Prime Minister. I did not play a part in the process at Number Ten by which candidates for peerages are considered and decided upon. I did acknowledge that I had recommended or supported recommendations for peerages or other honours in the past – as many people do, sometimes successfully, sometimes not. Most importantly … I have never accepted a gift or a loan for the Labour Party as an inducement or reward for procuring or attempting to procure the grant of a peerage or any honour.'[7]

Levy suggests the solution should be state funding of political parties, but that is never likely to happen: it would inject a measure of extra-parliamentary control and oversight on expenditure. How would it ever be administered and what external constraints could there be on how the money is spent? Democracy remains a rough-hewn survival of the fittest – and who will fund it? Must parties, with ever declining and ageing memberships, be even more reliant on a few powerful billionaires? You can almost hear the shade of David Lloyd George justifying cash for honours a century on: 'You and I know perfectly well it is a far cleaner method of filling the party chest than the methods used in the United States or the Socialist Party.'

People with money will always buy advantage and flaunt status. Prime ministers sometimes find it useful to flatter them or to enhance their influence. While political parties exist, they will need to raise cash and there will be willing donors. The awarding of an honour, at least publicly, highlights their value to the prime minister and his party – and occasionally invites ridicule, as happened with some of Boris Johnson's appointments in 2022. What is imperative is that there should be limits on donations and that wealthy men (it is invariably men still) cannot buy elections as seems to be happening increasingly in the United States where the billionaire Elon Musk, owner of the social media company X (formerly Twitter), donated $277m to help get Donald Trump elected president in 2024 and was awarded a governmental advisory position in charge of cutting government waste. Musk had previously supported Democratic candidates. The US does not deal in honours, but it certainly deals in influence. Musk flaunts his role but perhaps many others – here as well as in the US – do not? Such expenditure makes Gregory's efforts pale in comparison.

What was needed then and is required now is the oxygen of publicity: that donations are declared and favours recorded. It happens, but slowly and not enough. Democracy dies in darkness. And perhaps that is how the rich and powerful and their political recipients like it.

BIBLIOGRAPHY

There have been three biographies of Maundy Gregory in the decades since his death. The first of these, by a journalist called Gerald Macmillan, was called *Honours for Sale* and came out in 1954, still close to the events and personalities that had been involved with Gregory, including the man himself, but not yet with access to many of the documents now held in open files at the National Archives.

The American journalist Tom Cullen's book *Maundy Gregory: Purveyor of Honours* was published in 1974 and was perhaps the fullest and most entertaining work about the old fraud, not least because he tracked down and interviewed a range of people who had interacted with him. These ranged from Elise Craven, the child star who appeared in the first pantomime that Gregory presented in Ipswich in 1907, to Ronnie Russell, the barman at the Hotel Meurice in Paris, and, crucially, Madame Anne Yvinec, the owner of the Hotel Belle-Vue at Chateauneuf-du-Faou in Brittany where he hid from the Germans for four months. All are now long gone: you would have to be well into your nineties to remember Monsieur de Gregoire and his yapping dog now and well past your century to have been tapped up for an honour by him in the 1920s.

The most recent book is Andrew Cook's *Cash for Honours*, published in 2008, which had access to the Gregory files in the

National Archives and diligently researched for the names of those who were awarded honours, perhaps after ringing the bell to seek admission to the Chief's inner sanctum in Parliament Street, which have long since been converted into MPs' offices.

I have made use of all three books and added more details from the National Archives and British Newspaper Library – whose staff were most helpful – about the politics and social milieu in which Gregory was allowed to operate. If he now seems almost a figure of fun as well as pretension – the image of him fleeing the Germans on a bicycle in 1940 is indelible – it is noticeable both how remote and yet how strikingly contemporary the saga of Arthur John Peter Michael Maundy Gregory remains.

Mark Adkin: *The Charge: The Real Reason why the Light Brigade was Lost,* Pimlico, 2000.

Richard Aldington: *Frauds,* Heinemann, 1957.

Herbert A. Asquith: *Moments of Memory,* Scribner, 1938.

John M. Barry: *The Great Influenza: The Epic Story of the Deadliest Plague in History,* Penguin, 2005.

Stephen Bates: *Asquith,* Haus, 2006.

Lord Beaverbrook: *The Decline and Fall of Lloyd George,* Collins, 1963.

Robert Blake: *The Unknown Prime Minister: The Life and Times of Andrew Bonar Law 1858–1923,* Eyre and Spottiswoode, 1955.

Michael and Eleanor Brock: *H.H. Asquith: Letters to Victoria Stanley,* OUP, 1982.

Anne Chisholm and Michael Davie: *Beaverbrook: A Life,* Pimlico, 1993.

David Clark: *Victor Grayson: The Man and the Mystery,* Quartet, 2016.

Colin Clifford: *The Asquiths,* John Murray, 2002.

Andrew Cook: *Cash for Honours: The Story of Maundy Gregory,* The History Press, 2008.

Colin R. Coote: *Editorial: The Memoirs of Colin R. Coote*, Eyre and Spottiswoode, 1965.

Don. M. Cregier: *Chiefs without Indians*, University Press of America, 1982.

Tom Cullen: *Maundy Gregory: Purveyor of Honours*, Bodley Head, 1974.

Gerard De Groot: *Blighty: British Society in the Era of the Great War*, Longman, 1996.

David Dutton: *Austen Chamberlain: Gentleman in Politics*, Ross Anderson Publications, 1985.

David Gilmour: *Curzon*, Papermac, 1995.

Robert Graves and Alan Hodge: *The Long Weekend: A Social History of Great Britain 1918–1939*, The Folio Society, 2009.

John Grigg: *The Young Lloyd George*, Methuen, 1978.

John Grigg: *Lloyd George: The People's Champion 1902–1911*, Penguin, 1997.

John Grigg: *Lloyd George: From Peace to War 1912–16*, Penguin, 1997.

John Grigg: *Lloyd George: War Leader 1916–1918*, Penguin, 2003.

Gerald Hamilton: *The Way It Was with Me*, Leslie Frewin, 1969.

Tim Harris: *Restoration: Charles II and His Kingdoms*, Penguin, 2006.

Roy Hattersley: *David Lloyd George: The Great Outsider*, Little Brown, 2010.

Simon Heffer: *Sing as We Go: Britain Between the Wars*, Penguin, 2024.

John Hostettler: *A History of Criminal Justice in England and Wales*, Waterside Press, 2009.

Samuel Hynes: *The Edwardian Turn of Mind*, Pimlico, 1991.

Lawrence James: *The Middle Class: A History*, Little Brown, 2006.

Roy Jenkins: *Baldwin*, Collins, 1987.

Roy Jenkins: *Churchill*, Pan, 2001.

Nigel Jones: *Tower*, Windmill, 2012.

Stephen Koss: *Asquith*, Allen Lane, 1976.

Stephen Koss: *The Rise and Fall of the Political Press in Britain*, Hamish Hamilton, 1981.

Lord Michael Levy: *A Question of Honour*, Simon and Schuster, 2008.

Frances Lloyd George: *The Years that are Past*, Hutchinson, 1967.

Gerald Macmillan: *Honours for Sale: The Strange Story of Maundy Gregory*, Richards Press, 1954.

Margaret Macmillan: *Peacemakers: The Paris Conference of 1919 and its Attempt to End War*, John Murray, 2001.

Ronan McGreevy: *Great Hatred: The Assassination of Sir Henry Wilson*, Faber, 2022.

Keith Middlemas and John Barnes: *Baldwin, a Biography*, Weidenfeld and Nicolson, 1969.

H. Montgomery Hyde: *Norman Birkett, The Life of Lord Birkett of Ulverston*, Hamish Hamilton, 1964.

Lucy Moore: *Anything Goes: A Biography of the Roaring Twenties*, Atlantic, 2008.

Kenneth O. Morgan: *Consensus and Disunity: The Lloyd George Coalition Government 1918–22*, Clarendon Press, 1979.

Juliet Nicolson: *The Great Silence 1918–1920: Living in the Shadow of the Great War*, John Murray, 2009.

Matthew Parris: *Great Parliamentary Scandals: Four Centuries of Calumny, Smear and Innuendo*, Robson, 1997.

Hugh Purcell: *Lloyd George*, Haus, 2006.

Robert Rhodes James: *Memoirs of a Conservative, J.C.C. Davidson's Memoirs and Papers 1910–37*, Weidenfeld and Nicolson, 1969.

Robert Rhodes James: *The British Revolution: British Politics 1880–1939*, Methuen, 1976.

Lord Riddell: *Lord Riddell's Intimate Diary of the Peace Conference and After 1918–23*: Victor Gollancz Ltd., 1933.

Kenneth Rose: *King George V*, Papermac, 1983.

The Rough Guide to Brittany and Normandy, 2022.

G.R. Searle: *Corruption in British Politics 1895–1930,* Clarendon Press, 1987.

Gary Sheffield: *The Chief: Douglas Haig and the British Army,* Aurum, 2011.

Mary Soames: *Winston and Clemmie: The Personal Letters of the Churchills,* Houghton Mifflin, 1999.

A.J.A. Symons: *The Quest for Corvo: An Experiment in Biography,* Quartet Books, 1993.

John Terraine: *Douglas Haig: The Educated Soldier,* Cassell, 2000.

The Times: *Great Lives: A Century in Obituaries,* Times Books, 2005.

Adrian Tinniswood: *The Long Weekend: Life in the English Country House Between the Wars,* Jonathan Cape, 2016.

J.C. Trewin: *Benson and the Bensonians,* Barrie and Rockliff, 1960.

Gavin Weightman and Steve Humphries: *The Making of Modern London 1914–1939,* Sidgwick and Jackson, 1984.

Stanley Weintraub: *Silent Night: The Remarkable Christmas Truce of 1914.* Simon and Schuster, 2001.

Geoffrey Wheatcroft: *The Randlords: The Men Who Made South Africa.* Weidenfeld and Nicolson, 1985.

John Wilson: *CB: A Life of Sir Henry Campbell-Bannerman,* Book Club Edition, 1973.

Trevor Wilson: *The Downfall of the Liberal Party 1914–1935,* Collins, 1966.

Denis Winter: *Death's Men, Soldiers of the First World War,* Penguin, 1979.

Newspapers
The Times
Daily Telegraph
Manchester Guardian
Daily Express

Daily Mail
Morning Post
Daily Sketch
Mayfair and Town Topics
Whitehall Gazette

Reference Books
Dictionary of National Biography
Who's Who and Who Was Who
British Newspaper Library
National Archives

ENDNOTES

Introduction

1. *Daily Express*: 'A Famous Figure in Whitehall by One Who Knew Him', 22 February 1933.
2. The purchasing power of one pound in 1922 is equivalent to approximately £47 today. Thus, £10,000 in 1922 would be worth the equivalent of about £475,000 now and £40,000 would perhaps be £1.9 million according to the Bank of England's inflation calculator. For a peerage with a seat in the House of Lords, £50,000 would equate to about £2.3million today. www.bankofengland.co.uk/monetary-policy/inflation/inflation-calculator
3. *Dictionary of National Biography*: Gregory and Cullen estimate p30. £30,000 equals roughly £1.4m in equivalent spending power today.
4. *Editorial: The Memoirs of Colin R. Coote*, Eyre and Spottiswoode, 1965, p88–89.
5. Gerald Macmillan: *Honours for Sale: The Strange Story of Maundy Gregory*, The Richards Press, 1954, p113.
6. Tom Cullen: *Maundy Gregory: Purveyor of Honours*, Bodley Head, 1974, p33.

Chapter 1

1. UK Parliament statistics.
2. LSE study October 2020: Martin Bayly: 'Fatalism and an absence of public grief: how British society dealt with the 1918 flu'. https://blogs.lse.ac.uk/politicsandpolicy/public-memory-1918-flu. My mother, aged eleven, and my grandparents went down with the virus in early November 1918 (her brothers were away at the war). She ever afterwards remembered on 11 November lying sick in bed listening to the sounds of drunken celebration and singing in the street outside.
3. Juliet Nicolson: *The Great Silence 1918–1920*. John Murray, 2009, p72.
4. Ronan McGreevy: *Great Hatred: The Assassination of Sir Henry Wilson*. Faber, 2022.
5. Figures quoted by Gerard DeGroot: *Blighty: British Society in the Era of the Great War*, Longman, 1996, p273–4.
6. *Farmers Weekly* article, 10 November 2018: 'How farming suffered post WW1 from the Government's great betrayal.'
7. Quoted in John Meynard Keynes: 'The Economic Consequences of the Peace' Chapter 5. Baldwin's own wealth came from an industrial background: the family ironworks in Worcestershire despite his carefully cultivated image as a countryman.
8. Gerard DeGroot, op cit., p292.
9. Gerard DeGroot, op cit., p298.
10. Quoted by DeGroot, p261: M. Petter: 'Temporary gentlemen in the aftermath of the Great War', Historical Journal vol. 37, p 150.
11. Coppard: '*With a machine gun to Cambrai*', Cassell, 1969, p133.

Chapter 2

1. Robert Lyvedon was a Whig politician who had served for a fortnight as Secretary at War in Lord John Russell's

cabinet in 1852 and somewhat longer as President of the Board of Control, overseeing the East India Company at the time of the Indian Mutiny in Lord Palmerston's government between 1855 and 1858, after which he received his promotion to the baronage.

2. A photograph shows the heavily bearded vicar wearing the cap which is a sort of floppy square Anglican version of the Catholic biretta.

3. Much of the biographical material in this chapter comes from Tom Cullen: *Maundy Gregory: Purveyor of Honours* (1974) and Gerald Macmillan: *Honours for Sale* (1954), both of whom had the opportunity to speak to people who knew Gregory.

4. The school closed in the 1920s, and part of its site was turned into the local speedway and greyhound racing stadium while another area of the grounds known as the Dell was to become the home for many years of Southampton football club.

5. This was an early attempt by Oxford to widen its student intake, deriving from an 1868 Royal Commission. It enabled less wealthy students to enrol and study for a degree without being attached to a college. Eventually, they became members of the St. Catharine's Society, named after the hall where they met. This would become St. Catherine's (sic) college which opened in 1962.

6. Andrew Cook: *Cash for Honours: The Story of Maundy Gregory*, The History Press, 2008, p8.

7. Gerald Macmillan: *Honours for Sale*, Richards Press 1954, p98.

8. Cullen, op cit., p62. The reputation of the dramatist W. G. Wills has not fared well: even at the time one of his historical dramas was described as 'semi-poetic drivel'. *A Royal Divorce*, however, did tickle the fancy of James Joyce who mentions it several times in *Finnegan's Wake* – he may even have seen Maundy Gregory in it. Edith Cole, Kelly's

wife, played Josephine in the play many times and was financially successful enough to found a home for stray dogs in Liverpool: she came to a sticky end from burns while trying to clean a pair of gloves with petrol in 1927.

9. Sir Seymour Hicks, another contemporary actor manager, wrote in his memoirs: 'I have heard, though I cannot vouch for the story, that Sir Frank's contracts with his artists were always worded: "To play the Ghost in Hamlet and keep wicket," or "To play Laertes and field cover-point"; and that no Polonius need apply unless he happened to be a first-class wicket-keeper."' Hicks: *Me and My Missus*, Cassell,1939.

10. J. C. Trewin: *Benson and the Bensonians*, Barrie and Rockliff, 1960, p153.

11. Cullen, op cit., p65.

12. Cullen, op cit., p72.

13. This would have been Susan Margaret St. Maur, wife of the 15th Duke and author of the popular book *Impressions of a Tenderfoot during a Journey in Search of Sport in the Far West* (1890), which was a travel account of a train journey across Canada with her husband. The couple had no children.

14. Despite her name, which derived from her German husband, the princess was born Lady Anne Savile, and she would achieve a little posthumous fame by becoming the first woman to die while flying across the Atlantic in 1927.

Chapter 3

1. His godmother was apparently the famous Jersey-born actress Lillie Langtry, 'the Jersey Lily'.

2. Birkenhead's poverty was relative: apart from the yacht, he had six motor cars, three chauffeurs, eight horses and grooms, a townhouse in Grosvenor Gardens, Belgravia, and a country house in Northamptonshire.

3. *F. E. Smith* by John Campbell, Pimlico, 1983, p260.

4. Cullen, op cit., p136.

5. Cullen, op cit., p127–8.

6. Cullen suggests this may have been as much as 500 guineas, though of course the young MP Colin Coote said he was offered a cartoon and write-up for £50.

7. Colin Coote, the future *Telegraph* editor, who knew Bottomley, said of his wartime recruitment speeches: 'He had two types of speech, one materialistic and the other emotional. The latter he called "The Prince of Peace" and used to say: "I always charge fifty guineas for the Prince." His face was a slab with a slit of a mouth which opened to imbibe great quantities of champagne ... he kept no commandments, not even the eleventh.' Editorial, op cit., p104: the eleventh commandment speaks against bearing grudges or seeking vengeance and adds: 'love your neighbour as yourself', *Leviticus 19:18*.

8. Newton eventually served three years in prison for misappropriating a client's funds after being convicted in 1913 and was struck off. Somerset, who was an equerry to the Prince of Wales (later Edward VII), fled abroad and lived the rest of his life with his male partner in France.

9. Macmillan, op cit., p106.

10. National Archives: Arthur John Maundy Gregory file KV2/340.

11. *Mayfair and Town Topics*, 11 July 1914: 'Visitors at Claridge's Hotel include: HRH Prince Christopher of Greece, HH Hakki Pasha, HH Princess of Monaco, Prince and Princess of Castagneto, Viscount and Viscountess Yarnock, Lord and Lady Rothermere ... Mrs J.L. Dugdale.' Pity poor ordinary Mrs Dugdale, perhaps lucky to make the cut at all – surely an incentive for hubby to acquire a title. Such lists for the main hotels filled a page.

12. The grand, ornate late Victorian gothic hotel on the north side of the square next to the Empire was eventually restored to its former glory after years as an office block and became a Premier Inn, though it was boarded

up again in the autumn of 2024. The building is next door to the former Empire Theatre (in those days a notorious pick-up spot for sex workers), then a cinema since 1927, now run by Cineworld.

13. Hattersley: *David Lloyd George: The Great Outsider*, Little Brown, 2010, p352.

14. *Mayfair*, 19 September 1914.

Chapter 4

1. DeGroot, op cit., p12.

2. DeGroot, op cit., p 191.

3. *Daily Express*, 21 and 22 August 1914, cited in Stephen Koss, *The Rise and Fall of the Political Press in Britain*, Hamish Hamilton, 1981, p 695.

4. Stanley Weintraub: *Silent Night: The Remarkable Christmas Truce of 1914*, Simon and Schuster, 2001, p141–2.

5. The inherent unlikelihood of the story, not least that the snow would not have melted during several days at sea in September, does not appear to have occurred to the German generals, or to British gossips when they heard the story.

6. Professor Christopher Andrew: Espionage and counter subversion essay at MI5.gov.uk.

7. Samuel Weber: article 'First as Tragedy, Second as Farce: Executing German Spies' in Voces Novae, volume 4, number 1 (2013).

8. *Dictionary of National Biography*: Sir Basil Home Thomson.

9. Cullen, op cit., p89–90.

10. National Archives, MI5 Gregory file KV2/340.

Chapter 5

1. *Mayfair and Town Topics*, 8 August 1914.

2. Moderations is the name given to the first university examination that Oxford students sit in their subjects before proceeding to Finals. Dr Pope evidently believed that this alone qualified Gregory to be an officer.

3. 'More a great poster than a great man' said Asquith's wife Margot characteristically waspishly, mindful of the famous 1914 pointing finger recruiting poster: 'Your Country Needs You'.

4. Quoted in Grigg, *Lloyd George: From Peace to War 1912–16*, Penguin, 1985, p438. Lindsay, a Tory politician, had recently succeeded his father as 27th Earl of Crawford, but had served early in the war as a private in the Royal Army Medical Corps.

5. Quoted in Gary Sheffield and John Bourne: *Douglas Haig War Diaries and Letters*, BCA, 2005, p228. It was on this visit that Asquith met his son Raymond for the last time, ten days before he was killed.

6. Montagu was Jewish, and, although that did not deter Asquith from promoting him to the cabinet, he insouciantly called him 'the Assyrian', though probably not to his face. Asquith was particularly shocked when Venetia Stanley agreed to convert to Judaism.

7. Frances Lloyd George: *The Years that Are Passed*, Hutchinson, 1967, p89.

8. Lloyd George: *War Memoirs volume 1*, Odhams, 1938, p602–3. The settling of scores against Asquith and Field Marshal Haig came after their deaths.

9. Quoted by Roy Hattersley in *David Lloyd George: The Great Outsider*, Little Brown, 2010, p35.

10. Quoted in John Grigg, *The Young Lloyd George*, Methuen, 1973, p67–8. The letter was undated, but Grigg speculated that it was written in 1886 or 1887. The letter, which survives, indicates that it was written in pencil at 1.30 on a Sunday morning.

11. Frances Lloyd George: *The Years that are Past*, Hutchinson, 1967, p40–42.

12. John Grigg: *Lloyd George: From Peace to War 1912–1916*, Methuen, 1985, p44–66.

13. George Cadbury, of the chocolate manufacturing family, was a Quaker and wanted to buy the paper, originally

started by Charles Dickens, to campaign against the Boer War. Through mergers, it eventually became the left-leaning *News Chronicle* and was closed in 1960, after which it was absorbed into the *Daily Mail.*

14. Hattersley, op cit., p329.
15. Roy Jenkins, *Asquith*, Chilmark Press, 1964, p360.
16. Frances Lloyd George: *The Years that are Past*, p89.
17. This was a bit rich coming from Robertson, the son of a Lincolnshire village tailor. He was, however, the only man ever to rise from the ranks as an enlisted soldier all the way to Field Marshal.
18. Lloyd George: *War Memoirs volume 2* (Odhams Press, 1936), p 2014.
19. Jenkins, op cit., p430.
20. Hattersley, op cit., p409.
21. Quoted in Colin Clifford: *The Asquiths*, John Murray, 2002, p386. *Nash's Magazine* was a British monthly mainly publishing short stories by well-known writers. It merged with *Good Housekeeping* magazine in 1937.
22. Frances Lloyd George, op cit., p90.

Chapter 6
1. Hattersley op cit., p437, quoting Stevenson's diary for 1 March 1917.
2. In the event she outlived him by 27 years, dying in 1972 aged 84. She had had two abortions during their relationship and one daughter, Jennifer, was born in 1929, though she may have been the offspring of Thomas Tweed, Lloyd George's chief of staff, with whom Frances had a brief affair.
3. G.R. Searle: *Corruption in British Politics 1895–1930*, p318.
4. Kenneth O. Morgan, *Consensus and Disunity: The Lloyd George Coalition Government*, Clarendon Press, 1986, p27.
5. The original 'Broncho' Billy was actually a Jewish actor from Arkansas called Gilbert M. Aronson (1880–1971),

who had never been a cowboy but was previously an art-ist's model in New York. He was one of the actors in the first great western, *The Great Train Robbery*, in 1903. Sutherland, by contrast, was a hard drinking and swearing Scotsman who did not hesitate to mislead. He was closer to the Prime Minister than some ministers and he culti-vated close links with their editors.

6. The strike began in a factory in Rochdale where some of the men refused to show the new female employees how to operate the machinery and were sacked. When the directors refused to reinstate the men, disruption rapidly spread, jeopardizing munitions manufacture. See Grigg: *Lloyd George: War Leader*, op cit., p110–13.

7. Cullen, op cit., p103.

8. Robert Blake: *The Unknown Prime Minister: The Life and Times of Andrew Bonar Law 1858–1923*, Eyre and Spottiswoode, 1955, p385.

9. Hankey's diary 28 August 1918, quoted by Hattersley op cit., p473.

Chapter 7

1. Keith Middlemas and John Barnes, *Baldwin: a Biography*, Weidenfeld and Nicolson, 1969, p97.

2. Hugh Purcell: *Lloyd George*, Haus, 2006, p75.

3. No serving American president had ever left the mainland of the US before or met other world leaders while in office, and few had visited other countries even after leaving the White House.

4. Dictionary of National Biography.

5. Half a Crown was two shillings and six pence, an eighth of a pound, roughly equivalent to five or six pounds in 2024. The Gazette ran to as many as forty pages some-times but towards the end sank to about twenty.

6. Cullen, op cit., p101.

7. Macmillan, op cit., p147–49.

8. Cullen, opt cit., p100.
9. *Daily Telegraph*, 27 February 1970.
10. Macmillan, op cit., p134.
11. Coote, op cit., p92.
12. Cullen, op cit., p95.
13. Don M. Cregier, *Chiefs without Indians, University Press of America*, 1982, p113–16.
14. Cullen, op cit., p96. The lord mayor in question was not identified, but the only one with a baronetcy during the recent period was Sir George Lunn, who was the city's mayor from 1915–17. Did he pay for his honour or did it come more or less with the job?
15. *Morning Post*, 29 August 1922. The *Post* eventually merged with the *Daily Telegraph* in 1937.
16. Cullen, op cit., p103.
17. *Morning Post*, 28 August 1922.
18. Coote, op cit., p89–90.
19. Robert Rhodes James: *Memoirs of a Conservative: J.C.C. Davidson's Memoirs and Papers 1910-37*, Weidenfeld and Nicolson, 1969, p279. J. C. C. Davidson, the Conservative MP for Hemel Hempstead, was close to both Bonar Law and Baldwin, successive party leaders, serving as a parliamentary private secretary and adviser to both in turn through the 1920s. At the time of his conversation with Lloyd George, which he noted down in a memorandum the following day, he was Conservative party chairman.
20. Cullen, op cit., p104–5.

Chapter 8

1. Patrick Balfour: *Society Racket: A Critical Survey of Modern Social Life*, John Long Ltd., 1933.
2. Rose, op cit., p258.
3. Cook, op cit., p276–96, 312 and 328–31.
4. Searle, op cit., chapter seven.

5. Though, to be fair, Lord Northcliffe allegedly turned down the first offer of a peerage he received saying that if he wanted one 'he would buy it like an honest man'. He accepted his peerage however at the age of 39 in 1904.
6. Hansard, House of Commons debates, 28 May 1919.
7. The notorious Lord Dawson of Penn, who would quietly finish the King off with an injection of morphine sixteen years later, so that news of his death would appear in the respectable morning newspapers such as *The Times* not London's rackety evening papers, or so he reasoned. The clerihew which went round at the time, therefore, was perhaps more accurate than its authors knew: 'Lord Dawson of Penn/ Has killed many men/ That's why we sing/ God save the King.' News of Dawson's action only came to light in 1986.
8. Cullen, op cit., p111.
9. Searle, op cit., p354–5.
10. Hansard, House of Commons, 28 February 1921.
11. The title is still extant in 2024 with the third baronet being Sir Andrew Rowland Hodge, a former estate agent. Among Hodge's other descendants are his granddaughter Vicki Hodge, an actress, model and former girlfriend of Prince Andrew, and the East End tough guy John Bindon, and his great granddaughter, the supermodel Jodie Kidd.
12. The letter is quoted in full in the appendices to Lord Beaverbrook's book *The Decline and Fall of Lloyd George*, published 10 years later by Collins in 1963, p241-3.
13. Letter 27 August 1927, quoted in Cullen, op cit., p151.
14. David Dutton: *Austen Chamberlain: Gentleman in Politics*, Ross Anderson Publications, 1985, p178–9.

Chapter 9

1. After Sir Eric Geddes, the businessman brought into the government by Lloyd George during the war, and after it tasked with fellow business leaders to find huge savings

in expenditure. It recommended £87m cuts out of more than £600m government expenditure, though in the end the cabinet agreed on reductions of £57m to the defence, education, health and pensions budgets. Cuts on such a scale did not entirely have the effects intended (sound familiar?), budgets were reduced at a cost to economic growth and productivity. Increased unemployment diminished public services, especially education, and led to the abandonment of many of the government's post-war electoral promises, including homes fit for heroes. See Simon Heffer *Sing as We Go: Britain Between the Wars*, Penguin 2023, p74–78.

2. Hattersley, op cit., p517.

3. *Lord Riddell's Intimate Diary*: op cit., p164.

4. Hattersley op cit., p550.

5. The Vesteys seem to have been expert in using tax loop-holes. In 1980, the *Sunday Times* revealed that two years earlier Vestey Brothers, the largest retailers of meat in the world at that time and the largest privately owned company, paid virtually no tax. It was revealed that the company had paid just £10 tax on profits of £2.3 million in 1978. As Edmund Vestey said: 'Let's face it, nobody pays more tax than they have to. We're all tax dodgers aren't we.' Some more than others.

6. Robinson's name was first submitted by Winston Churchill in 1906 because the South African magnate had agreed to staff one of his mines with white contract workers rather than imported Chinese labourers. Robinson was furious when he did not get a baronetcy that year, but he received the honour two years later from Asquith's government, after Campbell-Bannerman's death. See John Wilson: *CB*, Constable, 1973, p582–3.

7. Geoffrey Wheatcroft: *The Randlords*, Weidenfeld and Nicolson, 1985, p31. Robinson eventually ruined Cohen by suing him for libel and then, having been awarded limited

damages, instituted further proceedings for perjury against him which led to Cohen being jailed for three years.

8. Searle, *Corruption in British Politics*, op cit., p358.

9. Hansard House of Lords debates, 22 June 1922.

10. Hansard House of Lords debates, 29 June 1922.

11. Kenneth Rose: *King George V*, Macmillan, 1983, p252.

12. Ashley, somewhat later Baron Mount Temple, would later become one of Hitler's British appeasers as chairman of the Anglo-German Fellowship in the 1930s. He was the father of Edwina Mountbatten, Lord Louis Mountbatten's wife.

13. Family hangers-on had been rewarded too: Hildebrand Harmsworth, the famously useless younger brother of Northcliffe and Rothermere, was made a baronet for unspecified public services in the 1922 honours list. Cecil King, his nephew, commented that he 'had never done a stroke of work in his life' and when the announcement was made the family sent him a telegram sardonically cheering: 'At last, a grateful nation has given you your due reward.' Hildebrand did not enjoy it for long: he died of cirrhosis of the liver in 1929 aged 57.

14. Searle, op ct., p359–61.

15. Northumberland two years later headed the consortium which bought *The Morning Post* to save it from the clutches of Lord Rothermere, but he was no longer alive when it was finally absorbed into the *Daily Telegraph* in 1937.

16. Burking: old slang term meaning to suffocate. Allegedly after the nineteenth-century Edinburgh murderer William Burke of Burke and Hare infamy.

17. Hansard, House of Lords debate, 17 July 1922.

18. Mary Soames: *Winston and Clementine: The Personal Letters of the Churchills*, Houghton Mifflin, 1999 p256.

19. Information on the debate and commission, see Searle, op cit., chapter VIII.

Chapter 10

1. See Morgan, *Consensus and Disunity*, op cit., p342. Roy Hattersley, the former deputy leader of the Labour Party, devoted only four pages of his 700-page biography of Lloyd George to the honours scandal, despite once telling my former *Guardian* colleagues over lunch that he believed that he was the most corrupt prime minister in Britain's history.
2. *Daily Chronicle*, 18 July 1922.
3. Cregier, op cit., p124.
4. Riddell, op cit., p381.
5. Middlemas and Barnes, op cit., p115.
6. The Carlton Club gathering originated the Tory backbenchers' regular parliamentary meetings, still known as the 1922 committee for that reason.
7. Middlemas and Barnes op cit., p123.
8. Blake, op cit., p457.
9. Searle, op cit., p392.
10. Middlemas and Barnes, op cit., p98.

Chapter 11

1. The so-called Zinoviev letter election, when the *Daily Mail* four days before voting published a faked missive, supposedly from Grigory Zinoviev, the head of the Communist Comintern in Moscow, ordering the British Communist Party to engage in subversion to undermine the country. The press blamed the Labour government for wanting better links with Russia and the letter probably cost it support though it was faltering anyway. The letter certainly confirmed Labour supporters in the view that the right-wing press would use any means to do the party down: a situation confirmed at election times ever since.
2. The nearest has been 72 in the 2024 general election.
3. Cregier, op cit., p142.
4. Davidson played a large part in Baldwin's rise having suggested his name to Law for his first ministerial job as a

junior treasury minister. The two men became firm friends, with Davidson becoming Baldwin's loyal and diligent parliamentary private secretary. Baldwin made him chairman of the Conservative Party in 1927.

5. Robert Rhodes James: *Memoirs of a Conservative*, Weidenfeld and Nicolson, 1969, p280.

6. Bennett himself was awarded a baronetcy in the wake of the 1929 general election but was forced to stand down the following year following bankruptcy.

7. This would have been George V, who was Duke of York from 1892 to 1901.

8. Rhodes James, in editing the book 45 years later, did not name the man to spare embarrassment to his heirs and family. The story is told on pages 281–2 of *Memoirs of a Conservative*.

9. Now Ashridge Business School.

10. Searle, op cit., p406.

11. Hansard Commons Debates, 24 July 1925.

Chapter 12

1. The author's own parents entered a mixed marriage in the late 1930s, agreeing to these rules. My CofE father's mother was hostile to her son marrying my mother because she was a Catholic and she made her views clear. Both my parents were devout and observant members of their respective faiths, and in nearly 43 years of marriage never worshipped together. Their three children were brought up as Catholics and went to Mass but were sent to secular or Church of England schools.

2. Farrow's story is recounted in Cook, p211–12 and Cullen pages 169–70, based on an affidavit filed by Farrow in March 1934. O'Sullivan and Farrow remained married until his death in 1963.

3. National Archives: KV2/340 MI5 files: Maundy Gregory.

4. i.e. Catholic patriarch not Greek Orthodox patriarch, both of which claimed authority over the Holy Sepulchre, the site of Jesus's burial – and their successors still do.

5. The terrace itself no longer exists, having been replaced by one of two matching large art deco apartment blocks called Albion Gate.

6. National Archives MEPO2/ 9147.

7. A solitary telephone was subsequently installed connecting the club to the Houses of Parliament.

8. Macmillan op cit., p165.

9. The Ambassador Club article in *The Whitehall Gazette* is quoted extensively in Macmillan op cit., p133–7. Serge Voronoff, mentioned here, was a Russian-born French surgeon who in the 1920s became famous for what was called xenotransplantation: inserting monkey gland tissue into men's testicles as a supposed anti-ageing procedure. It made him a great deal of money, but did not work. Perhaps it took one conman to recognise another.

10. National Archive KV2/340.

11. Cullen, op cit., p137.

12. Campbell, op cit., p599.

13. Cullen, op cit., p150.

14. Horwood became known as the Chocolate Soldier at Scotland Yard in 1922 after he was poisoned with an arsenic-infused walnut whip, part of a boxful sent in by an ill-wisher. He also declined to discipline two officers who forcibly tried to extract a confession from a young factory worker named Irene Savidge, who they had seen being accosted by Lloyd George's former parliamentary private secretary Sir Leo Chiozza Money, again in Hyde Park, earlier that year.

15. Cook op. cit, p118.

16. Dorking Museum website.

17. Deterding's honorary knighthood, awarded in 1920, was for supplying petroleum to Britain during the First World War.

18. National Archives op cit., KV2/340.

19. Von Alvensleben was conservative but was not himself a Nazi. He narrowly escaped assassination during the Night of the Long Knives in 1934, when Hitler ordered the execution of the leaders of the Brown Shirt movement, and spent time in prison during the Second World War on charges of defeatism. He certainly never made use of his free membership of the Ambassador Club.
20. Macmillan, op cit., p123.
21. Account in A. J. A. Symons *The Quest for Corvo: An experiment in Biography*, Cassell and Co., 1934, Chapter XX. A. J. A. stood for Alphonse James Albert. His Corvo biography is innovative because it indeed recounts his search to understand the author, his life and work.

Chapter 13

1. The company peaked with more than a thousand shops selling mainly dairy products across the country in the mid-1920s. It was the first company to promote the sale of margarine (originally called Butterine) and owned a factory in Southall churning out 100,000 tons a year. When Sir George died in July 1930, he was worth £2 million. The chain is now part of the Morrisons supermarket group.
2. Cullen, op cit., p177.
3. The couple were not actually divorced.
4. National Archives, MEPO2/9147 about Mrs Rosse including the relationship with her niece. Chief Inspector Askew, investigating Gregory's activities the following year, interviewed Ethel and despaired: 'She is a most garrulous person and I found her very difficult in keeping to the point,' he wrote. The file also contains police statements and other documents relating to what happened next.
5. Cullen, op cit., p184.
6. Kidney disease.
7. *Daily Express* interview, 19 July 1933.

8. Macmillan, op cit., p180.

9. The All Saints, Bisham website lists several worthies buried in the graveyard, including the famous Edwardian actors Oscar Asche and his wife Lily Brayton, which would no doubt have pleased Gregory. Edith gets a mention in the list, too, as 'Suspected murder victim'. https://4u-team.org/churches/all-saints-bisham/

Chapter 14

1. Details taken from Billyard-Leake's statement to the police in National Archives file T527/432.

2. Billyard-Leake's statement said his father, Charles, had hoped for a baronetcy after the war for allowing his mansion and 250-acre estate at Harefield Park in Hillingdon just outside northwest London to be used as a hospital by Australian and New Zealand troops, but had turned down the knighthood which had been offered instead. Harefield is now internationally known as a specialist heart and lung transplant hospital.

3. An order founded in the nineteenth century and awarded by the Bey of Tunisia to eminent Tunisians, French citizens, or those with a connection to the country. It is difficult to know how Gregory qualified under any such heading. It was abolished in 1957.

4. Cook, op cit., p208–09.

5. One was a Lady Rathbone, according to Billyard-Leake's later statement, but there was no Lady Rathbone. She did not exist.

6. Sir Francis Hopwood, Lord Southborough, was one of Gregory's lunching cronies and a very valuable one to have as he was a former senior civil servant who had worked on confidential missions and negotiations for successive governments for more than thirty years before his retirement in the early 1920s. He was supposedly a paragon of discretion and also was well-known to successive ministers including Austen Chamberlain and Churchill. In the words of *The Times'* obit-

uary on 17 January 1947, Southborough was: 'a civil servant all the time, and a very correct one, whose personal views and contributions to discussions or action were never trumpeted in public. He had a fine presence and a quiet, dignified, yet friendly manner, behind which lay deep resources of knowledge, wisdom, and strength of character. He was not easy to know well, for his temperament was cool and he never 'gave himself away'. Such attributes would have appealed to Gregory, though Southborough does not seem to have exercised similar discretion in his dealings with him.

7. National Archives file TS27/432.
8. Cullen, op cit., p34. Also, Cook, op cit., p214–15.
9. H. Montgomery Hyde: *Norman Birkett, The Life of Lord Birkett of Ulverston*, Hamish Hamilton, 1964, p353–59.
10. Cook, op cit., p219.
11. Rhodes James, op cit., p88.
12. Court reports; *Daily Telegraph*, 22 February 1933; *Daily Mail*, 23 February 1933 and Montgomery Hyde, op cit., p357.
13. Cullen, op cit., p195.
14. *Daily Sketch*, 22 February 1933.
15. Cullen, op cit., p196.

Chapter 15
1. The Economic League remained active until the early 1990s.
2. Rhodes James, op cit., p288.
3. Half-crown: an eighth of a pound in pre-decimal currency, perhaps closer to £5 today.
4. *Daily Sketch*, 23 February 1933.
5. *Daily Express*, 24 February 1933.
6. *Daily Express*, op cit., 19 July 1933.
7. National Archives MEPO 2/9147 Mrs Rosse.
8. Cook, op cit., p198.
9. National Archives MEPO2/9147. Ethel's full statement is in the file.

10. National Archives file MEPO 2/9147.
11. Cook, op cit., p238–40. The details of Gregory's creditors run to several pages in the Board of Trade files BT226/4757, Gregory May 1933 accounts in the National Archives.
12. Cullen, op cit., p201.
13. Cullen, op cit., p201.
14. Hansard, 28 July 1933.
15. Cullen, op cit., p203–10.
16. These were 26 bottles of chemicals, including mercury, nitric acid and lead nitrate but neither housekeeper knew anything about them or what they were doing there and they seem to have played no further part in the investigation.
17. Cook, op cit., p242–45. See also *Lethal Witness: Sir Bernard Spilsbury* by Andrew Rose, Sutton Publishing, 2007, which does not mention the Rosse case but casts doubt on the reliability of Spilsbury's witness evidence in other famous cases.
18. Cullen op cit., p217.

Chapter 16

1. Cullen, op cit., p225. Much of the information in this chapter derives from Chapter XVI of *Maundy Gregory: Purveyor of Honours*, p221–36.
2. Evidently a Papal knighthood, though Gregory probably did not bother to explain the difference to the regulars at the American Bar.
3. Mickey's father, Marcel, who was Gregory's particular friend, was in the French Resistance but was captured by the Germans in 1944 and killed with a lethal injection.
4. National Archives KV2/340.
5. William Joyce, an American-born former supporter of Oswald Mosley's British Union of Fascists, fled to Germany just before the outbreak of the war and was used by the Nazis to broadcast propaganda to Britain, where his sneering tone earned him the nickname of Lord Haw-Haw. He

was hanged for treason in January 1946 on the basis that he had had a British passport at the time of fleeing.

6. National Archives KV2/340. The man who took Gregory's watch (and witnessed his will) was actually called Benzion Samuel Hormesky, who survived the war and went on to work for the United Nations Relief and Rehabilitation agency afterwards.

Chapter 17

1. Gerald Macmillan op cit. Appendix II.
2. *see* H. J. Hanham: *The sale of honours in late Victorian England* in Victorian Studies, March 1960. Lionel at least had his Austrian title, Freiherr, to fall back on as a hereditary Baron. Queen Victoria relented enough for his son Nathan to become the first Jewish peer in the House of Lords in 1885.
3. Hooley was declared bankrupt four times and served two prison sentences, but even so became the party's candidate for Ilkeston where he had an estate in 1897, shortly before he became ineligible to stand because of his latest bankruptcy.
4. Truth volume XXXVIII, 1895.
5. Hansard, 8 May 1900.
6. Not entirely ended: Harold Macmillan was made an earl two years before his death in 1984, more than twenty years after he stood down as prime minister and twenty-three years since the previous hereditary peerage had been created. Subsequently, Willie Whitelaw, Margaret Thatcher's deputy, and George Thomas, the 1980s Commons Speaker, were both made viscounts. Margaret Thatcher's husband Denis was made a baronet in 1991 – the first created since 1964 – shortly after she resigned. His son, Mark, has succeeded to the title following his death in 2003.
7. Lord Michael Levy: *A Question of Honour*, Simon and Schuster, 2008, p244.

INDEX

10 Downing Street 39, 68,
    70, 196, 201
10 Hyde Park Terrace 26,
    161, 182, 194, 199,
    201, 213, 217
43 Club, Gerrard Street 164
8 Rue d'Anjou, Paris 219

Abbey Lodge, St John's
    Wood 24, 26, 161
Ablett, Noel 86
Ackroyd of Lightcliffe,
    Sir William 101
Addison, Christopher 74
Aitken, Max *see*
    Beaverbrook, Lord
Albemarle Investment
    Syndicate 33
Alfonso XIII,
    King of Spain 31
All Saints, Marlow 189
Allenby, General 100
Alleyne, Barbara (Elise
    Barbara Alleyne
    Barrett) 18–19
Ambassador Club, Conduit
    Street 34, 90, 149,
    158, 161, 162–7, 170,
    173, 176, 197–8, 201,
    207, 213
Amery, Leo 53, 78
Anglesey, Lord 55
Anne, Queen 230
*Around the World in Eighty
    Days* 159
Ashley, Colonel Wilfred 127

Askew, Chief Inspector
    Arthur 199–200, 203,
    212, 214, 218
Asquith, Herbert 39, 47,
    51–4, 59, 60–1, 62–5,
    68, 70, 77, 79, 90, 93,
    100, 103, 104, 146
Asquith, Margot 52, 65
Asquith, Raymond 52–3
Astor V, John Jacob 137
Astor, Waldorf 70
Athlumney, Lord 41
Atkinson,
    Sir Edward Tindal 198
Augusta-Victoria of
    Hohenzollern 31
Austin, Sir Herbert 86

Baden-Powell, General
    Robert 56
Balaclava, Battle of 9
Baldwin, Lucy 140
Baldwin, Stanley 4, 81, 102,
    135, 139–41, 142–3,
    145, 147–8, 150–2, 208
Balfour, Arthur 78, 90
Balfour, Patrick 99
Banister Court,
    Southampton 11
Bar, James 104
Barlassina, Monsignor Luigi
    157, 160
Barnes, Phyllis 44
Barrett, Elise Barbara
    Alleyne *see* Alleyne,
    Barbara

Barrie, J. M. 56
Barrowman, Doug 236
Battle of Dorking, The
    (1871) 37
Beardsley, Aubrey 174
Beaufort, Duke of 55
Beaverbrook, Lord (Max
    Aitken) 64, 71, 80, 88,
    93, 128, 143, 167
Belgium 40
Belle-Vue, Chateauneuf-du-
    Faou 223
Belloc, Hilaire 75, 104
Benjamin, Barbara *see*
    Alleyne, Barbara
Benn, William
    Wedgwood 132
Bennett, Albert 148
Benson, Frank 15–17
Berlin 173–4
Berry, William (Lord
    Camrose) 152
Bethell, Baron 101
Billyard-Leake, Lieutenant-
    Commander Edward
    Whaley 192–8, 200,
    202, 212
Birkenhead 16
Birkenhead, Lord (F. E.
    Smith) 25, 90, 91, 100,
    124–6, 163, 166
Birkett KC, Norman 200,
    201, 202–3
Bissett, Arthur 170
Blackpool 12
Blair, Dr 183, 184, 185

Blumenfeld, Ralph 39
Bogota 58–9
Bonar Law, Andrew 63–4,
     69, 78, 80, 96, 99, 100,
     103, 107, 108, 110,
     112, 113, 116, 134,
     139, 141–2
Borthwick, Algernon (Lord
     Glenesk) 232
Borwick, Baron 101
Borwick, Sir Robert
     118–19
Bottomley, Horatio 29–30,
     32, 38, 88, 107
Bow Street Magistrates'
     Court 200, 212
Bowes-Lyon, Elizabeth 91
Bramley, Tom 7, 207
Breeckow, Georg 40
Brighton 27, 176
Bristol Grill,
     Cork Street 170
British Legion 3
Brixton Burglary, The 14
Brown's Hotel 161
Buccleuch, Duke of 55
Buckingham, Duke of 230
Buckingham Palace 2, 26, 65
Burke's Landed Gentry 26,
     90, 170
Burrage, Alfred 5
Buxton, Earl 122

Cadbury, George 59
Cameron, David 106
Campbell-Bannerman,
     Sir Henry 103, 119, 235
Carlton Club 139, 140,
     142, 233
Carlton Hotel, Haymarket
     161, 183, 194, 196,
     202, 209, 214
Carroll, Lewis 29
Carson, Edward 63
Casement, Sir Roger 43
Cash for Honours 100
Caterham 49
Chamberlain, Austen 96,
     99, 101, 103, 113–14,
     127, 136, 140, 141,
     162, 163
Chamberlain, Joseph 113
Charles I 230–30
Charles II 230
Chester, Betty 192

Childers, Erskine 38
Church of the Immaculate
     Conception,
     Mayfair 157
Churchill, Clementine 133
Churchill, Winston 44,
     52, 55, 60, 64, 69, 72,
     90–1, 93, 110, 115,
     133, 137, 139, 162,
     169
Clark, David 72, 73
Clemenceau, Georges 82
Cleopatra 20
Clynes, J. R. 90, 162
Cobden, Richard 231
Coffin, Charles Hayden
     20–1, 22
Cohen, Louis 119
Colchester,
     Father Francis 157
Cole (later Kelly), Edith 15
Colletta, Madam 34
Combine Attractions
     Syndicate 20–22
Connaught, HRH Duke
     of 85
Cooch Behar, Maharajah
     of 31
Cook, Andrew 100, 102,
     103, 211, 217
Coote, Captain Colin 86,
     88, 91, 92, 97, 218
Coppard, George 6
Corvo, Baron 27, 175–6,
     177, 200
Cowdray, Lord 84
Crawford, 27th Earl of
     1124
Crewe, Lord 105
Criccieth 54, 59, 78
Crippen, Dr 32
Croft, Sir Henry Page
     105–8, 110
Cromwell, Thomas 229
Cullen, Tom 15, 17–26
     passim, 33, 44, 75, 86,
     109, 134, 160, 167, 170,
     174, 199, 201, 203, 214,
     215, 218–25 *passim*
Curzon, Lord 69, 116–17,
     138, 140, 142

D'Roubaix family 221, 226
D'Roubaix, Mickey 221,
     226

D'Roubaix-Bulger,
     Marcel 226
Daily Chronicle 135–6,
     137–8
Daily Express 39, 71, 183,
     187, 190, 204, 205,
     209, 214, 226, 228
Daily Mail 38, 70, 88, 91,
     96, 136, 143, 214, 220
Daily News 59
Daily Sketch 204–5,
     209, 212
Daily Telegraph 109, 152,
     205, 215, 237
David, A. J. 151
Davidson, Harold 'Jumbo'
     11–12, 19–20, 22
Davidson, J. C. C. 145,
     147–51, 201, 207,
     208–9
Davidson, John 97
Davidson, Molly 19–20
Davies (later Rosse), Edith
     Marion (Vivienne
     Pierpont) 23, 161–2,
     180–90, 199, 209–13,
     214–17
Davies, Ethel 181–2,
     186–7, 209, 211–12,
     215–16, 217–18
Davies, Fred 181–2, 185,
     186, 210, 211, 212,
     215–16, 217
Davies, J. T. 110
Davies, Joseph 70
Davies, Mrs Timothy 57
Debs, Eugene V. 86
Deepdene Hotel, Dorking
     34, 168–70, 173,
     180, 201
DeGroot, Gerard 4
Delius, Frederick 24
Desert Song, The 199
Deterding, Sir Henri 172
Dewar, Sir Thomas 110
Dieppe 220–2, 227
Disraeli, Benjamin 169
Donald, Sir Robert 137
Dorothy 20–1
Douglas, Lew 91
Doxford, Ernest 95
Dracula (1897) 38
Drancy internment camp 224
Drughorn of Ifield,
     Sir John 118

Duchess of Somerset 20
Duff, Sir Patrick 196
Duncan, Isadora 15
Dunedin, Lord 133–4

Eade, Percy 227
*East Anglian
    Daily Times* 18
Edward III 195
Edward VIII 2, 25
Edwards, Mrs Catherine 57
Elizabeth I 229, 230
Elizabeth II 166
Ellaby, Christopher 11
Era, The 17
Evening Standard 137
Exeter College, Oxford 12
Eyres, Lottie 183–4

Farrow, John Villiers 157–9
Ferdinand,
    Archduke Franz 34
Ferdinand,
    King of Bulgaria 86
Fevrier 223, 226
Financial Times 152
Finny, Captain A. J. 51
Fisher, H. A. L. 77
Fitch, Inspector Herbert 33
Flemwell, George 73
Foch, Marshal 76
Frampton, Walter 215, 216
Fremantle, Sir Sydney 195
Fulton, Eustace 200, 203

Gaiety Theatre orchestra
    21, 23, 24
Gallipoli 60, 72
Garibaldi, Giuseppe 27–8
Garter King of Arms 9
Geddes, Sir Eric 69, 168
George I 230
George II King of the
    Hellenes 31, 161–2,
    163, 183, 186, 194, 197
George III 231
George IV 163
George V 2, 34, 102, 109,
    111, 117, 120–1, 122,
    126, 129, 131, 142, 149
George VI 85, 91, 149,
    166, 222
Germany 34, 37–42, 48,
    79, 89, 132, 173–4
Gilmour, Sir John 215

Gladstone, Lord Herbert
    146
Gladstone, William 233
Gleason, Arthur 5
Glenarthur, Baron 100
Graham-Campbell, Sir Rollo
    191, 202, 203
Grant of Forres,
    Sir Alexander 101
Grayson, Victor 71–3
*Great War in England in
    1897, The* (1894) 38
Greece 138–9
Greene, Sir Wilfred 147
Greet, Ben 14
Gregory, Edward 11, 13
Gregory, Rev. Francis
    Maundy 10
Gregory, Michael 11
Gregory, Stephen 11, 13
Gregory, Ursula *see* Mayow,
    Ursula
Grey, Lord 231
Grigg, John 59
Groombridge, Detective
    Sergeant 227–8
Guest, Captain Freddie 71,
    84, 91–3, 97, 98, 108,
    111, 112, 117–18,
    137–8, 235
Guinness, Sir Arthur 232
Gwynne, H. A. 'Taffy' 128,
    142–3

Hadrian VII 175
Haig (1st Earl Haig), Field
    Marshal Douglas 52,
    62, 75–6, 85, 100, 109
Haldane, Viscount 39
Hale, James 224
Hall, Admiral
    'Blinker' 195, 207
Halsey, Sir Lionel 195, 196
Hanbury-Williams, Sir John
    161, 163
Hankey, Sir Maurice 45,
    69, 70, 75, 78, 79, 116
*Hansard's Parliamentary
    Debates* 163
Hardinge, Charles 37
Hardy, Thomas 56
Harington, Sir Charles
    Harington 138
Harker, Colonel 166–8, 172
Harmsworth, Esmond 143

Harris, Lord 121
Hattersley, Roy 60, 117
Haw-Haw, Lord 227
Henderson, Arthur 69,
    133, 136
Henry IV 9
Henry VIII 229
Henry, Ainley 15
Hetman of Ukraine *see*
    Skoropadsky, Pavlo
Hewart, Gordon 100
Hitler, Adolf 89, 173
Hodge, Sir Rowland
    110–12, 102, 118
Hogg, Sir Douglas 153
Honours Gazette 126
Hooley, Ernest Terah 233
Hope, Thomas 169
Hopkin-Morris, Rhys 153
Horwood, General
    Sir William 167–8, 171
Hoskins, Percy 209, 228
Hospital of St. John of
    Jerusalem, Venerable
    Order of the 159–60
Hotel Lotti, Paris 208,
    215, 219
Hotel Meurice 219–20
Howard, Mrs Hilda 185, 186
Hulton, Edward 128
Hurwitz-y-Zender,
    Ludovico 42
Hyde Park 2
Hylton, Jack 164

Inskip, Attorney General
    Sir Thomas 200, 201
Invasion of 1910, The
    (1906) 38
Iphigenia 192
Ireland 3, 34, 43, 47–8, 62,
    77, 79
Isaacs, Godfrey 58
Isaacs, Michael 198
Isaacs, Sir Rufus (Lord
    Reading) 58–9, 146–7
Italy 117

James I 95, 229–30
Jekyll, Audrey 19
Jellicoe, Admiral 11, 100
Joel, Solly 120, 121, 125
John Bull 30, 32, 38
John of Gaunt 9
John XXIII 156

Johnson, Boris 110, 238
Jones, Mrs Lizzie 57
Jones, Thomas 70
Jowett, Fred 104
Joynson-Hicks,
    Sir William 114

Keen-Hargreaves, Arthur 27
Keen-Hargreaves, Harry
    27, 32–3
Keen-Hargreaves, Jack
    'Baron' 27, 67
Keen-Hargreaves, Jack
    senior 27–8
Kell, Vernon 40, 42, 195
Kelly, Captain Richard
    207–8, 222, 227
Kelly, William Wallace
    14–15, 17
Kelvin, Lord 232
Kemal, Mustafa
    (Attaturk) 139
Kennedy-Cox, Reginald 20
Kent, Walter 102
Kerr, Philip 70
Keynes, John Maynard 65
Kiggell, General
    Launcelot 62
Kipling, Rudyard 143
Kitchener, Lord 51, 60, 62
Korostovetz, Volodymyr
    171–3
Kruger, Paul 123

Lane-Mitchell, William 106
Lansdowne, Lord 105
Lava, Thelma de 168
Le Beau, Monsieur 219–20,
    222–3, 223, 224
Le Mans 223
Le Queux, William 38
Lee, Arthur 52
Levi, Mr David 186
Levy, Lord Michael 229,
    237–8
Liddell, Major Guy 227
Light Brigade, Charge of
    the 9
Lindsay, David 52
Linford Gwyer, Sir Maurice
    197, 198
Little Red Riding Hood 18
Llewellyn of Bwllfa,
    Sir David 101
Llewellyn, Roddy 101

Lloyd George, David 4,
    6, 34, 53–65, 67–71,
    74–80, 81–3, 85, 88,
    91, 93, 95, 96–8, 99,
    100–1, 103, 104,
    108, 111–13, 115–17,
    121–2, 123, 124–33,
    135–42, 146–7,
    152, 167, 194, 201,
    235–6, 238
Lloyd George, Gwilym
    138, 147
Lloyd George, Margaret
    see Owen, Margaret
Lloyd George, Megan
    57, 141
Lloyd, George 152
Lloyd, Richard 54, 68
Lody, Carl Hans 41
London Gazette 117, 124
Long, Walter 114
Loos, Battle of 51
Loraine family 13–14, 32
Loraine, Harry 13
Loraine, Ida, Vivien and
    Florence 13
Loraine, Robert 13–14
Luton News 102
Lutyens, Edwin 163
Lyceum, Ipswich 18
Lyndhurst 13, 32
Lyvedon, Lord Robert 9

Macdonald, Ramsay 101,
    136, 196
MacKinlay, Mrs Dagny 181
Maclay, Sir Joseph 69
Maclean, Sir Fitzroy 31
Macmillan, Gerald 87, 89,
    174–5, 176
Man and Superman 13
Manchester Guardian 94
Manuel II, King of
    Portugal 31
Marconi 58–9, 60, 83
Marlborough, Duchess of
    169
Marlborough, Duke of
    156, 162
Marple, G. S. 84
Marsh, Eddy 110
Mata Hari *see* Zelle,
    Margarethe
Maurice, General Frederick
    75, 76–7, 138

Maxton, Jimmy 154
Mayfair and Town Topics
    28–32, 34, 38, 48, 67,
    83, 85, 111
Mayow, Lieutenant Colonel
    George Wynell 9
Mayow (later Gregory),
    Ursula 9–10, 13
Mazzina, Francesco 33, 165
Mazzina, Peter 33, 165–6,
    169, 170, 186, 213
McCurdy, Charles 97,
    117, 134
Messina, Italy 21
Meston, Baron 100
Meyrick, Kate 164
MI5 40, 42, 43–5, 50
Miller, Ruby 20
Millionaires' Club, Cork
    Street 170
Mills, Frederick 112–13
Milner, Lord 69, 70, 78
Moffatt, James Douglas
    94, 103, 130, 191–3,
    196, 202
Mone, Michelle 236–7
Montagu, Edwin 52
Montenegro 89
Montenegro, Prince of 31
Morgan, Kenneth O. 135
Morley College,
    Winchester 13
Morning Post 95, 96, 128,
    135, 142
Moseley, Oswald 173
Mountbatten of Battenberg,
    Prince Louis 39, 192
Murray, Alexander (Alick)
    Master of Elibank 'the
    Master' 58–9, 83, 84,
    91, 103
Murray, Gilbert 56
Musk, Elon 238
Mussolini, Benito 89, 161,
    173, 194

Narcissus 161, 175
Nash's Magazine 64
National Union of
    Ex-Servicemen 3
Naylor-Leyland, Captain
    Herbert 234
News of the World 75, 91
Newton, Arthur 32
Nicholas II, Czar 2

Nicholas, Grand Duke 31, 90, 195
Nicholson, Harold 54
Nivelle, General Robert 76
Noon, Gulam 237
Northcliffe, Lord 63, 70, 88, 137
Northumberland, 8th Duke of 129–31
Northumberland, Duke of 95

O'Sullivan, Maureen 158, 159
Observer, The 70
Oddie, Samuel Ingleby 215–16
Orlando, Vittorio 82
Other Club 91
Owen (later Lloyd George), Margaret 55, 56–7, 68, 141
Owen, Wilfred 5

Palmerston, Lord 231
Paris 157, 208, 215, 219–22, 224
Parish, Mrs 84
Parsons-Smith, Dr Basil 186, 218
Passchendaele 76, 77
Patagonia 59
Pease, Jack 103, 104
Peel, Sir Robert 231
Peel, Viscount 152
Pengelly, Benjamin 160, 180, 188, 214
People 143
Percy, Harry 9
Peterborough, Bishop of 233
Phipps, Captain Bertie 219–20, 221, 222
Pierpont, Vivienne *see* Davies, Edith Marion
Pip 29
Pirie-Go, Mrs Mabel 26
Pitt the Younger, William 230–1
Pius XI 195
Playfair, Nigel 15
Plumer, General 100
Plummer, Dr Edgar Curnow 183–4, 185–6, 187, 210, 212, 214, 215–16, 218

Plymouth, Rev. 50
Ponsonby, Arthur 103
Ponzi, Charles 86
Pope, Dr. R. 50
Porter, Hilda 72–3
Pounder, Professor Derrick 218
Pratley, George 210
Preston, Sir Harry 26
Prince of Wales Theatre, Southampton 14
Protocols of the Elders of Zion, The 160
Punch 85, 163
Pym, Francis 236
Pyman, Walter 95

Quest for Corvo, The 176

Rawlinson, General 100
Reform Club 95
Rhodes James, Robert 147–8
Rhondda, Lord 69
Riddell, Lord George 75, 91, 109, 116, 129, 132, 138, 167
Riddle of the Sands, The (1903) 38
Rimbaud, Arthur 174
Robertson, Sir William 62, 75–6
Robey, George 53
Robinson, Sir Joseph 119–26, 134
Roche Lynch, Dr Gerald 214–15, 216
Rolfe, Frederick *see* Corvo, Baron
Rosebery, Lord 90, 133, 234, 234
Rosenberg, Alfred 173
Rosse, Edith *see* Davies, Edith Marion
Rosse, Fred 21, 23, 90, 181, 186, 187, 211, 212, 214
Rothermere, Lord 91, 128, 137, 143
Rothschild, Lionel de 232
Royal Albion Hotel, Brighton 26
Royal Divorce, A 14
Russell, Ronnie 220, 225
Russia 2

Saki 38
Sales, J. Rowland 17–18, 19, 21, 22
Salisbury, Marquess of 104, 120, 129
Sanders, Robert 118
Sarajevo 34
Savery, Bill 16
Scotsman, The 128
Seely, General Jack 158
Selborne, Earl of 104
Selborne, Lord 97, 122–4
Self-Condemned 12–13
Seymour Cocks, Fred 215
Sforza-Cesarini, Duchess of 175
Shakespeare, William 13, 14, 15
Shaw, George Bernard 13, 82
Shaw, Harry 94–5, 102, 129
Sheppard, Harry 23
Simon, Sir John 162
Sitwell, Edith 156
Skegness 12
Skoropadsky, Pavlo (Hetman of Ukraine) 171, 173
Smith, F. E. *see* Birkenhead, Lord
Smuts, General Jan 69, 91
Soeurs de la Retraite du Sacre Coeur, Paris 157
Somerset, Duke of 55
Somerset, Lord Arthur 32
Somme, Battle of the 61
South Africa 13, 119, 126
Southampton 10–11
Southborough, Lord 171, 196, 197
Spilsbury, Sir Bernard 214–15, 216
Sports Club, St. James's Square 193
Stage, The 22
Stamfordham, Lord 112, 120–1, 129
Stanley, Sir Albert 69
Stanley, Venetia 52
Stern, Sydney (Lord Wandsworth) 233–4
Stevenson, Frances 57, 61, 65, 68
Stewart, Sir William 109

Stiffkey, Norfolk 11–12
Stoker, Bram 38
Stowe House,
    Buckinghamshire 94–5
Stratford-upon-Avon 15
Strindberg, August 13
Suffield, Lord 233
Sunday Times 135, 152
Sutherland, William 'Bronco
    Bill' 70, 74–5, 94, 129
Sydney Mirror 72
Symons, A. J. A. 176–7

Tabard 85
Tarzan the Ape Man 158
Taylor, Peter 219, 222
Teck, Prince Alexander
    of 21
Temple, John 95
Tennyson, Lord 232
Terry, Ellen 19
Thames Ditton 24–5, 26,
    73, 181, 188
The Times 63, 70, 76, 88,
    137, 139, 189, 200
Thick of It, The 75
Thirty-Nine Steps, The
    (1915) 38
Thomas, Jimmy 162
Thomas, Sir Godfrey
    194, 196
Thomson, Basil 33,
    42–3, 45, 72, 86, 87,
    168, 173
Tree, Sir Herbert Beerbohm
    18, 91
Trevethin, Baron 100
Trump, Donald 238
Truth 234
Turkey 138–9

Ukraine 171–4

Vanity Fair 29
Vanity Fair, Thames Ditton
    24–5, 26, 181

Vernon family 9
Vernon, Courtenay Percy
    (3rd Baron Lyveden)
Vestey, Sir William 118
Victor Emmanuel II,
    King of
    Piedmont-Sardinia and
    Italy 28
Victoria, Queen 10, 231,
    232, 233
von Alvensleben, Werner
    173, 174

Waldorf Astor, William 234
Wales 55, 79
*War in the Air,
    The* (1907) 38
War of the Worlds, The
    (1897) 38
Ward, Leslie 'Spy' 29
Waring, Sir Samuel 118
Watson, Sir George
    179–80, 187,
    191, 194
Watson, Sir Thomas 102
Watson-Armstrong,
    William 234
Waugh, Evelyn 6, 156
Webb, Beatrice 67
Weissmuller, Johnny 158
Wells, Captain 94
Wells, H. G. 38
Wells, Mrs Kate 155, 183,
    185, 199
Wertheim, Louise 42
What's On 16
*When William Came: A
    Story of London under
    the Hohenzollerns*
    (1913) 38
White, John Baker 164,
    167–8, 207
White, Leonard 225
*Whitehall Gazette and
    St. James's Review,
    The* 84–90, 92, 102,

149, 162, 164, 166,
    168, 170, 173, 193,
    213, 227
Whitelaw, William 102
Whiteley, George 103
Whitgift School,
    Croydon 12
Who's Who 193, 198
Wickham Steed,
    Henry 128
Wilde, Oscar 174, 220
Wilhelm II, Emperor of
    Germany 35, 82
William and Mary 230
William the Conqueror 9
Williams, Graham 40
Williams, Harcourt 15
Williamson, Sir Archibald
    (Baron Forres) 118
Williamson, James (Lord
    Ashton) 233–4
Wills, William Gorman 14
Wilson, E. Holt 45, 70
Wilson, Field Marshal
    Sir Henry 3, 121
Wilson, Leslie 96, 127
Wilson, President
    Woodrow 82
Wodehouse, P. G. 29
Wolkonsky, Prince of
    Ukraine 90
Woolf, Virginia 65
Wyndham's Theatre 20

Yates, John 237
York, Duke of
    see George VI
Younger, Sir George 99,
    110, 112, 118, 141
Ypres 76
Yvinec, Madame Anne 223,
    224, 226

Zaharoff, Basil 71
Zelle, Margarethe 'Mata
    Hari' 42–3